Clinical Biofeedback: A Procedural Manual

Clinical Biofeedback:
A Procedural Manual

By Kenneth R. Gaarder, M.D.

Department of Psychiatry, University of Texas Health Science Center at San Antonio and the Audie L. Murphy Memorial Veterans Administration Hospital, San Antonio, Texas

and Penelope S. Montgomery, M.S.

Department of Psychiatry, University of Texas Health Science Center at San Antonio, Texas

with four contributors.

The Williams & Wilkins Company • *Baltimore*

Library of Congress Cataloging in Publication Data

Gaarder, Kenneth R
    Clinical biofeedback.

    Bibliography: p.
    Includes index.
    1. Biofeedback training. 2. Psychotherapy. I. Montgomery, Penelope, joint author.
    II. Title.
RC489.B53G3   616.8'914   76-41264
ISBN 0-683-03400-6

Composed and printed at the
Waverly Press, Inc.
Mt. Royal and Guilford Aves.
Baltimore, Md. 21202, U.S.A.

Dedicated

to our mentors:

GARDNER MURPHY
MARJORIE L. BROWN
ROBERT H. BARNES

Foreword

Biofeedback is unique among medical treatments. Psychiatry, before now, had nothing comparable. Biofeedback represents the blending of ancient wisdom — the control of bodily function through meditation or suggestion — with newer relaxation and behavioral therapy techniques within the context of the doctor-patient relationship in a modern scientific laboratory where rigorous measures can be applied and experimental design can either prove or disprove the claims of the therapists. Best of all, biofeedback is under the patient's control. He is not a passive recipient in the procedure and elaborate instrumentation, but he is his own therapist who must learn, understand, and apply the techniques of therapy on his own behalf. Biofeedback should have happened a long time ago.

It is to this unique situation that this book is addressed — how to help the patient learn not something mystical, but a valid program which can be measured with scientific instrumentation. The book addresses the art and science of helping the patient learn to control and reverse pathophysiological processes. It enables the healer to enter an exciting new area of therapy and bring his patient along as a partner. It provides the clinician with the basic background, methods, and technique to enter into the treatment program with his patient.

Dr. Gaarder is a psychoanalyst who can bring his knowledge in this area to bear on the newer biofeedback techniques. This background allows him to apprize the role of the doctor-patient relationship in biofeedback therapy. Biofeedback is opening new approaches to the understanding of this relationship and stimulates thinking in new directions. The depth in which the doctor-patient relationship is treated and its importance in biofeedback illustrate why biofeedback therapy must be supervised by professionals with an understanding of the totality of physiological and psychological processes. He helps the reader distinguish the place of one and another treatment method for a given patient. Ms. Montgomery is one of the little known pioneers in biofeedback research. She helped to develop the present facility as one of the earlier laboratories to explore the process. In these explorations, she has resisted the temptations inherent in investigation of new therapies to proclaim them as the latest panacea.

This is more than a procedural manual. It talks about important concepts and sets procedures in proper context of a therapeutic relationship. Who knows, a major contribution of biofeedback may be to significantly improve our understanding of psychotherapy.

ROBERT L. LEON, M.D.
San Antonio, Texas

Preface

This book has a simple purpose, which is to supply enough information about the use of biofeedback in clinical practice so that a trained practitioner can learn the details of use and introduce it into his practice and so that his technicians will be able to learn the details of doing the therapy. To achieve this goal we have adopted a particular style of using a great deal of redundancy while avoiding repetition. Our aim is to try to say our important points in several different ways so as to be sure they are understood. The book is written for graduate practitioners, but at the same time we have attempted to make the language simple enough so that less trained technicians will find it useful. Our aim has been thoroughness and we have made every effort to cover all aspects of our topics. In giving every step of every procedure, we have written much that is already known or will be easily learned by particular individuals. Therefore, many readers will find that they are soon able to ignore many of our steps and details. However, we are confident that it is important to have these same details for other readers. By no means do we feel that we have described a final method or necessarily the best method of those available and used. Rather, what we describe is what we have done ourselves, used extensively, and found to give good results. At this time it is not possible to compare it objectively with different methods.

Likewise, we do not feel that much of what we describe is original. Many of the details have been learned from others and are widely used. Regretfully, we have not been able to give full credit for this, because the sources have not always been known or have sometimes been forgotten. We have not attempted to make a critical or comprehensive survey of clinical biofeedback literature in our writing. This would not have furthered our purpose of teaching methods to practitioners who wish to learn the use of biofeedback. Likewise, we have avoided the tangled issue of why biofeedback is effective. We feel certain that the appropriate attention to the details of application are important in the effectiveness of treatment, but have not felt that this is the place to debate these issues extensively.

Some feel that biofeedback should be used only in research until more extensive clinical trials have been done. We do not agree with this except as an idealized position. We know of few currently used functional treatment methods which have developed out of completely tested procedures and consider it grossly unrealistic and over-idealistic to make this demand of biofeedback. Biofeedback is unique in the very little risk of harmful effects. We feel that the methods as we describe them and as we and others have used them are simple and effective and can be applied by competent and conscientious practitioners without great difficulty.

We intend that our book might function at the interface of past, present, and future. From the past, we have sought both to utilize what has already been done with biofeedback by ourselves and others, and to immerse ourselves in the general principles of therapy as they have evolved, hopefully avoiding more than minimal re-discovery through trial and error. In the present, we have attempted to present techniques which will enable practitioners to offer help to patients whose conditions often respond poorly to conventional management. For the future, we hope to be part of an evolution toward more effective and better defined treatment.

The book is organized with chapter titles which are self-explanatory. The more theoretical and abstract material is presented near the beginning of the book and the more practical material near the end. Practitioners might focus more heavily upon the early parts and technicians more upon the latter parts. *Chapters are divided into a few main headings which are unnumbered and whose titles are centered on the page. The next lower division is section headings which are designated by chapter number and sequentially by section number within the chapter. Thus, section 7.11 is the 11th section within Chapter 7.*

KENNETH R. GAARDER
PENELOPE S. MONTGOMERY

Acknowledgments

This book is very much a product of the Department of Psychiatry at the University of Texas Health Science Center at San Antonio and could not have been written without the support and collaboration of our colleagues and co-workers within the department. The life span of this new school and the life span of clinical biofeedback are virtually identical and our laboratory was started by Robert Barnes and one of the authors with the help of Barbara Brown soon after the school opened. Peyton Bland, as electronics engineer, and Richard McKenzie, as acting head for a period, were also crucial to the laboratory's development. The other major institutional support has been provided by the Veterans Administration at the Audie L. Murphy Memorial Veterans Hospital where Edward Kollar as Chief of Psychiatry has supervised our program's development. Richard Filer at the Veterans Administration Center Office has been important by seeing that there is widespread awareness of the potential provided by biofeedback and Joseph Baker by endorsing the Clinical Psychophysiology Laboratory. The detailing of the procedures described in the book was undertaken in part for the purpose of establishing treatment methods for veterans and to carry out research supported by Veterans Administration Merit Review Awards. However, the actual writing of the manuscript has not been at any government expense. Other work upon which the book was based was done with Institutional Grant support from the Health Science Center.

All of the staff and adjunct staff of our two laboratories have contributed heavily to the ideas and work we present. This includes Steven Burns, Richard Flickinger, George Garza, Jack Johnson, Mary Kurtz, Don Mayfield, Nancy Migl, Augustine de la Pena, and Diana Slaughter. The physical medicine techniques of Chapter 10 could not have been developed without the help of Arthur Grant, Leonel Fuentes, and their staffs.

Another important influence has been the opportunity provided by John Sparks to participate in the development of a biofeedback program at Wilford Hall USAF Hospital at Lackland Air Force Base in

San Antonio. This program was begun by Fredrick Brown, Kenneth Rylee and John Gormly.

It was a privilege of the senior author to have been a member of the invisible college which existed before biofeedback became institutionalized and to have had the opportunity at that time to get to know John Basmajian, Barbara Brown, Thomas Budzynski, Roland Fischer, Elmer and Alyce Green, Thomas Mulholland, Barry Sterman, and Johann Stoyva. Since then, there had been further influence by Craig Cleaves, Robert Coursey, Bernard Engel, Bernard Frankel, Joe Kamiya, William Leaf, Wolfgang Luthe, Steven Padnes, Dali Patel, Alan Roberts, Jesse Rubin, Harold Russell, Gary Schwartz, Daniel Sheer, Edward Taub, Harold Wiener, George Whatmore, and Redford Williams.

This book did not develop *sui generis* and much of its value comes from contact with these and other colleagues. Its limitations, however, must be our responsibility.

Part of the material in Chapter 1 is adapted from two articles published in the *Archives of General Psychiatry 25:* 429–441, 1971. The articles are entitled "Control of States of Consciousness. I. Attainment through Control of Psychophysiological Variables"; and "II. Attainment through External Feedback Augmenting Control of Psychophysiological Variables." These are adapted with the kind permission of the American Medical Association by whom there was copyright in 1971. Most of the quotations at the beginning of chapters are from M. B. Strauss, *Familiar Medical Quotations,* Little Brown, Boston, 1968.

Finally, both in spirit and in context, biofeedback and our book show the influences of W. Ross Ashby, whose interest in psychiatry can come full circle, and Gardner Murphy, who rarely misses the essence of anything.

Contributors

Mary Bieker, B.S., is the first therapist trained by the comprehensive method described and has justified the undertaking by her competence. Practically, her contributions were to Chapters 5 and 11.

Charles G. Burgar, B.S., Electronics Engineer at the Department of Psychiatry, University of Texas Health Science Center at San Antonio, made contributions that were invaluable in the specifications and recommendations set out in Chapter 12.

John Gormly, Chief Biofeedback Therapist at the Audie L. Murphy V.A. Hospital, provided closure on some details of Chapters 7, 8, 9, and 10.

Richard Sherman, Ph.D., Research Physiologist at the Audie L. Murphy V.A. Hospital, contributed significantly to Chapters 3, 4, and 10.

Contents

Figures

Tables

Surely every medicine is an innovation; and he that will not apply new remedies must expect new evils; for time is the greatest innovator, and if time of course alters things to the worse, and wisdom and counsel shall not alter them to the better, what shall be the end?

Sir Francis Bacon
"Of Innovations," Essays

CHAPTER 1

Scientific foundation of biofeedback therapy

§1.1 Introduction. Biofeedback rests upon a particularly secure foundation and once the foundation is examined its firmness becomes clear. The first corner of that foundation is the general principle of feedback, which is a major tool of control theory. This is briefly examined in Section 1.2. The history of biofeedback and other parallel developments and the simple technology of biofeedback are considered in Sections 1.3 through 1.8. Another corner of the foundation is then examined in the consideration of homeostatic adaptive control systems (Secs. 1.9–1.20), a great biological generalization of enormous power. It is shown how the state of any organism may be controlled by control of the state of the inputs to the components of the systems making up the organism (Secs. 1.21–1.34).

A third corner of the foundation of biofeedback is the consideration of disease as deranged homeostasis (Secs. 1.35–1.37) and biofeedback as a direct impingement upon that homeostasis (Secs. 1.38–1.41). Finally, an essential part of any therapeutic method is to relate it to the general principles of therapeutics (Secs. 1.42–1.48) and some of the particular strengths of biofeedback emerge here, along with a lucid perspective from which to re-examine therapeutics.

THEORETICAL AND ABSTRACT CONCEPTS OF BIOFEEDBACK

§1.2 Cultural Zeitgeist. Any particular unique treatment method or clinical point of view can be conceived as arising out of a particular cultural context which must be right for the method or point of view to arise. This seems especially true of biofeedback because of its discovery by many individuals and its rapid acceptance by many others. The fact it was simultaneously discovered by numerous individuals (Brown, 1974; Stoyva, 1976) is best explained by recognizing that biofeedback represents a special instance of the concept of *feedback* (Mayr, 1970) which has become widely and concretely understood since World War II. The concept is pivotal to modern electrical engineering control theory

3

and indispensable to understanding physiology. Primitive people—who have no inkling of such concepts as the wheel, the use of fire, metal, or counting—have to structure their world without the power provided by these relevant concepts and their material representation. By the same token, until the last few decades, we have structured our world without much explicit reliance upon the concept of feedback. Now this situation has changed drastically and most people recently trained in technical disciplines can be expected to have some understanding of feedback, while for many the concept is vivid, explicit, and deeply understood.

§1.3 **Early History of Biofeedback.** Such an easily achieved goal as the artificial closing of an external feedback loop has occurred many times over the ages without the formal logic of its occurrence being necessarily appreciated. One such early example is Narcissus seeing himself mirrored in the pond and becoming self-absorbed. The feedback provided by a mirror is used daily when men shave and women apply makeup and is used by a school of German physiotherapists to train self-awareness.

Completing an external feedback loop electronically has been practical for about 50 years, and it is of interest that one of the first things Adrian did with the EEG was to observe his own alpha rhythm and how it was affected by eye movements (Mulholland, 1968). Likewise, Jacobson (1938) reports closing a feedback loop verbally by telling his subjects how they were doing while he observed their electromyograph (EMG). Another example of early use of feedback was by Margolin and Kubie (1944) who placed a microphone to pick up a patient's respiration and heart beat and used the amplified playback to induce a hypnoid state. In all of these instances, the use of feedback was incidental to other concerns of the investigator, and it usually cannot be told from what is written whether there was awareness of the explicit power of the concept of feedback.

§1.4 **Current History of Biofeedback Research.** It is not easy to do justice to all of the investigators involved in describing the current use of external feedback. One reason is that much current knowledge has not yet been published. Another is that new facets of the early work keep turning up. Some of these have been reported by Brown (1974) in her new book, and others are mentioned by Stoyva (1976). A third reason is that current feedback work has emerged from different scientific disciplines. Finally, most of us are now fully aware that history, as well as beauty, is in the eye of the beholder. This forces us to acknowledge limitations to the scope of our vision of a scene in which we stand. In making a best effort, however, it seems valid to divide the current history of biofeedback into three phases. In the first phase, several investigators used the principles of external feedback without an explicit recognition that a new principle had been discovered, while in the second phase, it began to become clear to these investigators and to others that new principles did indeed exist, and the explicit recognition of the principles became an end in itself. One of the earliest uses of feedback was in the work of Whatmore and Kohli (1974) who used the EMG as a means to feed information back to patients in teaching muscle relaxation in the early 1950's. Another early worker was Kamiya (1969) who, in the late 1950's while studying alpha rhythm, found that his subjects were able to control a signal he was providing them of the presence of their alpha rhythm. Although his work was not published in definitive form, Kamiya's findings became widely known, and he is now credited by many with founding the study of biofeedback. Hefferline (1958) was another of the earliest workers who used feedback in an experiment where the subject was not aware that he was controlling his muscle tension.

The second phase of biofeedback work began during the early part of the 1960's as a number of other people became interested in the study of biofeedback, and each may be credited with having had creative insight into the recognition of a new principle. Among these people were Mulholland (1968), Green, et al. (1969a), Murphy and Leeds (1975), Stoyva (1970), and Brown (1974). It appears valid to see feedback as another instance of simultaneous discovery of an idea whose time of birth had come. In the latter part of the 1960's, many more people began to study external feedback. In 1969, the Biofeedback Research Society was formed at a scientific meeting held in Santa Monica, California, to bring together people doing research in the area. Meetings are now held yearly and membership in the society is over 800. In addition, the Society for Psychophysiological Research, the American Psychological Association, and the American Psychiatric Association, among other scientific societies, devote sections to reports of biofeedback.

The third phase of biofeedback work has been one in which there has been the widespread growth of clinical use of the new techniques by many clinicians throughout the country and the rest of the world. This began in earnest in the first part of the 1970's. There are now more than a half-dozen reputable small companies marketing professional quality portable biofeedback equipment and many more advertising to the lay public. Newspaper and magazine articles abound, patients suffering from otherwise untreatable illnesses seek out treatment from universities, from reputable private clinics, and from a growing number of charlatans attempting to cash in on a popular craze. Conscientious practitioners are concerned to see that what is valuable in the methods is not lost in the confusion and misunderstanding.

The next phase of the development of biofeedback is hard to predict. Many hope that it will contain a consolidation of the diffuse knowledge generated thus far. This book has been written in that spirit, to attempt to define in detail the clinical methods found of use by us. Two developments which would help greatly are the evolution of criteria for evaluating the clinical use of a technique, and the emergence of control theory principles as a framework for understanding what happens in biofeedback learning. Presently, any clinical evidence presented can be faulted on methodological grounds, so that there is a stalemate in evaluating clinical results (Blanchard and Young, 1974). In particular, there is a standoff between clinicians and experimenters, with each unsatisfied with the position of the other. Clinicians rightly feel that each case must be treated individually for best results, whereas experimenters rightly feel that firm conclusions cannot be drawn about the results of a small sample of patients treated by heterogeneous methods. A partial answer to the problem may be found in compromise, with experimenters coming to recognize that "pure" treatment procedures do not exist, and clinicians learning to define their procedures operationally in testable algorithms with describable decision points (see Secs. 1.42–1.48). Then, heterogeneous methods with a limited number of components might be applied in a specified way. Control groups are also necessary to ascertain whether comparable results could be obtained with easier methods, while piecemeal evaluation of the steps of an algorithm can be used to form a composite picture of a treatment method. Control theory can help here when it is possible to manipulate the parameters of a feedback to make it ineffective or counter-effective, thereby allowing the use of the altered feedback as a control for the effective feedback (Powers, 1973). Beyond that, control theory would predict that there are as yet unimagined highly effective uses of biofeedback awaiting discovery.

§1.5 Feedback Framework versus Operant Framework. The above history of external feedback reflecting the work of people who explicitly recognize feedback has not included a parallel development in another field. This is the evolution of operant conditioning, which can be viewed as a form of feedback. Upon careful reflection, it becomes evident that operant conditioning meets the requirements of a feedback (Fig. 1.1). For example, if it is desired to train a pigeon to tap a key, he is gradually "shaped" into tapping the key by rewarding any activity which brings him closer to the key or to tapping the key. This is a feedback because doing the thing which is desired (i.e., internally initiating an activity) produces external information (in the form of a reward) which is different from the information produced by not doing the desired thing (i.e., from alternative internal states). The fact, however, that operant conditioning is a form of feedback is often not recognized and it is only recently that there has been much cross-fertilization between the field of operant conditioning and the field of feedback. Even so, there is not yet widely accepted rigorous and comprehensive analysis of operant condi-

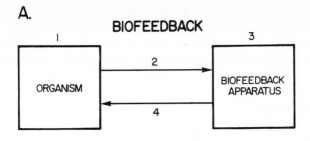

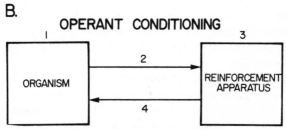

Figure 1.1. Similarity of biofeedback and operant conditioning. *A*. In biofeedback, an organism (*1*) (usually a human) is functioning in a setting [i.e., structured environment (*2, 3, 4*)] where some particular behavior or physiological variable of the organism is picked up, and carried (*2*) to a biofeedback apparatus (*3*) which measures and processes it and in some form feeds back a signal derived from that behavior or physiological variable (*4*). *B*. In operant conditioning, an organism (*1*) is likewise functioning in a setting [a structured environment (*2, 3, 4*)] where some particular behavior of the organism is likewise picked up and carried (*2*) to an apparatus, in this case a reinforcement apparatus (*3*), which measures, processes, and in the form of a reward or punishment feeds back information leading to what is desired for the next step (*4*).

tioning in terms of control system concepts (Powers, 1973; Barnwell and Stafford, in press).

The most relevant early work in operant conditioning was from Neal Miller's group (1969). Miller is another worker who is credited by many with having founded the field of biofeedback. Parallel to the development of biofeedback referred to above, Miller and his co-workers did extensive work with animals showing that psychophysiological variables which had been thought by some to be uncontrollable can in fact be controlled. The essence of the technique is as described above: a variable is measured, and if it moves in the desired direction, reward is given and information is thereby fed back (alternatively, punishment for the variable moving in the undesired direction may also be used). Using this technique, Miller's group has found it possible to control many autonomic variables. Thus, heart rate, intestinal motility, blood pressure, and skin temperature of selected body regions have been controlled.

One major factor appears to differentiate the feedback of operant conditioning from other feedback. That factor is what might best be called the valence of the feedback. Whereas in other techniques (which are used mainly with humans), the information is usually fed back in "neutral" form on a dial or other display, in operant conditioning (which is usually with animals), the information is fed back in the form of a compelling reward or punishment and thereby given a motivating value to the subject. Although it is true that the human subject in an ordinary feedback experiment is influenced by his own motivation to succeed at the task or by the social reinforcement of approval from the experimenter or therapist, these influences lack the compelling quality of food to a starved animal or electric shocks. When we understand how to provide the kind of compelling valence to feedback information which is achieved in conditioning experiments without treating the subject in a demeaning manner, some important advances in the use of feedback might be expected.

§1.6 Foundations of Biofeedback. All of the work categorized as biofeedback relies upon a simple idea – to provide subjects or patients with information about what is going on inside their bodies. Given this information, they have a chance to control the process about which the information is provided, whereas without the information, control would be impossible. This idea rests upon two principles. The first of these is the principle of feedback (DiStefano, et al., 1967; Mayr, 1970; Gaarder, 1975), of which biofeedback is a specific instance, while the second is the "great truism of information theory." This principle of Ashby's (1963) can best be stated as follows: *a variable cannot be controlled unless information about the variable is available to the controller*. This is a truism because it is a self-evident statement within the context of control system principles. It is an important truism and becomes axiomatic, however, because unrecognized the world has one shape, and recognized it has another. When the variable to be controlled belongs to the controller and when information about the variable is processed and presented back to the controller, a feedback loop is completed. An elementary understanding of this truism can be gained by a study of the error-controlled regulator in Ashby's *Introduction to Cybernetics* (1963; see also Conant, 1969). Although some beginnings have been made at providing a more rigorous analysis of psychophysiological feedback than the elementary one just given (Mulholland, 1976), there is not yet a great deal more known about the matter. We have just considered the essence of the general concept of feedback. Several branches of engineering carry the rigorous analysis of feedback many steps further. Much of this work has been done to study feedback in nonliving systems such as electronic circuits or naval gunfiring control systems. From this work, many general laws have been derived, many of them in the form of mathematical equations. It is now possible to make many generalizations about feedback which apply to living as well as non-living systems; however, the laws governing living systems are often much more complex and are not now understood in many instances.

Some of the properties of feedback systems which are important to consider include: (1) block diagrams can be used to represent feedback systems for purposes of analysis; (2) feedback systems are closed loop systems; (3) negative feedback tends to promote stability whereas positive feedback tends to promote instability; (4) feedback systems have steady state and dynamic descriptions; (5) feedback systems are affected by time delays; (6) feedback systems have particular stability characteristics; (7) feedback systems are limited by their channel capacity; (8) feedback systems have linear and non-linear properties.

It is not necessary for the practitioner to understand these properties of feedback in order to use biofeedback. On the other hand, the researcher extends his understanding both in breadth and depth by being acquainted with them. Elementary understanding is available from several sources (DiStefano, et al., 1967; Wender, 1968; Gaarder, 1975). More advanced works are also available (Jones, 1973; Powers, 1973). However, a major challenge still facing the field of biofeedback is the application of the general principles of feedback to the understanding of biofeedback.

§1.7 **The Term "Biofeedback."** The term *biofeedback* has come into widespread use to designate the process which is the main focus of this book. A more precise term would be *external psychophysiological feedback,* since the prefix *bio-* only means "living," and, as we shall shortly see, every living organism functions by virtue of hundreds of internal feedback loops mediating homeostasis (Secs. 1.12–1.33). All of these could logically be called "bio"-feedback. However, popular usage has resulted in the term *biofeedback* being widely used and commonly understood to be limited to external psychophysiological feedback. Furthermore, precise terms are unwieldy and we therefore will use the term biofeedback in the usual way (Secs. 1.8 and 1.38), accepting it in spite of its limitations.

§1.8 **Methods of Feeding Back Signals for Biofeedback.** The general method of biofeedback can best be summarized by saying that it is deceptively simple and that in that simplicity lies much of its success or failure. When a particular psychophysiological variable is continuously measured, usually the resultant measurement is a fairly complex signal containing a great deal of information. Most often simply presenting the raw signal to the subject as a feedback would overwhelm him with irrelevant information. Thus, in EEG feedback control, progress was begun by filtering the raw signal for alpha rhythm to feed back to the subject the simple information of whether alpha rhythm was present or not. Here again, however, the method is not as simple as it would appear since alpha rhythm is not just present or absent. Instead, one must have recourse to an elementary classification of signals to designate them as continuous (analog) or discontinuous (digital). Then, among the alternatives are feedback signals which: (1) merely say whether an immediate criterion level of alpha is present or not; (2) show both the presence of alpha and its amplitude; (3) show the amount of alpha in a recent short epoch; or (4) show the per cent of time a criterion level of alpha was present in a recent short epoch. Even these alternatives do not fully exhaust the possibilities for signal processing. When it is further recognized that the signal may be fed back in one of several sense modalities—such as sight or hearing—and that the signal may be scaled into one of several dimensions of that modality—such as pitch or volume—it can be seen that the problem of choosing a feedback is not simple at all. At the present time, many investigators have chosen slightly different methods of feedback and comparative studies have only begun to be undertaken, so that there is often only a small basis for comparing one investigator's work with another.

Another problem has been mentioned above (Sec. 1.5)—for the most part the feedback information in human experiments has been relatively neutral or lacking in valence, so as to lack a compelling quality. Also, it is necessary to prescribe a context within which feedback is used—whether in timed sessions or ad lib; whether with other techniques or alone; whether alternating feedback trials with no feedback trials to accelerate learning, etc. These research questions, as yet not well understood, will someday have important impact upon the clinical use of biofeedback. For the present, however, the empirical fact of its effectiveness supersedes such considerations.

HOMEOSTATIC ADAPTIVE CONTROL SYSTEMS

§1.9 Introduction. The idea of feedback is not only a foundation for biofeedback, it also leads into the study of homeostasis, the major means by which the body maintains itself in health. Homeostatic mechanisms are always feedback mechanisms. We will begin this section by a simple description of the homeostatic systems of the body (Secs. 1.10–1.20). Then, we will describe how a physiological state may be controlled by control of the information content of the channels (Secs. 1.21–1.34). Having done this, we will conclude by showing how homeostatic imbalance can be seen in disease conditions (Secs. 1.35–1.37).

§1.10 Homeostatic Adaptive Control Systems (HACS). Since the time of Claude Bernard, there has been a gradually increasing awareness of the importance of homeostatic mechanisms (Langley, 1965). The necessity of using feedback-mediated adaptive control mechanisms as a cornerstone of physiology is well recognized, even though much work remains to be done on the specifics of such mechanisms. Taken broadly, the homeostatic adaptive control systems (HACS) idea can be thought of as saying that one overriding purpose of all psychological and physiological mechanisms is to ensure the survival of the organism or of its own kind (Ashby, 1963). The major means used by the HACS is to have feedback control the value of essential psychophysiological variables to keep them within critical limits. Thus, from the viewpoint of homeostasis, any understanding of a physiological or psychological mechanism is incomplete if it does not explain how the mechanism is adaptive, how it uses feedback, and how it maintains essential internal variables within acceptable limits. [Perhaps one reason the HACS view has been so long in coming is an apparent inadequacy with which we are not yet prepared to deal fully: the failure of HACS ideas to make lucid why and how behavior in adapting to a new situation so often results in a drastic change from the previous state. Here we are confronted with the paradox of stasis versus kinesis – that in order to maintain some things the same inside, it is necessary to change others drastically. Thus, a naked man turned outside on a cold day must run very fast (kinesis) in order to maintain his body temperature (stasis). This means we are dealing as much or more with a dynamic system (homeokinesis) as with a static (homeostasis) system (see Iberall and Cardon, 1969; Zeeman, 1976; Barnwell and Stafford, in press).]

In order to translate the generalities dealt with above into more concrete terms, we may make use of diagrams which summarize the HACS functions of the organism in the form of information flow diagrams. Although over-simplified, these diagrams can be thought of as specifying the relationship between the organism and the environment (Fig. 1.2) and between the designated components of the organism as well (Fig. 1.3). (In control system terminology, this is saying that the diagrams are homomorphic with the organism and the environment.) Each box in the diagrams represents a particular system, and each

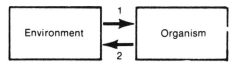

Figure 1.2. Block diagram of the relationship between the organism and the environment. Channel 1 represents the flow of information from the environment to the organism and Channel 2 represents the flow of information from the organism to the environment. This diagram is homomorphic with Figure 1.3.

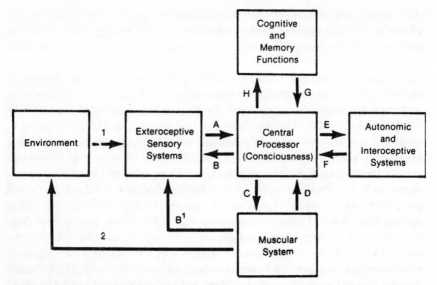

Figure 1.3. Simplified block diagram of the components of the homeostatic adaptive control system. See text for description of Channels A through H.

arrow represents the communication channels between two systems. Since all organs of the body may be put in one or another of the boxes as appropriate, the diagram is complete. The most important parts of the diagrams, from the view of the HACS, are the arrows, which represent channels which communicate information between the various components. At a gross level of analysis, it can be appreciated that any one channel—for example, the channel carrying information from the sensory systems to the central processor—may vary greatly in what it carries. Thus, if one is sitting in a quiet room with one's eyes shut, the channel from the sensory system is carrying relatively little visual and auditory information to the brain compared to its activity while watching television, in which a great deal of visual and auditory information must be transmitted.

Although it has long been appreciated that purely physiological systems, such as the heart-lungs-blood-tissue system, are in a state of dynamic equilibrium, it is less familiar to impose upon ourselves the idea that the same must also be true of the information-processing system just described (Fischer, 1971). This is, however, the demand placed by logic. This requires that we imagine each box (with its component subsystems) to have particular rates of input and output of information with particular compositions which must somehow or other result in the system as a whole being adaptive, being in homeostatic equilibrium, and being able to exert appropriate control. These unfamiliar strictures will be utilized below.

§1.11 State and Transformation. Having stated the idea of a balance within the HACS diagrammed, it becomes possible to carry the analysis a bit further and to consider two additional descriptors of the system — state and transformation. The first of these — state — is taken to be the momentary state of the system, with the moment being appropriately long enough to define a particular state but not so long as to encompass change of state. [Here again, we simplify as we skip over the way in which hierarchically higher units of behavior which require longer times for completion can be designated as states occupying increasing lengths of time (see Sec. 2.27 and Chap. 4).] The concept of state is elaborated by Ashby (1963), who has shown how the state of a determinate system can be defined by knowing the last value of each variable of the system, plus the last increment of input to the system. This means that at any moment, the state of our HACS is defined by the values of the variables in the boxes, plus the value of the information just received over the arrows. (Again, simplifying, we assume the organism is a determinate system because there is enough truth in the assumption so that we may take advantage of it.) While recognizing that the power of this particular idealized situation is not matched by our knowledge of any organism at any moment, we may, nonetheless, hold onto the method of analysis because of what it will provide for us later.

Once knowing the state of the HACS and the value of the new input, we are able to identify what the new state will be. The process of reaching the mental state is transformation — the going from one state to another. In a broad sense, the history of the HACS is a chain of states — S_1 S_2 S_3 . . . S_n — with the change from one state to the next being the transformations — STSTST. . . . Merely noting that sometimes the transformation may be from a particular state to the same state allows for a flexible notational system covering enduring states as well as constantly changing ones.

We have now arrived at a basis for representing the behavior of an organism as a chain of psychophysiological states with the changes between states being represented by transformations. Any particular state may be defined by the process of designating the values of the variables of the systems in the boxes and the nature of the information in the arrows representing information channels between the boxes.

Having identified the HACS in a state of dynamic equilibrium as one frame of reference describing an organism, and the chain of states and transformations as another frame of reference with a different perspective, we are now in a position to go back and examine the components of the HACS a bit more closely. Our method will be that of defining the control links or information channels, as shown in Figures 1.2 and 1.3, with the description of the subsystems joined by the channels being implied in the definitions.

§1.12 **Environmental Influences (Channel 1, Figs. 1.2 and 1.3).** These involve everything in the environment which impinges upon the organism, whether primarily as energy or as information. Seeing and hearing a fire engine drive by is primarily an informational issue even though the information is transmitted by the energy of light and sound. Although for the most part the environment impinges as information as diagrammed, there are, of course, also the impingements as energy per se. Thus, the jet airliner carrying a man from Chicago to New York or the brickbat knocking another man unconscious have energic properties which transcend their informational content. We will only concern ourselves with the impingement of the environment as energy carrying information, however, and it is, of course, the purpose of the exteroceptive sensory systems to convey this information.

§1.13 **Sensory Input Channel (Channel A, Fig. 1.3).** A major determinant of the content of the sensory input channels is the impinging environment. If nothing is "there," little is transmitted, and if too much is "there," it may be nearly impossible to turn it off. Since the sensory systems are interposed between the environment and the central nervous system, these channels only convey from the external environment that to which the sensors are capable of responding.

§1.14 **Sensory Input Feedback Channels (Channels B and B¹, Fig. 1.3).** Feedback mechanisms to control sensory input are now being studied at the neurophysiological level (Gaarder, 1975). One manifestation of these mechanisms is the capacity to focus attention selectively from one sensory modality to another and to attend selectively within a particular modality to a particular part of the environment. Thus, a person fixating his gaze on a point is nevertheless able to attend selectively to one or another quadrant of his vision or centrally or peripherally, as he chooses.

§1.15 **Muscle Effector Channel (Channel C, Fig. 1.3).** The commands of the brain to the muscular system are carried over this channel. An example of differences in *quantity* of information transmitted over a channel is provided by comparing the activity of muscle nerves while relaxing versus the activity during motor tasks. An example of differences in *quality* of information transmitted over a channel is provided by the enormous difference in requirement for complex control between maintaining posture and tonus with the expenditure of considerable energy versus the expenditure of the same amount of energy in a highly complex motor task where the information must be contained in a more complex structure. Thus, standing stiffly at attention might expend the same energy as playing the violin, and although the quantity of nerve impulses is identical, the quality and complexity would be higher in the latter. To understand an extreme degree of inactivity, it should be recalled that no muscle nerve firing at all is possible, contrary to old notions of constant tonic firing (Basmajian, 1974).

§1.16 Feedback to the Environment and Effector of the Environment (Channel 2, Figs. 1.2 and 1.3). Once the commands to the muscular system are transformed by the muscles into muscular actions, they then impinge upon the environment as information (e.g., in speech and gestures) or as energy (e.g., in moving an object). Our diagrams show concretely the often unappreciated truth that almost the only output of the brain to the world is muscle movement, which is power amplified and therefore apt to be disjunctive. Certainly, there is much to ponder and reflect upon in this and in the simple observation that the awake human rarely fails to make movements several times a minute.

§1.17 Muscle Feedback Channel (Channel D, Fig. 1.3). Channels for the feedback of muscle performance exist in proprioceptive fibers in muscle, as well as in other interoceptive and exteroceptive receptors which reflect what the muscle has done. An example of how this operates is provided by the so-called stretch reflex. By passively flexing a joint so as to stretch a muscle, muscle firing can be elicited in the muscle. This means that a positive feedback has been established, since increased tension on the muscle is signalled centrally, causing the central nervous system to "order" a still further increase in the tension by muscular contraction. An example of change of state is provided by the decoupling of the muscle feedback so that during sleep or deep relaxation no such reflex contraction occurs.

§1.18 Autonomic Effector Channel (Channel E, Fig. 1.3). Central control of various autonomic functions is exerted through the autonomic control channels. Thus, heart rate, skin temperature, gut motility, tear secretion, pupillary response, and other autonomic functions are regulated. Since there are both sympathetic (ergotrophic) and parasympathetic (trophotrophic) systems, there are often *two* channels of control to an organ rather than just the one pictured. As the term *autonomic* indicates, there is also a great deal of autonomous or local control of these functions as well.

§1.19 Interoceptive and Autonomic Feedback Channel (Channel F, Fig. 1.3). These are the nervous channels which convey information about the state of visceral functions to the central nervous system. Although these channels are well known from experimental evidence, they do not for the most part directly impinge upon consciousness. Evidence from autogenic training (Schultz and Luthe, 1959), yogic training (Koestler, 1961), operant studies (Miller, 1969), and the Soviet literature (Razran, 1961), however, makes it appear that this is because of a lack of discriminative learning and not because of an intrinsic incapacity to perceive visceral function.

§1.20 Central Nervous System Information Flow Channels (Channels G and H, Fig. 1.3). In diagramming the HACS, certain arbitrary distinctions have been made. Thus, analogy to current computer technology has led to designating a "central processor" to carry out the major functions of the central nervous system. At the same time, the content of the stream of consciousness elaborated by William James (1960) is highly reflective of a part of the functioning of a central processor. Because of the capacity of the stream of consciousness to vary in its cognitive and mnemonic contents and because of the alternation of these contents with sensory and motor contents in the shifting of attention, we have placed the cognitive and mnemonic functions in a separate system with connecting links to the central processor. Thus, Channel H represents the command of the central processor calling for cognitive and mnemonic activity and Channel G represents the elicited cognitive or mnemonic material presented for central processing and is associated with consciousness of thought or memory.

CONTROL OF INPUT

§1.21 Introduction. Having proceeded from the recognition of a HACS to the acknowledgment of momentary states of the HACS and transformations between those states, our next task is to show how psychophysiological state and state of consciousness are defined by and controlled by the information channels between the subsystems in the boxes of Figure 1.3. Ashby (1963) has shown in his "law of experience" how a system can be brought to a desired state by controlling the input over a sequence of particular steps (i.e., through several states and transformations). By simply using a chain of input steps (i.e., controlling the information channel in a particular way) we can, therefore, bring any particular subsystem to the state we wish, and we may ignore concern for the particular state of the subsystem from which we start. Thus, we may concentrate on control of the information channels (input parameters to a particular component) as the major mechanism in control of state. We will show how unique psychophysiological states can be created by the control of the input parameters of the subsystems (Secs. 1.22–1.34).

Although Ashby has given proof of his law of experience, we will merely provide examples to illustrate the law without demonstrating proof. We will first give examples in which a single channel is altered and discuss the effect of this upon the state of the organism. Later, we will see that more than one channel is always affected, when examples of complex change of channels to achieve change of state are given. One reason that all channels are always affected is that we are dealing with a homeostatic system where changing one variable has far reaching effects on most other variables.

§1.22 Control of Sensory Input (Channel 1 and Channel A). The extensive literature on sensory deprivation is concerned with methods which reduce the input to the exteroceptive sensory systems (Channel 1) and thereby reduce the output of these systems (Channel A) to the central nervous system. The profound effects of this upon the psychophysiological state and the state of consciousness have been well documented (Ludwig, 1966; Rasmussen, 1973).

A less known method of reducing exteroceptive sensory input is through the use of a drug [phencyclidine (Serny)] which has a specific blocking effect on the thalamic nuclei, where sensory input (Channel A) is received by the central processor. Again, a profound alteration of the state of consciousness is produced (Bakker and Amini, 1961). Another method of controlling exteroceptive sensory input is by sensory overload, where all modalities are maximally stimulated. An example of this would be the so-called psychedelic environment where flashing colored lights and loud rock music bombard the senses. Ashby's law of experience is operative when trance-like states are produced with stereotyped rhythms which absorb the mind.

§1.23 Control of Sensory Feedback (Channel B). Thus far, the examples have controlled sensory input by controlling the external environment to provide specific input or by controlling the input channel capacity by drug blockage. Another method of controlling sensory input is by controlling the feedback to the sensory system. One example is selecting the content of the visual world by means of the feedback of eye movements (Gaarder, 1975). Thus, in order to absorb the sensory input of a printed page, one must engage in a highly programmed feedback activity of scanning the page with eye jumps and fixations. Without the use of this feedback control, the structured input cannot exist. Further examples are provided by selectively attending to or excluding areas of the visual environment. Thus, shown a nude, some people look at, and others look away from, the genital areas. Feedback control is involved in the focusing of attention on sensory modalities or within sensory modalities, although the linkages have not yet been worked out. Thus, the capacity of the human to hear one speaker selectively at a cocktail party where there are others speaking more loudly is certainly mediated by feedback mechanisms. What is not generally recognized, however, is that by using sensory feedback in this particular way, a person is altering the balance of information flow so as to produce a particular unique psychophysiological state.

§1.24 Control of Muscle Tension (Channel C). The range of issues in the control of muscle tension extends from the use of the muscular system for complex motor tasks, includes the use of muscle tension in the maintenance of character armor (Reich, 1949; Braatoy, 1954), and reaches to the achievement of (nearly) total relaxation in Jacobson's (1938) deep muscle relaxation therapy as practiced by himself and those modifying his efforts (Whatmore and Kohli, 1974), and to the total muscle relaxation universally achieved in sleep. Basmajian (1974) finds that total muscle relaxation with no muscle bundle firing in a particular muscle is indeed possible and does occur, and that single muscle units can be taught to fire selectively, thus showing ideals of no activity and of precise control of activity of anatomical units.

It is worthwhile to point out again that a specific behavioral state is a unique state of psychophysiological organization: e.g., that the state of executing a highly complex motor task (such as a quarterback carrying out a football play or a tennis player returning a ball) is uniquely different from all of the other states to which we refer. In particular, we can describe Channel C during complex motor tasks as having a large informational content and a low entropy (i.e., a high degree of organization). In other words, a complex motor task is programmed from a large set of alternative possibilities in its own specific way.

Reich (1949) and Braatoy (1954) have shown how some individuals virtually live their lives within a particular state of muscle tension commonly involving specific rigidity of postural tone and facial expression. Murphy and Leeds (1975) also review how muscle tension chronically inhibits the flood of painful memories which return if the individual relaxes. Thus, in these individuals, we see two distinct states — "before" and "after." Before the relaxation the memories are not accessible to consciousness, and after relaxing a psychological reorganization takes place.

Jacobson (1938), Schultz and Luthe (1959), Wolpe (1973), and Whatmore and Kohli (1974), using various frames of reference, have endorsed the beneficial effects of deep muscle relaxation and have arrived at an empirically valid finding which may someday be recognized as of the highest importance. This is the fact that anxiety cannot exist in the presence of deep muscle relaxation. Thus, minimal activity of Channels C and D precludes the existence of anxiety, and empirical treatment of anxiety consists of simply reducing muscle tension. This appears to be a stable cornerstone upon which important neurophysiological and therapeutic structures can be built.

Sleep is the other state in which complete muscle relaxation is achieved and is readily seen to be a unique psychophysiological state with its own unique organization. Many interesting transformations are regularly programmed — the change from waking to sleeping state and the changes from one state to another within sleep — i.e., from one stage of sleep to another. It is good to remind ourselves that the adaptive function of sleep is not yet known (Gaarder, 1966).

§1.25 Control of Muscle Feedback (Channel D). Although we have just dealt with the question of control of muscle tension, we have done so by the oversimplification of ignoring that one of the most potent methods of controlling muscle tension utilizes the monitoring of proprioceptive feedback from the muscular system. Self-observation and the findings of Jacobson and others imply that the reason we are not able to control muscle tension is that we are not able to recognize it. This is an example of the "great truism of information theory"—that a variable cannot be controlled unless information about it is available to the controller (Sec. 1.6). It means that one of the major functions of muscle relaxation training is the discriminative learning of the recognition of muscle tension level (Feldenkrais, 1949). Biofeedback techniques take advantage of this issue to provide another way of learning control more rapidly.

§1.26 Control of Autonomic Variables and Control of Interoceptive and Autonomic Feedback (Channels E and F). Apart from the biofeedback studies to be noted, artificially considering a single autonomic channel in isolation does not provide starkly simple examples of control such as those given above. Therefore, we will first consider both channels of the autonomic loop together. By the very token of these functions being autonomic—i.e., relatively automatic and involuntary—they tend to be outside of consciousness and, therefore, their feedback is not readily available to consciousness without discriminative training which most of us have forsworn. Likewise, because many of these automatic functions—such as cardiac-respiratory-vascular regulation and digestive regulation—must be carried on in one form or another regardless of other activity, and because their activity does not usually set the stage for the state of the organism as a whole as vividly as do sensory and motor activity, clear examples of domination of the organism by autonomic functioning are not seen. Even the autonomic aspects of sexual and excretory activities are closely related to the function of the organism as a whole.

Yogic control (Koestler, 1961) is a major instance of autonomic control which is being frequently verified by experimental observation, so that conscious voluntary control of heart rate, skin temperature, intestinal peristalsis, and so forth by trained yogis is now readily acknowledged.

Deranged control of autonomic variables as an operationally valid concept is also evident in such diseases as essential hypertension, where a useful understanding can begin by thinking of the disease as primarily a regulating mechanism somehow set at the wrong level (Secs. 1.36–1.37).

§1.27 Control of Cognitive and Mnemonic Variables and the Control of Their Feedback (Channels G and H). Because these variables are not yet available to direct observation through any agency other than introspective consciousness, not as much can be said of them as of the other systems. Also, as with the autonomic variables, we are now into the area in which the other systems can readily be made to dominate (for the moment, and in any single instance) this system by their activity. Thus, one may say with considerable confidence that no single line of poetry has ever been composed by a quarterback while getting a pass off to a receiver nor has any sprinter ever remembered anything outside the scope of his race while halfway down the track. These trite examples serve to illustrate the unappreciated truism that cognitive and mnemonic functions are highly dependent on the state of the sensory and muscular systems. Indeed, one can define as necessary for cognition and memory a lowering of sensory and motor activities below critical limits which would interfere too much.

§1.28 Control of State through Complex Control of Information Channels. By now the point has been well established that the earlier examples of control of state through control of a single channel are oversimplified and that in every instance the true nature of the situation is better defined by a specification of the information on all of the channels. In addition, it can be seen that some physiological variables which reflect overall activity, such as arousal level, are appropriately considered as being made up of an "average" of the activity in many of the channels. Thus, in high arousal such as fleeing an attack, many channels have a great deal of activity, in contrast to low arousal, such as in quiet relaxation, where most channels have little activity. Finally, some therapists consider control as a central issue of the treatment. This is especially true of behavior therapy (Bandura, 1969; Wolpe, 1973). We will now look at some examples of states where consideration of several channels is essential.

§1.29 Yogic Asanas. In the typical yogic asana (posture), particular muscle groups are placed under tension. This elicits the stretch reflex, which consists of: (1) the stretching of the muscle through assuming a particular posture; (2) the feedback proprioceptive signal of the stretch (Channel D); (3) the central processing of this information; and (4) the "reflex" of muscle nerve firing in the same group, resulting in muscle activity in that group (Channel C). Thus, the asana has an alerting effect through the effect of this cycle of activity on the reticular activating system.

§1.30 Yogic or Zen Meditation. Meditation not only has the effects of the meditative asana just discussed, but in addition, the sensory system (Channel A) is put into a state of relative deprivation and stereotypy by being in a quiet calm environment and by using sensory feedback control (Channel B) to focus on a single potential input in a single way.

Furthermore, cognitive and mnemonic functions are consciously controlled by voluntarily limiting the content of thought, usually in a stereotyped way.

§1.31 Yogic Autonomic Control. Once all of the above preconditions are fulfilled, it appears possible to focus the attention consciously upon a specific autonomic function and thereby gain control of it (Koestler, 1961; Tart, 1969). The fact that lack of training makes these things virtually impossible for most of us should not keep us from acknowledging their reality in others.

§1.32 Free Associative State. It is by now obvious that any mental state has a unique psychophysiological state accompanying it, which can be fairly well defined by defining the content of the information channels. This is true of the psychoanalytic free associative state. Thus, Braatoy's (1954) work on muscle relaxation as a precondition for recall of painful memory defines the content of the channels to and from the muscular system (Channels C and D) and the quiet, softly lit room (Channel 1) helps to determine the sensory input (Channel A). The defining characteristic of the free associative state would be ready availability of free floating thought and memory (Channels G and H), but it is apparent that it cannot be achieved without first controlling the muscular and sensory systems.

§1.33 Control of State through Biofeedback. Most of this book is concerned with another method of gaining further control of the state of the organism, which is to provide an external artificial feedback channel by measuring a particular psychophysiological variable and providing information about the variable to the organism (Secs. 1.38–1.41).

§1.34 Further Concepts Implied by the HACS Model. Our study so far has put us on the verge of dealing with some other concepts which we will now only briefly mention. These concepts form much of the basis for the later consideration of structure (Secs. 2.24–2.27; Chap. 4). These concepts have to do with: (1) the time duration of a state, with the definition chosen determining whether one is dealing with a time domain of the order of a "moment" (Harter, 1967; Gaarder, 1975) or of higher units of time; (2) the hierarchy of time-defined units becoming informational units (Sec. 2.26) in a way analogous to the informational hierarchical structuring of language into *letters-words-sentences* (Polanyi, 1968; Gaarder, 1975); (3) the programming of these units into chains with algorithmic structure (Sec. 2.25); and (4) the structure of these informational-behavioral chains as action cycles (Secs. 4.2–4.12).

HOMEOSTASIS IN HEALTH AND DISEASE

§1.35 Disease as Deranged Homeostasis. In all instances which come to mind, disease conditions can be defined by the fact that some homeostatic mechanism is deranged. Most often, this will mean that the values of physiological measures are outside of their normal limits. Thus, hypertension is diagnosed when blood pressure is above certain limits and stroke results in it being impossible to send nerve impulses down a motor nerve and to receive proprioceptive information about the effectors. These examples both have to do with variables we can try to control with biofeedback. There are also countless other instances of disease where a quantitative variable is outside of its normal limits, but where the variable is not suitable to use as a feedback parameter. Simple examples are elevated white blood cell counts in infections and elevated blood sugars in diabetes. Qualitative variables are also abnormal in other conditions – the heart sounds in valvular disease and the thought content in schizophrenia.

We should not lose sight of the fact that we are dealing with a situation which is circularly defined. Thus, for there to be disease, there must be sign of disease, and if there is sign of disease, there must be disease. However, the concept of normal homeostasis defines the limits of normal variation, whereas deranged homeostasis is indicated by excessive variation of physiological and psychological variables which defines illness.

Although derangement of homeostasis always defines disease, only part of the time does it define the cause of disease, and likewise, correction of the derangement only part of the time cures the disease. There are other instances where the deranged homeostasis which we detect is a secondary effect of the illness and where its correction does not cure.

§1.36 **Stress as a Cause of Derangement.** By reconsideration of how the homeostatic balance of a system is maintained (Sec. 1.10), we can see that external environmental stress, which can sometimes be considered too much or too little environmental stimulation, will lead to changing the values of various homeostatically mediated physiological parameters beyond their normal limits. Also, when the stress becomes chronic, the homeostatic mechanism can "reset" itself at the new, abnormal value and remain there even after the stress is removed.

§1.37 **Nature of Stresses.** When individual disease conditions are studied, especially the psychosomatic conditions, the role of stress in the preconditions leading to the disease is widely recognized (Kiritz and Moos, 1974; M. T. Singer, 1974; Benson, 1975). Thus, in peptic ulcer, arthritis, hypertension, diabetes, migraine, and tension headaches, examination has uniformly led to the recognition of stress as a pre-condition for the emergence of the disease.

Holmes' group (Holmes and Rahe, 1967) have reversed this sequence of inquiry by determining major life events and noting the incidence of illness in relation to them. They list all of the major life events which can occur in a person's life and then note the occurrence of illness in relationship to them. These life events include such things as graduation from college, taking a new job, getting married, having a child born, losing a job, getting divorced, losing a parent, etc. They found a much higher incidence of illness at the time of these events, compared to times when the individual's life was relatively more quiet. Surprisingly, they found that events which are usually considered "happy" or positive, such as the birth of a child or getting a new job, contributed almost as much to the likelihood of disease emerging as the obviously negative events such as being fired from a job. Other studies show that certain kinds of ubiquitous stresses, such as environmental noise, also contribute to the pre-conditions of disease.

BIOFEEDBACK AS DIRECT IMPINGEMENT ON HOMEOSTASIS

§1.38 **Re-Examination of the Concept of Biofeedback.** The things we have considered thus far allow us to look once more at the concept of biofeedback and see it in relationship to the patient who might use it. We have examined the concept of feedback and covered the concept of homeostasis, which is based upon internal feedback mechanisms of the organism, and finally we have seen how disease can be thought of as involving the derangement of homeostatic feedback mechanisms and how treatment may consist of correcting the deranged homeostasis.

Biofeedback can be conceived as a way of imposing an additional external feedback loop upon the already existing feedback loops of the homeostatic adaptive control system. This is a parallel channel (see Fig. 1.6). The principle of external feedback may be understood concretely by referring to Figure 1.4. Here is shown the homeostatic adaptive control system of the body with the crucial addition (designated by the heavy arrows) of feedback loops completed between an internal process and the sensory input system. Thus, Channel 1 completes the loop between the central nervous system and sensory input by means of EEG while Channels 2 and 3 complete feedback loops with the muscular and autonomic systems, respectively, as described next. Each of these heavy arrows should be considered separately as if the other two were not there. Each of the three heavy arrows, therefore, represents a biofeedback channel which feeds back information about the system from which it originates. Assume that the biofeedback channel is a unit consisting of physiological transducer, amplifier, signal-reducing element, and signal display as described in the next paragraph. Channel 1, conveying information from the central nervous system, could be feedback of the EEG, such as alpha rhythm. Channel 2, conveying information from the muscular system, could be feedback of frontalis EMG.

Channel 3, conveying information from the autonomic and enteroceptive systems, could be feedback of heart rate or skin temperature.

Typically, a biofeedback system consists of these elements: *transducer, amplifier, signal reducer,* and *signal display* (Fig. 1.5). A *trans-*

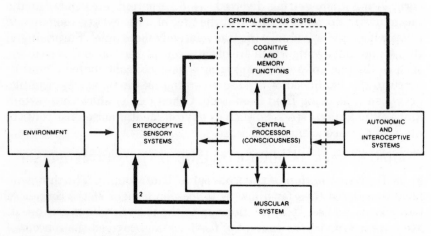

Figure 1.4. Psychophysiological feedback. Three examples of closing feedback loops are shown by the heavy arrows superimposed upon the homeostatic adaptive control system diagram. In each instance, it is assumed that the heavy arrow represents a unit consisting of physiological transducer, amplifier, signal-reducing element, and signal display. Channel 1, feedback of the EEG; Channel 2, feedback of the EMG; Channel 3, autonomic feedback, such as heart rate or skin temperature.

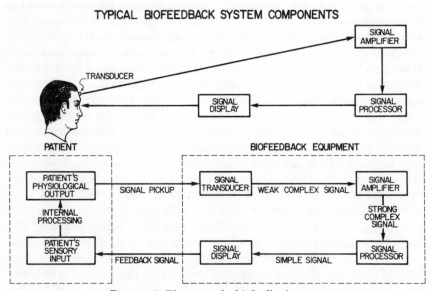

Figure 1.5. Elements of a biofeedback system.

ducer is something which receives signals from a patient and converts them into a form measurable by instruments. Examples are skin electrodes or a temperature probe. The *amplifier* converts the electric signal into an electrically manageable quantity by amplifying it. The *signal reducer* then extracts some part of the information conveyed in the signal and "filters out" and discards the rest of the information not needed. Finally, the *signal display* converts the energy of the reduced signal into some form of stimulus or varying sensation available to the subject, such as a variable light or a variable sound.

Obviously, the biofeedback system is a feedback to the subject who produces the original signals being fed back. In other words, a subject or patient – to produce the original signals, to perceive the feedback, and to react to the feedback – is the essential reason for needing the biofeedback system in the first place, and the subject completes the feedback loop.

§1.39 Biofeedback Directly Effecting a Psychophysiological Variable. From the above description, it is easy to visualize the most obvious therapeutic use of biofeedback – to use it to measure a psychophysiological variable which is related to the cause of a particular disease in order to enable a patient to learn to change the variable in the desired direction and thereby relieve the condition (see Sec. 3.11). If there is a defective, undeveloped, or non-existent internal channel, the biofeedback provides a parallel channel (Fig. 1.6).

Such is the case in the use of blood pressure biofeedback to treat essential hypertension. There is now widespread agreement that the damage done by the disease of hypertension is due to the elevated blood pressure and that lowering the blood pressure prevents the damage. Therefore, if patients are able to learn through biofeedback to lower their blood pressure, they are protected from the damage they otherwise would face. There are other instances in which it is or will become possible to measure physiological variables directly related to diseases and train the patient to control the variable in the desired direction. Prominent among them are cardiac arrhythmias and sphincter dysfunctions, and Engel (1975) has been one of the principal investigators pursuing the treatment of these directly involved variables.

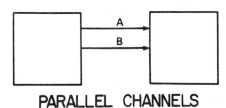

PARALLEL CHANNELS

Figure 1.6. Block diagram of parallel channels.

§1.40 **Stress Relief through Biofeedback.** Earlier (Secs. 1.35–1.37), we examined the fact that stress in the form of environmental overstimulation can lead to disease states resulting from and characterized by hyperarousal. This can best be conceptualized by considering the HACS as chronically having to process excessive quantities of information over its various channels and the treatment is obviously to reduce the amount of information chronically in transit. Such a conceptualization fits well with the clinical syndrome of chronic anxiety, which is accompanied by generalized hyperarousal. It also describes some more localized syndromes such as tension headaches, where the scalp muscles contract more than necessary, with accompanying pain from the excess muscle activity leading to overactivity of the proprioceptive feedback as well. Benson's (1975) description of the "relaxation response" provides a lucid answer to the problem presented.

Furthermore, it is obvious that biofeedback adds an additional dimension to the treatment of these conditions, because the patient does not have to rely solely upon his own perception of his state of relaxation, but can have immediate, objective, inescapable, easily discriminable information in the form of a feedback signal such as EMG muscle tension readings or finger temperature.

§1.41 **Control Systems Analysis of Biofeedback Procedures.** Here we have briefly and superficially examined the impingement of some biofeedback treatments upon the deranged homeostatic adaptive control system of diseased conditions. In doing so, we have superficially utilized some control system principles (see Chap. 9). However, at the present time, more sophisticated control systems analysis of biofeedback treatment is only beginning. A few examples are in the work of Mulholland (1976), Pope and Gersten (1975), and Brudny et al. (1974b), in which consideration is given to such questions as conceptualizing circuit diagrams, evaluating feedback loop gain, compensating for broken internal loops, allowing for time lags, and estimating the information content of signals. We have found that effective clinical practice is possible without better understanding of these issues and we will not explore them further here. However, it is good to recognize that the future development of biofeedback may depend in large part on how our understanding of control systems progresses.

BIOFEEDBACK AS THERAPEUTIC METHOD

§1.42 **Introduction.** Any therapeutic method must be understood and evaluated in terms of several frames of reference, including: (1) the general science of therapeutics (Sec. 1.43); (2) the pathophysiology of the condition treated (Sec. 1.44); (3) the special consideration of a particular technique (Sec. 1.45); (4) the overall evidence of the efficacy of the method (Sec. 1.46); (5) the piecemeal evidence of the efficacy of a treatment component (Sec. 1.47); (6) practical considerations of the use of the overall method (Sec. 1.48). Each of these will be considered in turn in this section.

§1.43 **General Science of Therapeutics.** For the intellectual mastery of a process to be considered scientific, a minimum requirement is that the process be rigorously described, with its regularities and invariances substantiated and its exceptions and variations noted. Such is barely the case for the general science of therapeutics, which covers all things done for the hopeful benefit of patients (Modell, 1955). Part of the reason for this lack of development is the fact that there is such diversity in the conditions treated and the therapeutic actions undertaken. Thus, within conventional medicine, the spectrum covered includes a plethora of drugs with specific actions upon a host of conditions. Furthermore, there are diverse surgical methods, from the lancing of boils through cardiac valve replacement, often with a highly particular and well reasoned alteration affecting some specific function. Then there are multiple physical methods ranging from the application of heat, cold, or various radiations through massage, manipulation, and exercise. Finally, psychotherapeutic methods with divergent rationales use a wide range of interpersonal techniques to influence patients, and it is widely agreed that all of the just listed techniques require effective interpersonal management within the framework of the therapeutic method to be effective (Strupp, 1973). It is small wonder that a general science of therapeutics is so rudimentary.

Such a science must be based upon general laws of process. This means that certain things must be known of the condition treated and of the treatment, including the expected natural history of the condition treated (Feinstein, 1967), the expected effect of the treatment upon the condition, and means of observing the actual effect. Also, as a general proposition, it must be expected that any treatment has a particular cost relative to the resources of the person or organism treated, including economic cost, cost of time, and cost in terms of undesirable or unexpected side effects of the treatment. Implicit in all of the above is the concept of any treatment as a unitary algorithm within time. In other words, every treatment has a beginning, a middle, and an end which must be transversed in the correct order to expect good results—the various elements of the treatment must be applied in the proper sequence to achieve the desired end (see Secs. 2.24–2.26; Chap. 4).

All of the above considerations apply to biofeedback and will be dealt with later in considerable detail. The single most crucial of the above is the ability of any particular technique to cause or lead to change. Change of the condition treated is the ultimate goal, although at times the therapist will settle for the moment for substantial change in another system which eventually leads back to change of the condition treated. Next in importance is recognizing the importance of the therapeutic relationship (see Chap. 2), and third would be the importance of recognizing the algorithmic structure (see Chap. 4) of treatment.

§1.44 Pathophysiology of the Condition Treated. Whenever a particular condition is to be treated, there must be a detailed elaboration of what is known about the condition (Feinstein, 1967). Sometimes this knowledge is complete enough to suggest a desirable path of treatment clearly, while sometimes therapeutic rationales develop empirically.

§1.45 Special Consideration of a Particular Technique. The therapeutic method of biofeedback is based upon the concrete provision of otherwise unavailable information, following Ashby's laws of requisite variety (Ashby, 1963) (see Sec. 1.6). The treatment of any particular condition may either provide information directly related to the condition or information about another physiological parameter indirectly related to the condition (see Sec. 3.11). Furthermore, as explained above, particular techniques are constrained on the one hand by the general laws of control systems which partly determine the effect of a particular feedback and on the other by the laws of behavior which determine how the information provided is used by the organism in a particular instance.

§1.46 Overall Evidence of the Efficacy of a Method. A particular method of therapy must prove useful according to a number of criteria, including primarily how much the undesired effects of the treated condition are removed, how permanent is the removal, how difficult it is to remove and keep away the treated condition, what are the cost and side effects of treatment, and similar questions.

§1.47 Piecemeal Evidence of the Efficacy of a Treatment Component. Measuring therapeutic effectiveness is extremely difficult because of a justifiable therapeutic pressure toward the differentiation of a treatment method into different components. Thus, it is uncommon to find a well designed therapy which has a single component—rather, the overwhelming likelihood is that a particular method will consist of a number of components which must be correctly combined in the proper sequence to be most effective. When such is the state of affairs, one of the most common questions to arise is whether or not a particular component plays a significant role in the effect of the method. We know that often something is done as *part* of an effective treatment which does, in fact, not actually contribute to the effectiveness of the treatment—i.e., if eliminated, the treatment would still work. The contribution of the experimental method at this point may be to demonstrate whether or not a particular component of treatment is capable of a particular limited effect—i.e., whether it causes a particular change. It must be recognized that the answer to this limited question usually does not illuminate the previous question of the overall efficacy of treatment. Examples of this issue abound in the biofeedback literature. An instance is in the study of blood pressure control by biofeedback. The overall question may be whether biofeedback can usefully help a patient with essential hypertension to keep his blood pressure down. This is a large question requiring answers to such issues as whether the blood pressure remains down between treatment sessions and whether it remains down for a reasonable period after treatment is terminated. A piecemeal question may involve precise information about whether a patient is able to use feedback information reliably to raise or lower blood pressure during a training trial.

Evidence concerning a method is made of a composite of these piecemeal bits of information with more holistic data about the whole treatment method. Rarely is a complete picture of evidence available. Rather, there are almost inevitably huge gaps in the information which must be bridged by inference.

Since the treatment methods consist of several components, there is the inevitable need to decide how much each component contributes to the success of the method. The particular component of the interpersonal therapeutic relationship is especially complex, because of the diversity of qualities which may be contributing (see Chap. 2). Thus, the therapist's conveying personal qualities of trustworthiness, competence, empathy, authority, mastery, certainty, comprehension, concern, flexibility, and watchfulness—to mention but a few—have an enormous effect upon treatment which is difficult to quantify. In addition, these qualities or their lack are also easily attributed by the patient to certain actions of the therapist. For example, if the therapist must follow the rigid and apparently meaningless sequence of procedures of a research protocol unrelated to the particular case, the patient will likely question the therapist's qualities of trustworthiness, competence, and flexibility. Likewise, if a therapist is detached, the patient will doubt empathy, concern, and watchfulness. If a procedure enlists the patient's aid, it may be well accepted, whereas if it ignores the patient's needs, it may have a negative impact upon treatment.

§1.48 **Practical Considerations of an Overall Method.** Whether a particular method is worth using depends on a range of practical questions of scope beyond those already considered. These include whether the method can be taught to others, whether patients are willing to use it, whether a better method is available, whether the time and effort are commensurate with the gain achieved, how the method fits with the rest of the practice of the therapist, whether insurance covers the treatment, and many others. Biofeedback methods must be judged within the framework of these questions as well.

§1.49 **Summary.** This chapter has examined the scientific foundation of biofeedback as an idea whose time has arrived. The concrete concept of feedback is largely derived from engineering and has become widely understood since World War II (Sec. 1.1). Biological homeostasis is largely mediated by internal feedback mechanisms and biological feedback mechanisms lead naturally to the idea of external psychophysiological feedback (biofeedback). The history of biofeedback is briefly considered (Secs. 1.2–1.4) and the background in current control theory is reviewed (Secs. 1.5–1.8).

Homeostatic adaptive control systems are next examined at some length with emphasis upon specific channels (Secs. 1.9–1.20). Then, it is shown how the state of the organism can be controlled by the information flow in these specific channels (Secs. 1.21–1.34). When this perspective is taken, disease can be seen as deranged homeostasis (Secs. 1.35–1.37). Biofeedback has its power because it can teach people to affect the homeostatic level of psychophysiological variables directly (Secs. 1.38–1.41). The use of biofeedback as a therapeutic method is then examined from the frame of reference of therapeutics (Secs. 1.42–1.43) and the special facts of the particular situation encountered (Secs. 1.44–1.48).

*One of the essential qualities of the clinician is interest in humanity,
for the secret of the care of the patient is in caring for the patient.*

> Francis Weld Peabody
> The Care of the Patient

*You can cultivate the disposition, and it will work its way through to
the surface, — nay, more, — you can try to wear a quiet and encouraging
look, and it will react on your disposition and make you like what you
seem to be, or at least bring you near to its own likeness.*

> Oliver Wendell Holmes
> "The Young Practitioner," Medical Essays

*To see another human being with any understanding involves a
relationship, and into this relationship our feelings will inevitably
enter. The important thing is for us to try to become aware of our
feelings, and when they are so intense that they cloud or distort our
judgment or lead us into blunders, we must try to face ourselves
squarely and look for the trouble spots there.*

> Carl Binger
> Harper's Magazine

*Make it a rule never to be angry at anything a sick man says or does to
you. Sickness often adds to the natural irritability of the temper. We,
therefore, bear the reproaches of our patients with meekness and silence.*

> Benjamin Rush

CHAPTER 2

The therapeutic relationship in biofeedback treatment

§2.1 Introduction. This chapter will focus upon the therapeutic relationship which must be cultivated in furthering the work of biofeedback treatment. This is done in five major sections. The therapeutic relationship (Secs. 2.2–2.7) is first described as a distinct entity. Next, the therapeutic contract (Secs. 2.8–2.19) is added as a major vehicle of the relationship and the work of the relationship. Biofeedback in the therapeutic relationship (Secs. 2.20–2.21) can then be considered as one of the unique components of biofeedback treatment, with non-biofeedback procedures (Secs. 2.22–2.23) being the other. Finally, another frame of reference for understanding the therapeutic relationship is provided by the introduction of the concept of structure (Secs. 2.24–2.27).

§2.2 Establishing the Patient-Therapist Relationship. In all forms of therapy, it is widely recognized that treatment will not do well unless careful attention is paid to the relationship between patient and therapist (Houston, 1938; Watzlawick, et al., 1967; Strupp, 1973; Bowden and Burstein, 1974). Extensive experience in our own clinic and in the work of other biofeedback therapists has found this equally true in biofeedback treatment. In almost every instance, this relationship will be a crucial determinant of the success of treatment. There are cases of patients who are unusually stable, self-directed, and motivated toward treatment who will do well without any particular attention being paid to the relationship. Usually, however, the therapist's best tool is the careful use of the relationship with the patient. First of all, we will describe this relationship in terms of some of its qualities. However, a fuller understanding of the relationship also requires consideration of the therapeutic contract, the place of biofeedback in the relationship, the non-biofeedback procedures, and the concept of structure.

§2.3 Terminology of Professional Roles. An important first issue is to determine who is carrying out treatment with the patient. Because biofeedback is a new field and professional roles are not yet firmly established by custom, terminology to describe these roles will vary from one setting to another. We use the following terms, but recognize they may be used differently elsewhere.

Practitioner. This is the physician, psychologist, or other professional with an advanced degree and training who is responsible for the overall biofeedback treatment of the patient. The practitioner is licensed to practice if in private practice, and if practicing in an institutional setting licensed as required and delegated the responsibility for overall biofeedback treatment of patients.

Biofeedback therapist. This is someone whose training and experience have been extensive enough so that he can work independently and largely autonomously with patients when delegated this responsibility by the practitioner. The practitioner is available for consultation when special situations warrant and will evaluate the patient for treatment, but most of the time the biofeedback therapist will see the patient for treatment without continuous consultation. The biofeedback therapist will usually have at least several years of experience with both biofeedback and other psychotherapeutic techniques.

Biofeedback technician. This is someone who has been trained in the techniques of biofeedback therapy, but who does not have the experience to be able to work independently and autonomously with patients. In his work he is closely supervised by the practitioner or an experienced biofeedback therapist. There will be some contact with the supervisor about each treatment session and the supervisor will have a good overview of what is happening in the treatment.

Therapist. We use the general term *therapist* to designate any of the above persons in their role of working with the patient. When used without the specific modifier *biofeedback therapist,* the term *therapist* can refer to the practitioner, biofeedback therapist, or biofeedback technician. The term is often used herein to refer to a therapist using completely non-biofeedback methods of treatment as well.

§2.4 Delegation. Biofeedback therapy involves long practice sessions which need to be monitored by someone on the therapeutic team. Because of the relative costs of time, practitioners will usually delegate this job. Briefing, debriefing, instructing, and interviewing patients during therapy sessions are also usually delegated. In these circumstances, therapeutic relationships are established with each member of the team who has contact with the patient. When there is frequent contact with the practitioner, the patient-therapist relationship may be largely focused upon the practitioner. When there is less contact as treatment progresses, the therapeutic relationship may be focused largely upon the biofeedback therapist or biofeedback technician. Patients will usually be intuitively aware of whether or not there is a good collaboration on the therapeutic team and will form their relationships accordingly. It should be strongly emphasized that the quality of treatment will be directly related to the quality of the working relationships within the therapeutic team, especially in treating patients who are psychologically labile. Extensive experience on therapeutic teams has documented amply that it is exactly around the intra-team conflicts that the breakdown of difficult treatment will occur and that the smooth functioning of the team improves the quality of care (Stanton and Schwartz, 1954). It is particularly important for the highly trained specialist to be aware of the feelings of subordinates, to respect their knowledge, to allow them latitude for personal growth in their work, to recognize the limits of his own knowledge, but at the same time maintain adequate control of the therapeutic setting and be sure the treatment is done as he wishes it.

§2.5 Characteristics the Therapist Should Cultivate. In order to do the best job possible in the therapeutic relationship, therapists from any of the professional roles should cultivate certain traits in themselves. A *cheerful, positive, friendly, encouraging attitude* is the chief of these (Lain Entralgo, 1969). The patient has a difficult job to do in surmounting deeply ingrained patterns and can use all of the encouragement the therapist can provide. After the therapist has acquired *orderliness* and *competence,* it is important that he also convey a sense of these traits to the patient. *Concern* for the patient and *empathy* are also important traits. High *moral* and *ethical values* in the professional relationship are also necessary (Houston, 1938).

Even though these are general traits a therapist should possess, there are individual variations in the personalities of different therapists which need to be studied and utilized. The therapist's personality is the major tool used in the therapeutic relationship and to a large extent we are all limited in certain directions by our personalities. We must attempt to capitalize upon our personal strengths and minimize our weaknesses to achieve the best results in our work. Thus, for example, the individual who is not naturally cheerful may compensate for this by allowing his concern for the patient to show. Self-study is necessary to know one's strengths and weaknesses. When thoughtfully pursued, this can be of personal benefit to the therapist as well as helpful in his work (Havens, 1974).

§2.6 Cultivation of the Patient-Therapist Relationship. One of the therapist's long range goals should be his own study of the patient-therapist relationship and how to strengthen it. This includes awareness of the state of rapport, sensing and generating enthusiastic collaboration, and aligning oneself with the patient against the symptom.

Awareness of the state of rapport requires particular attention to hidden messages. If the patient is suddenly critical of other therapists or other authority, if the patient appears superficially over-cooperative while not making progress, if the patient is suddenly detached or shows depression, rapport is usually deteriorating. Attention to the rapport will often enable the therapist to turn the situation around to enthusiastic collaboration, which is facilitated by the therapist's own involvement and infectious ability to see the positive side of the situation. In contrast to psychotherapy, where ultimate success may come through fully experiencing and living through despair, this form of treatment will usually be derailed by more than minimal experience of failure or by allowing despair to interfere with the effort of practice. This correctly implies that so far biofeedback has not been found useful by most clinicians in coping with depression (see Sec. 3.4). Aligning the therapeutic pair against the symptoms is largely achieved by the therapist's attitude toward the patient, toward the patient's healthy part, toward a goal of a more adaptive life for the patient, and away from the acceptance of the symptoms as necessary to the adaptation. Cultivation of this form of relationship for biofeedback therapy and of the personal traits necessary for the therapist should not be taken as a devaluation of opposite ways of relating and opposite traits in other forms of treatment where they may be appropriate. Differently structured forms of biofeedback therapy may also use other ways of relating. We merely refer to the importance of these dimensions in the particular therapy we are describing.

§2.7 **Elements in the Therapeutic Relationship.** It requires courage and toughmindedness to look unblinking into the true nature of the patient-therapist relationship. It is much easier to do now because of the work of those who have gone before, notably psychoanalysts and other psychotherapists. However, biofeedback and other new techniques are now in turn having an influence on the therapeutic relationship which demands full re-examination of the relationship once more. This is mainly because biofeedback techniques have been found clinically to be useful with a number of conditions which have been resistant to other forms of treatment, while at the same time it has not been clear whether the biofeedback techniques themselves were as responsible for the results of the treatment as was the therapeutic relationship. It seems now that both share in the efficacy of the treatment and that treatment is the poorer for the elimination of either factor. At the same time, however, we are enabled to obtain a new perspective on the therapeutic relationship by examining its evolution as recapitulated in biofeedback treatment. Later on (Chaps. 4–9), specific recommendations for carrying out biofeedback treatment which includes the management of the therapeutic relationship will be made. Here, however, we will go into some of the elements of the therapeutic relationship whose importance has been re-emphasized by biofeedback therapy.

The most important of these are the patient's faith and wish to trust. These can be considered a universal need which is not banished by disillusionment or cynicism. On the contrary, this need may often be plainly seen as even stronger in those who attempt to suppress it. The need becomes one of the therapist's strongest tools, but once mobilized, there must be some place for the therapist to move in making use of it. It is here that the therapist's alternatives for effective action, mentioned elsewhere (Secs. 1.43, 2.13) become important.

The patient's faith and wish to trust are concretely manifested in the power of suggestion, another of the elements in the therapeutic relationship which biofeedback forces us to re-examine. Suggestion can be defined as the property humans possess of being able to do unanticipated things when asked if the relationship with the one asking is strong and positive. While it has long been known that unusual degrees of control of the body exist, before the advent of biofeedback it was usually not easy to make any systematic use of this fact for therapeutic purposes (Koestler, 1961). A related element of the therapeutic relationship is the role played by ritual. Until recently, ritual has been devalued and treated with scorn as a vestige of superstition. Now, however, it is possible to see that not only is it a concrete method of focusing the power of suggestion, but that in and of itself it leads to the entrainment of psychophysiological states for the purpose of working toward a desired end state (see Sec. 1.43).

These elements are sometimes conceived as manifestations of the placebo effect (Stroebel and Glueck, 1973). Rather, however, it is the other way around and it is the placebo effect which is made up of these elements as a special limited case of the combination of the elements. Placebo effect has likewise sometimes been scorned as the foolishness of gullible patients influenced by the wickedness of megalomanic charlatans, rather than recognized as a limiting instance of universal forces within us which we dare not acknowledge (Houston, 1938; Modell, 1955; Lain Entralgo, 1969).

These interrelated elements have long been recognized to have great potential within themselves. However, experience over the years has been that therapies based upon them have been elusive. Thus, powerful hypnotists have emerged, achieved marvelous results, and then failed badly in simple cases (Kaufman, 1961). Early psychoanalysts were careful to minimize some of these elements in their therapy as a method of holding them constant. Many physicians go to great lengths to argue that these elements play no part in their treatment.

What makes the effective use of these elements more understandable is the recognition that they must be combined and utilized over time. Thus, it is never too hard to muster up one of them on special occasions in the therapeutic relationship, but it may be quite difficult to keep them working over the longer haul. This issue is repeatedly manifested in a simple sequence which is universally known: a patient faces a minor crisis, and with the help of the therapist, is able to muster up the courage to overcome pathological behavior. Then, after things have gone well for awhile, without realizing it, suddenly one day the patient finds himself back as deeply as ever in the pathological behavior. Two conditions where this is common are pathological drinking and eating — alcoholism and obesity — where cycles of remorse, resignation, determination, and relapse abound. The important thing about such vignettes is that they represent a sequence or a time-structured chain or a series of events rather than a single picture. In this example, the therapist would, through experience, attribute less relevance to the minor crisis and more relevance to the close monitoring of events after the crisis. This is by no means the only such sequence and is given only as an example of the need to be aware of time sequences (see Sec. 2.27). Easy cases are distinguishable from difficult cases by the degree to which time sequences are overt and easy to manage, while skilled therapists are distinguished from unskilled therapists by their ability to recognize and deal with time sequences. More will be said about this later (see Chap. 4).

THERAPEUTIC CONTRACT

§2.8 Concept of Contract. Sociologists have taught us that any relationship between individuals can be conceived of as a "contract" (Parsons, 1951). This means that each individual has agreed to certain rules in the relationship and has the expectation that the other individual will abide by certain rules as well. This agreement may be formal or informal, explicit or implicit. Most social contracts are informal and implicit in most of their details. The details of the contract are based on the needs of the individuals involved and the social context within which the contract is made.

A simple example of a social contract is the events which transpire when a person drives his car into a gas station. There is a wide range of expectations on the part of both the car driver and the service station attendant which are based on social context. Thus, the driver assumes that the station is selling gas, will offer it to him, will offer to clean his windshield and check his oil. The service station attendant, on the other hand, assumes that the driver wishes some of these services and will pay for them after they are delivered. The explicit part of the contract will include the driver saying exactly how much gas he wishes and the attendant being paid the correct amount for that gas.

The needs of the car driver are taken care of by his receiving the amount of gas he needs as well as the other services for his automobile. The needs of the service station attendant are taken care of by receiving salary from the payment for the service. This particular simple social contract is merely provided as an example so that the concept can be grasped.

§2.9 Therapeutic Contracts. The contract between therapist and patient in providing biofeedback therapy is a particular instance of a social contract which has its own special distinguishing features. First of all, it is a therapeutic contract and therefore is in the same category as other therapeutic contracts. However, just as the patient-therapist relationship in biofeedback therapy is a special instance of the general category of patient-therapist relationships, so is the contract likewise a special instance. These relationships and contracts are based on the patient having come because of some symptom or complaint and the therapist offering a service to help relieve the symptom or complaint. The need for relief from the complaint is the major need of the patient.

The major need of the therapist from the patient is usually that the patient provides him with an opportunity to pursue his vocation. Interaction provides the major part of the medium within which therapists pursue their vocation. Needs include the therapist's wish to help (altruism), wish to master a problem (curiosity), and wish to achieve recognition (power) (Bean, 1975). If the therapist is a private practitioner, the patient will probably pay a fee for the service, whereas if the therapist works in an institution, the patient will somehow be entitled to the service and the therapist will be paid a salary for providing the service. The direct payment of fee to the therapist would be somewhat more personal than a salary arranged by other parties to the contract (Menninger, 1973).

There is an elaborate social context of the relationship based on a number of factors, including the profession and specialty which the therapist is practicing, what role the therapist plays in the therapeutic team, and whether the therapy is provided in an institution. Other important factors affecting the therapeutic contract include the particular conceptions of disease held by patient and therapist, and their particular conceptions of their own and the other person's role in the treatment of the disease. Thus, in routine medical practice, doctor and patient often conceive of the cause of the disease arising out of factors which are the doctor's business and with which the patient need not concern himself. Likewise, the doctor will provide treatment and all the patient need do is take the pills offered. Overall then, the patient has relatively little responsibility for treatment. In other therapeutic contexts, the concepts of the disease may be quite different and this instance is mainly offered as an example (Parsons, 1951).

§2.10 Contract in Biofeedback Therapy. As biofeedback treatment has evolved over the past 10 years or so, there has grown with it a unique conception of the patient's illness which has resulted in a particular kind of therapeutic relationship. Although the therapeutic relationship still belongs under the general heading of therapeutic relationships as considered above and elsewhere, and although therapeutic approaches in the past have sometimes utilized the same conception of illness, biofeedback treatment has highlighted and especially utilized this conception in a unique way.

The particular concept of the patient's illness which is implicit in biofeedback treatment is that the patient's illness has come about as a result of something going on within the patient (breakdown of homeostasis) and that the patient has work to do in achieving a cure and a major responsibility in achieving a cure. Furthermore, this means that the therapeutic relationship is an especially important one in which the patient will be learning about his own internal bodily processes with the help of the therapist. In other words, the therapist functions toward the patient as a coach. This results in a particular kind of contract and a particular kind of therapeutic relationship.

§2.11 Coaching Contract and Relationship. Coaching is the general concept which applies to the teaching of physical skills. Thus, athletics, dancing, singing, acting, and meditation are skills which involve the use of the body in a highly skilled manner to achieve some result unattainable without training. Coaching differs from other teaching in that there is greater emphasis on the bodily skills learned. Even though there are many other forms of teaching, such as teaching handwriting, which involve teaching a bodily skill, this is usually only incidental to some other end to which the physical skill is a means.

When two individuals enter into a coach-pupil relationship, there are certain aspects of the relationship and the contract expressing the relationship which are unique. In order to be coached, the pupil has to agree to give the coach control over the pupil's body. In some respects, this goes even further than a physical examination (Parsons, 1951), where the patient allows a doctor to examine his body, since the patient not only allows examination of his body by the coach as necessary, but also allows examination of performance by his body, and still more significant, allows the coach to give instructions in how to use his body — i.e., to have control over it. Thus, biofeedback treatment differs from most treatment because the coaching relationship, including its physical aspects, is utilized.

The coaching relationship is manifested in the social contract between coach and pupil, which includes the above rights of the coach to control the pupil's body. In addition, in the coaching relationship it is taken for granted that the success of the endeavor depends a great deal on the pupil. This requires the pupil's willingness and ability to allow the coach to control him, his diligence at practice, and the conscientiousness with which he follows instructions. All of these considerations apply to biofeedback therapy and tend to make it unique compared to many other therapeutic efforts.

§2.12 **Goals of the Contract.** In contrast to the situations in certain other therapeutic contracts, the biofeedback therapy contract can enable the therapist to utilize the strong position of having well defined goals. It is worth exploring this contrast in some detail in order to better understand it, because this provides another of the most important tools in the patient-therapist relationship.

When a general medical practitioner accepts a patient, in a certain sense he accepts the patient unconditionally. In other words, he agrees to be available to consider all of the patient's problems and to continue to accept a role in treating a problem even though the treatment may prove ineffective. Likewise, except for blatant refusal to follow instructions, the patient is usually not held particularly responsible for his complaints nor for the results of treatment. Thus, in the general treatment of obesity, the doctor will probably not dismiss a patient who fails to lose weight. One way of describing this situation is to say that the goals are not well defined, are not tangible, and are not operational.

In contrast, if the same patient were in biofeedback treatment, some goals of the treatment would be set, and if the goals were not achieved and could not be reasonably redefined, the treatment would be discontinued. How this is accomplished will be explained later (Sec. 2.18).

Another example of a therapeutic procedure with less well defined goals is conventional psychodynamic psychotherapy. Here, the symptoms being treated include hard-to-define emotional complaints from which the patient seeks relief. The treatment in part is to allow the patient to say whatever is on his mind and it is accepted that the relationship between his complaint and what he says may be obscure and difficult to interpret. By the same token, the goals are also often vague and intangible. In contrast, when the same patient is treated with biofeedback therapy, it is necessary to define some tangible goals, usually having to do with physical complaints, toward which to work. This might be the relief of a specified degree of insomnia or a specifiable lessening of chronic anxiety, but spelling out a goal would be part of the therapeutic contract.

This discussion is not meant to imply criticism of general practitioners or psychotherapists. On the contrary, they may successfully deal with a number of problems for which biofeedback has nothing to offer. Also, the general practitioner does not turn a patient away because his treatment will not cure him, while the psychotherapist is often able to treat and cure interpersonal problems which have little to do with the body.

The situation is complicated when biofeedback treatment is offered by a practitioner who also offers other forms of treatment and this presents a special problem to consider. Thus, if a general physician offers biofeedback treatment in his office, or if a psychotherapist uses it as an adjunct to his psychotherapy, the setting of goals by two different methods complicates the picture. This will be considered further later (Sec. 3.2).

§2.13 **Biofeedback Treatment Goals.** Biofeedback treatment has so far been mainly utilized by its practitioners in relationship to specific physical symptoms, such as migraine headaches or fecal incontinence. This makes it easy to define the goals of treatment in terms of the *state of the main symptom* by making the improvement of the symptom the goal of treatment. Likewise, it is then easy to define the relative success or failure of the treatment by how the symptom does. Treatment goals in biofeedback can also be defined in terms of *change of psychophysiological feedback parameters*. For example, forehead muscle tension level criteria may be set as an end point of a particular procedure. Another example is reaching a criterion level of finger temperature with temperature feedback. A third type of treatment goal is defined by the patient reaching a *criterion of relaxation training* without feedback (see Chap. 5; Secs. 7.11, 7.12, 8.2).

Having three kinds of goals adds flexibility to the treatment and allows the therapist to work for gains in one area while another area is stagnant. This often supplies the "therapeutic leverage" necessary for success. As long as something is happening and as long as the therapist is able to account for what happens and provides structure for the next step, there is hope for the treatment. Once there is a stalemate, it is usually better to give up.

Even though there are other treatment goals, it is really only to the goal of major symptom relief that a treatment is ultimately directed, and achievement of the other goals only postpones the time when symptom relief must be expected. When therapeutic movement fails to occur, thorough re-assessment is in order, especially of factors of motivation and ambivalence. Psychotherapy is often indicated in those patients who achieve physiological goals without symptom relief; however, many of these patients turn out to be treatment failures with most methods of psychotherapy also.

§2.14 **Patient's Responsibility in the Biofeedback Therapy Contract.** The first responsibility of patients is that they accept the fact that their symptoms may in some way be a result of their living patterns (Secs. 1.35–1.37; 2.10; 3.3). The patients who will not do this can probably not be treated. Such patients wish to see their symptoms as alien to themselves and visited upon them by a malign fate. They wish to do nothing about their symptoms themselves, but want to have someone else get rid of them. Although we all have such tendencies within us, most of us can see the unreasonableness of this view and accept when we have played a part in the generation of our own troubles. This does not imply blaming patients for their symptoms, and often one can readily acknowledge that given the circumstances it could not turn out differently. Likewise, it does not mean that the patient necessarily need openly acknowledge this issue immediately. Some patients initially cannot do so but later can. This test at the start of therapy is a good one though, and those patients who are outspoken in their certainty that all is well within themselves can usually be expected to be difficult to treat.

Once patients accept that their symptoms are a result of living patterns, two possibilities for alleviation are open. The first is to change the living patterns, and the second is to change the way the patients have of reacting to the stresses they encounter in their living patterns. Early in biofeedback treatment the patient is usually advised to consider thinking about both of these things and to consider the treatment as offering a concrete way of changing his reaction to the stress encountered in his life. When the patient accepts this formulation, the treatment has one cornerstone of its potential success.

The next responsibility of the patient is to agree to the conditions of treatment. Thus, regular appointments, fees, practice sessions, and home practice have to be agreed upon. The home practice is particularly crucial as it gives the patient an important tangible role in his own treatment and it gives the therapist a good indicator to follow in evaluating the patient's cooperation.

§2.15 **Therapist's Responsibility in the Biofeedback Therapy Contract.** Aside from the usual responsibilities toward patients, therapists using biofeedback approaches have an additional responsibility imposed by the special requirements of the treatment—that is the responsibility to maintain the structure of the treatment. In contrast to psychotherapy, for example, where the therapist need not remember the details of the last session, the biofeedback therapist must remember as much as possible about the progression of the patient's symptoms and the patient's progress in his home practice. This can be facilitated by good brief progress notes (Appendix B). In addition, the therapist must maintain a concept of the anticipated structure of treatment, including alternative steps to be undertaken in the event that difficulties arise. As will become apparent later (Secs. 2.24–2.27), structure is especially important in this form of treatment.

§2.16 **Problems in the Therapeutic Contract.** One of the main reasons that the therapeutic contract is important and that definite goals in the contract are important is that problems arising in the contract can be so regularly anticipated. It is in the assessment of these problems that the therapist has the best guide of the progress of treatment, and it is in the resolution of the problems that the therapist has one of the strongest therapeutic tools. Problems can be anticipated in almost every treatment. In a few instances, their resolution will be simple or even automatic, but most treatments will require that the therapist pay close attention to seeing that the problems are recognized and dealt with (see Houston, 1938; Watzlawick, et al., 1967; Haley, 1967, 1968).

In one sense, any problem arising can be viewed in the context of a breach of the therapeutic contract. Therapists observe empirically that as long as the contract is observed, treatment usually goes well, and that when the contract is breached the treatment usually stops progressing. Rarely when the therapist is attentive and the patient is closely observing his end of the contract does treatment fail to progress. The most common breach of contract is failure to do home practice. This places the burden upon the therapist to maintain close contact with the patient about the progress of home practice – the most common failure of therapists is to neglect to question the patient carefully about home practice.

From another point of view, the failure of patients to live up to the contract can be viewed as resistance to giving up their symptoms. All patients can be seen as having arrived at an adjustment to their overall life stresses in which their illness is one part of their adjustment, and where it serves a function in their mental economy, even though they would be better off without it and might wish to get rid of it. Therefore, when their illness is better, there is strain upon their total equilibrium which can be relieved by a return of their illness, and there is a resistance to getting well. Thus, the same failure to carry out home practice can be viewed not only as a breach of contract, but also as resistance.

From a third point of view, the problems of treatment can be viewed as instances of self-fulfilling prophecies of the negative sort. According to this view, patients have become conditioned by failure to expect to be unable to control physiological processes and are ready to give up prematurely. It is on the basis of anticipated failure and negative thinking about their own capabilities that patients will justify their giving up and failing to practice, for instance.

Validity can be seen in all three of these different views, and different cases can be seen combining differing amounts of each. In practice, therapists will find themselves utilizing all three, and the way in which this is done will be important. Chapter 5 considers these problems in depth.

§2.17 Lack of Success in Practice. It would be distortion to see all failures in practice as due strictly to the patients' breaching of contract, resistance, or negative thinking, or as the therapist's failure to maintain the structure of the relationship. Often in spite of patients' cooperation they do not make progress. Here is one of the places where the therapist's resourcefulness becomes most important. It is particularly important to keep encouraging patients, but it is also important to keep close track of their difficulties, to have alternatives in mind, and to acknowledge the patients' discouragement and help them with it. This can be thought of as the importance of regaining "therapeutic leverage." Also, it is important to recognize that we are not yet able to tell whether a particular treatment plan uses the best biofeedback parameters and this may cause failure in practice. When treatment is not moving, the practitioner should be brought into the decision-making process. First, the obvious possibilities of improving home practice, clarifying misunderstandings, and dealing with psychological obstacles should be considered. After they have been ruled out, some changes in feedback parameters or training procedures should be tried. Close attention should be paid to the details of what is wrong and the changes made should somehow address themselves to these details.

§2.18 Therapeutic Failures. Sometimes, in spite of all efforts, with or without the patients' having breached the contract, shown intractable resistance or negative thinking, the treatment will fail. When there are breach of contract, resistance, and negative thinking as major factors, we owe it to our patients to let them know what we have observed, so that they have a better chance of success on subsequent attempts at treatment. Unless a new understanding can be reached, however, at this point treatment should be terminated. Where we do not detect these factors, it is important to acknowledge that treatment has failed but that we cannot tell why, so that the patient does not waste further time in futile efforts and so that we may eventually learn more about determinants of success and failure.

§2.19 Termination of Treatment. When a patient is successfully treated, there has been a strong bond developed between the patient and the therapist. Especially when treatment is successful, the patient becomes very attached to the therapist. It does not work well to terminate such treatment abruptly without careful planning which takes the patient's needs into account. There are a number of things to do to help the patient with the termination. First of all, testing the efficacy of the treatment by a trial period without treatment or by observation of performance under stress can help both patient and therapist to see how well the patient might do on his own. Secondly, it can help to encourage the patient to recognize the fact it is he and not the therapist in whom reposes the ability to overcome his symptom. Also, the door may be left open for the patient to return in the event that symptoms recur. Finally, when the patient has problems other than those dealt with by biofeedback treatment, it can be pointed out that the biofeedback treatment did what it was able to do, that it should not be expected to help the other problems, and that whatever effective action is necessary to deal with the other problems ought to be taken by the patient. Much of the termination process has to do with encouraging patients to have faith in their ability to get along on their own.

BIOFEEDBACK IN THE THERAPEUTIC RELATIONSHIP

§2.20 Biofeedback as Sole Therapeutic Agent. As an abstract model, biofeedback treatment might be seen as the application of biofeedback to a particular patient, with the relationship merely incidental and purely functional — merely assuring that the patient is at the right place at the right time and knows what he is to do in his practice session. We do not agree with such a model for most biofeedback treatment, considering it untenable both on the basis of what is already known about therapeutic relationships in general, and also on the basis of a great deal of empirical experience by many biofeedback therapists who have found the therapeutic relationship of importance. Once it is accepted that the therapeutic relationship is important in biofeedback treatment, it is then possible to construct an abstract model in which one component of therapeutic effect is derived from the biofeedback technique itself, and another component from the therapeutic relationship.

§2.21 Therapeutic Application of Biofeedback. When biofeedback is applied for therapeutic purposes, the relationship between the patient and therapist is closely related to the coaching relationship mentioned above (Sec. 2.11). The reason for this is that the patient is learning a physical skill and must rely on the coaching of the therapist as a guide to learning. The therapist usually works with the patient through the verbal medium of discussing the patient's symptoms, their waxings and wanings under various stresses, and in response to the procedures instituted. They also discuss other bodily reactions noted in connection with biofeedback practice, and the progress with the work with the biofeedback parameters. In clinical practice, the therapist will usually lose sight of the relative contributions to progress of the biofeedback work versus the therapeutic relationship, and indeed there is no need to know this to work effectively with the patient.

NON-BIOFEEDBACK PROCEDURES IN THE THERAPEUTIC RELATIONSHIP

§2.22 Necessity of Non-Biofeedback Procedures. By a non-biofeedback procedure we are referring to parts of a biofeedback treatment in which biofeedback is not used. Based on our own and other clinicians' experiences, we argue for the idea that most biofeedback treatment should include a part of the therapy where non-biofeedback procedures are used. One reason is that it is always important for the patient to be able to practice the skill he has learned with biofeedback when the biofeedback is not present. This has been called transfer of learning by experimentalists and carry-over effects by some clinicians. It is also essential to patients' self-confidence and belief in treatment that they are able to control physiological variables when the instrumental feedback is not actually present.

§2.23 Non-Biofeedback Procedures for Home Practice. A major practical reason for including some non-biofeedback procedures in most therapeutic regimes is that home practice is usually a desirable component of therapy and biofeedback instruments for home use are not yet widely available. Another reason that home practice is desirable is that it reduces the cost of treatment, the number of treatment sessions needed, and the time which treatment takes if part of the training is done at home. Still another desirable feature of home practice is that it gives the therapist an excellent opportunity to assess the state of the therapeutic relationship by seeing how the patients keep up their home practice and what difficulty they have with it. It is usually easier to determine patient cooperativeness with home practice since it is rare for there not to be enough motivation so that the patient appears fully participant during biofeedback session. On the other hand, home practice quite regularly elicits difficulties which can then be dealt with.

As a practical matter, home practice is apt to involve relaxation training using cassette tape recordings. Relaxation training is used because it is difficult to tailor a symptom-focused home practice to the many symptoms for which patients seek treatment, whereas relaxation will present a problem for most of our patients and will be related to the occurrence of later symptom relief. Cassette tape recordings as a method of presenting the relaxation training are practical because the instructions are presented uniformly. In addition, most patients find it easier to learn a relaxation procedure when someone's voice paces them through the procedure. This is equivalent to saying that the greatest obstacle to learning meditation is the problem of concentrating on the mantra. Obviously, this reflects dependency and the wish for help from an external source on the part of the patient, but fulfilling these needs enhances rather than detracts from the effectiveness of treatment.

STRUCTURE OF THE THERAPEUTIC RELATIONSHIP

§2.24 Elements. Earlier in this chapter, a number of the elements which make up therapy were briefly outlined. In biofeedback treatment, these include the therapeutic relationship, the biofeedback techniques, and the non-biofeedback procedures. These three can be considered the major components into which therapy is divided. The therapeutic relationship can be further divided into consideration of such elements as faith and the wish to trust, suggestion, ritual, placebo effects, the therapeutic contract, coaching, and the therapist's use of his personality. Other unmentioned elements may also be considered of greater priority by some therapists.

§2.25 **Structure.** When a number of elements are combined in a constrained manner, a structure results (Gaarder, 1975). Thus, when bricks and mortar are put together in a particular way, a building is created. The building is a structure. Likewise, when a group of alphabetic letters (elements or units) are combined in a string, a word is created. The word is structure. These matters are of importance to the biofeedback therapist because they help in learning that there is structure to the therapeutic relationship and structure to the therapy (Dollard, et al., 1953: Bandler and Grinder, 1975). This will be explained in greater detail below and used extensively in Chapter 4.

§2.26 **Time and Structure.** Structure is sometimes defined as something which exists over time. Thus, what is considered unique about a building—giving it structure—is the fact that its elements remain in the same relationship to one another over time. This view of structure is useful and is even sometimes hard to transcend. However, in order to understand the structure of the therapeutic relationship, it is not only important to have a concept of structure as enduring over time, but also to have a concept of structure as something *emerging* over time. This is easier to see for people who have been trained in computer technology or in linguistics, although it is a simple idea and self-evident upon reflection.

In order to understand structure emerging over time, we may consider as an example the structure of language. Thus, a sentence in written or spoken language consists of a string of words combined in a particular manner according to the rules of grammar. Once recorded in some way on audio tape or on paper, it is easy to think of the sentence as having structure which endures over time. However, if we consider either the production of the sentence or the process of registering the sentence in a reader or listener, the structure of the sentence can only *emerge* over time. In other words, the only way a sentence can be brought into existence is to write it or speak it in sequence over time, and the only way a sentence can be understood is to read it or listen to it in sequence over time. It is the serial relationship of the words over time which constitutes the emergent structure of a sentence.

Likewise, when we consider a human relationship, such as the therapeutic relationship, it is easier to conceive of its structure as something enduring over time, so that its structure lies in its constancy. However, upon reflection it is easy to see that from a different perspective, it has a structure which must emerge over time. Thus, for instance, the therapeutic relationship has a beginning, a middle, and an end. It cannot begin until the therapist and patient meet, and part of the beginning is for the therapist and patient to get to know one another and arrive at tentative agreement on how to proceed. Furthermore, the middle of the relationship cannot occur until after the beginning, and the end cannot occur until the middle has been traversed. Notice that this occurs over time, so that time is the dimension in which these aspects of structure of the relationship emerge.

§2.27 **Hierarchy in Structure.** In order to complete the understanding of the structure of the therapeutic relationship, it is necessary to consider the concept of hierarchy also. Again, this can best be done by considering an example, again the structure of language. The structure of written language is contained in a hierarchy in which the lowest level of the hierarchy consists of alphabetic letters. The letters are combined to make words, which is the next higher level of the hierarchy. The words are combined to make sentences, which is one step higher than words in the hierarchy. Higher levels also exist, but we will not examine them further here. Note that when structure is in the dimension of time, the lower levels of the hierarchy take less time and the higher levels of the hierarchy take more.

In the therapeutic relationship, there is a micro-structure occurring in short units of time, a macro-structure occurring in long units of time, and a number of levels in between. We have already considered the largest unit and the level just beneath it when we examined the total therapy as divided into beginning, middle, and end. A lower level beneath these is the individual session, which can likewise be divided into lower levels—the next lower level being the beginning, middle, and end of an individual session (Gaarder, 1975).

The micro-structure of the relationship enters at about this level. Although it is most important and is instinctively dealt with by good therapists, it is the most difficult to define and understand in explicit terms (Watzlawick, et al., 1967; Bandler and Grinder, 1975). Here are involved the series of individual transactions in which the therapist and patient either work together or pull apart, in which they either succeed in the therapeutic task or fail. Many of the events occurring in the micro-structure can be understood in terms of the contract and whether or not it is being fulfilled.

§2.28 **Summary.** This chapter has presented at length the arguments for the therapeutic relationship being the cornerstone of biofeedback treatment and for the biofeedback therapist having a detailed understanding of how this relationship progresses with each patient in order to achieve the optimal results of treatment.

A clinician is . . . one whose prime function is to manage a sick person with the purpose of alleviating most effectively the total impact of the illness on that person. . . . Clinical evidence is the basic material with which the clinician works. He gathers it from several sources: the history; the physical examination; laboratory studies and special technics (such as x-ray study); and consulting opinions.

Philip Tumulty
What Is a Clincian and What Does He Do?
(New Eng. J. Med. 283:1, 1970, 20)

There are various recommendations which a doctor gives to his patient, and which are very hard to get carried out. One of these is work for those who will not take it; another, rest for those who cannot get it; yet another is restraint of the appetites.

Sir Thomas Lauder Brunton

Inevitably, the doctor's work in the future will be more and more educational, and less and less curative. More and more will he deal with the physiology and psychology of his patient, less and less with his pathology. He will spend his time keeping the fit fit, rather than trying to make the unfit fit.

Thomas, Lord Horder

CHAPTER 3

Choice of patients for biofeedback therapy

§3.1 Introduction. Patients who seek biofeedback treatment themselves, are referred for biofeedback treatment, or are seen for other treatment by the biofeedback practitioner need to be evaluated as to whether biofeedback treatment should be undertaken. Each of the above situations of initial contact is slightly different and these differences can be briefly considered (Sec. 3.2). Once a patient is accepted for evaluation, a number of steps are undertaken to assess whether he is suitable for the treatment or not. These steps include assessment of the patient's response to the philosophy of treatment (Sec. 3.3); the patient's ego strength (Sec. 3.4); personality (Sec. 3.5); motivation (Sec. 3.6); the nature of the symptoms (Sec. 3.7); the possibility that other forms of treatment should be given priority (Sec. 3.8); experience the patient may have had attempting to obtain relief from his symptoms (Sec. 3.9); previous experience with other psychophysiological approaches and previous biofeedback experience (Sec. 3.10). The above considerations mainly relate to the patient as an individual. We may also consider the symptoms of the patient. This will be done by first considering symptoms in relation to biofeedback parameters (Sec. 3.11), where a classification system is introduced. Next, symptoms will be considered in relation to the previous use of biofeedback treatment by other clinicians (Sec. 3.12). Finally, a classification system of considering the nature of the disorder will be discussed (Sec. 3.13).

Although all of these factors are related to one another and the assessment of one will provide information on another, we will first take up each as a thing in itself. After doing so, we will briefly explore indications and contraindications of treatment and the initial decision-making process regarding a course of treatment (Sec. 3.14).

§3.2 Source of Referral. Depending upon the experience of the practitioner, type of practice, and the practitioner's relationship to other biofeedback practitioners locally and nationally, a fairly large part of a practice may be made up of patients who are self-referred. Often, these patients have excellent prospects for achieving good results from treatment. They are usually intelligent, well motivated, resourceful, discriminating, and hard working. They usually already have a good grasp of the principles of treatment from their reading and they know what they want. The above generalizations are occasionally not warranted in the case of a few eccentrics who seek treatment in relationship to a delusional or distorted belief system with largely magical qualities. Such cases often have to do with belief in some esoteric elaboration of parapsychology, the paranormal, and the supernatural. These few cases require especially careful evaluation if there is any basis at all for undertaking therapy. The major issue becomes whether they are open to any other explanations of their symtoms and could accept the therapeutic approach offered (see Sec. 3.3).

Before undertaking biofeedback treatment, the patient should be asked to clear his doing so with his primary sources of care, especially medical. If there are serious disagreements about undertaking biofeedback treatment, these need to be clarified. Sometimes the primary source of care will be unfamiliar with biofeedback and may dismiss it as a fad. At other times the source may have important information not available to the biofeedback practitioner which contraindicates treatment. This disagreement should not be dismissed lightly or disregarded. On the other hand, if treatment still appears indicated to the biofeedback practitioner, then the assent of the primary source of care, even though reluctant, should be sought. If such assent is not given, the patient has to decide whether to forego biofeedback treatment or seek another source of primary care. The biofeedback practitioner should probably not undertake treatment unless an assenting source of primary care has been obtained.

Patients referred from another source of care are usually the largest group seen. Often the referring source is well acquainted with biofeedback and has made a timely referral. Occasionally there is misunderstanding about biofeedback and the referral is inappropriate. Also, one needs to be alert to the possibility that the patient is referred because he presents an unusually difficult management problem. Sometimes we are able to detect and deal with this successfully, while other times the particular problem will overwhelm us also. We assume that when a patient is referred for treatment, the referring source will be contacted concerning the patient, informed of the results of initial evaluation, contacted as indicated during treatment, and informed of the outcome at termination unless there is reason not to do so.

Most biofeedback practitioners are also trained in other therapeutic methods: either medical, psychotherapeutic, or behavioral therapy. In the course of practice of their therapeutic discipline, a certain number of patients will be seen for whom biofeedback treatment appears indicated. These patients can be informed of the alternative of using the biofeedback approach, in order to decide about it for themselves. Since the practitioner will already know the patient, the assessment will be simplified. The biggest problem with this category of patient is that the two treatment approaches applied by the same practitioner may be incompatible. For instance, conventional psychotherapy is usually permissively structured, so that the patient chooses the direction of train of thought and may be allowed to wander, whereas biofeedback therapy is structured by the therapist and highly directed toward concrete goals. It is easier for this difference of approach to be pursued by different individual therapists, so a psychotherapist may find it preferable for someone else to do the biofeedback treatment. This can either be done by someone under the therapist's supervision or by a biofeedback practitioner to whom the patient is referred. On the other hand, some psychotherapists by nature will be easily able to combine the two roles of psychotherapist and biofeedback therapist and this will not be a problem for them. Also, as biofeedback therapy develops, techniques which are less structured might evolve.

§3.3 Compatibility with Treatment Philosophy. In the initial evaluation of a patient for biofeedback treatment, an explanation of the treatment and the philosophy of treatment is routinely presented to the patient. One of the most important indicators of whether treatment can be successfully undertaken is the patient's response to the explanation. Although such a presentation is part of the practitioner's obligation to patients, the special use of the response as a source of information in assessment makes structure of the presentation important. In particular, it is emphasized to the patient that the treatment is different, because its success depends upon the patient's efforts at learning something rather than upon the therapist doing something to or for the patient. Self-sufficient patients will welcome the chance to play the major role in their own treatment, whereas the overly dependent will resist the idea that they have any responsibility for themselves in therapy.

Depending upon the setting in which the treatment is given, the therapist should attempt to maximize the effectiveness of treatment by the way in which the issues of learning and patient responsibility are presented. Thus, if the practitioner is a physician, the emphasis can be upon biofeedback being a different form of medical treatment in which the patient has more responsibility for the outcome. On the other hand, if the practitioner is not a physician, the emphasis can be upon how this is different from medical treatment. Focusing upon this is important because even though there is a well recognized responsibility of patients in their own treatment, lay people generally do not recognize it. The importance of patient responsibility can be seen in a simplified way in the course of psychotherapy which may start with patients believing that the therapist is responsible for the patient's life and end when patients recognize that they are responsible for their own lives. Biofeedback therapy uses a method of self-practice which allows this distinction to be drawn before treatment is begun.

§3.4 **Ego Strength.** The concept of ego strength, derived from psychoanalysis, is used by psychotherapists to designate the strength of character of the patient. It is one of the most important dimensions of the patient to assess before deciding upon biofeedback treatment. Indications of a strong ego are common sense; independence; a history of coping well with stress; a sense of humor; good social, educational, and occupational adjustment; and a sustained capacity for directed dialogue dealing with important personal issues. The opposite qualities point toward a weak ego. From the perspective of homeostasis, a strong ego means stability, appropriateness, and moderation of response, whereas a weak ego means instability with poorly directed and excessive responses. Psychotic symptoms are extreme manifestation of a weak ego.

The reason for caution in treating patients with weak egos with biofeedback is that it is not easy to predict the effect of change, even change for the better, upon the patient's overall equilibrium. This follows the principle that changing one part of a system can cause changes in the rest of the system. It also follows the general experience of psychotherapists that change is especially stressful for the weak ego. When biofeedback treatment is considered for a patient with weak ego, a good rule to follow is not to undertake the treatment unless the patient is also under psychiatric care with someone with whom the biofeedback therapist can work closely. In lesser degrees of ego weakness, the collaboration with a psychiatrist is not necessary, but the therapist should be alert for signs of deterioration in the patient. Also, particular kinds of ego weakness are apt to present special problems. Thus, the alcoholic patient and other addicted patients present special challenges requiring special consideration.

Depression is a symptom related to ego strength requiring particular attention. Depression partly represents a feeling of inability to cope and always reflects some loss of ego strength. It is commonly masked by physical symptoms, especially some of those commonly treated by biofeedback, such as headaches (Diamond, 1973). As currently used, biofeedback procedures have not been very successful in dealing with the symptoms of depressed patients. If more than a minimal degree of depression is present, either biofeedback should not be undertaken or it should only be undertaken with concurrent psychiatric management.

The detection of depression or masked depression in a patient requires clinical judgment of a number of factors, including: the presence of recent loss in the patient's life; the expression of futility, discouragement, or apathy; the inability to mobilize hope; signs of insomnia, weight loss, intellectual deterioration; and, sometimes, hypochondriasis, physical preoccupation and passive-dependent dissatisfaction with treatment. Once treatment has begun, the depressed patient is apt to have many of the troubles with treatment referred to in Chapter 5. When it becomes evident that progress is stalled by depression, it is best to refer the patient to a psychiatrist for conventional management, continuing biofeedback treatment or not as indicated by whether therapist and patient can still define a common goal.

§3.5 Personality. A consideration of the patient's personality includes a wide variety of attributes which affect his chances of benefiting from biofeedback treatment. The assessment of this in detail is beyond the scope of this book, and we will restrict ourselves to the evaluation of which types of personality patterns are the most apt to benefit from biofeedback treatment. The two most important issues of personality have to do with whether the patient is able to form a good therapeutic relationship and whether he has much capacity to learn psychophysiological control. Regarding the first issue, the ability to form a good therapeutic relationship, many of the same criteria apply as with other forms of therapy. However, there are numerous instances where patients who do poorly with other methods have had good success with biobeedback therapy. Sometimes this is because the therapeutic relationship is better managed; sometimes it is because the therapeutic relationship is easier to manage with biofeedback treatment; sometimes it is because the attention to physiological processes provides a new focus to which the patient can relate; and sometimes the biofeedback per se is the crucial element.

A major dimension of personality is related to the ability to learn psychophysiological skills. Thus, some people are good athletes and physically courageous while others are not, and some people can learn high degrees of manual dexterity and others cannot. Likewise, some people have intuitive awareness of internal psychophysiological processes or can learn such awareness, while others find this difficult. Although the patient must have some minimal ability to discriminate psychophysiological states, it need not be developed, and some of the best successes come when latent ability is tapped in a patient who had been stunted in this area or who has neglected physical activity. Among those who have considered the problem, there is widespread agreement that our current complex urban culture is lacking in adequate opportunities for the expression of basic human needs of adult physical activity.

Many people, such as suburban housewives or office workers, do not have access to ways of recapturing the pleasure they had from childhood physical activity. Patients who had at one time developed particular physical skills should be considered as potentially especially good patients. Thus, athletics, ballet, or well developed musical skills from childhood should be noted encouragingly.

§3.6 Motivation. When a patient is poorly motivated, it is practically certain that treatment will fail. Therefore, its assessment in patients is crucial. Factors such as the response to the treatment philosophy, ego strength, and personality play a major role in motivation, but other factors must be considered as well. Of great importance here is whether there is secondary gain for the patient in remaining ill. Secondary gain is the reward a patient may receive for being sick – whether in the form of excuse from responsibility, unemployment insurance, added attention from a spouse, sympathy from others, or any other form. This is especially relevant when the patient is receiving some form of compensation which will terminate upon his getting well. The dilemma is: "stay sick and be taken care of, or get well and have to take care of oneself." Broad practical experience in medicine and psychotherapy has found that this particular factor is often nearly impossible to overcome and cases need to be carefully screened to avoid working with patients in whom the secondary gain of their illness is a major factor.

§3.7 Nature of Symptoms. Patients usually seek help because of symptoms, whereas the medical profession and other helping disciplines are oriented toward recognizing and dealing with causes. Seeking causes is practical when there is concrete medical pathology involved, but in the majority of cases, a combination of psychogenic factors and external stresses is of major importance, even though hard to identify and hard to weigh on a relative scale. In addition, these factors must be evaluated in relationship to explanatory theories which are tentative, untestable, and controversial. It is small wonder that many practitioners seek and find comfort in certainty, even at the price of distorting the facts of the situation. Thus, there is strong temptation to deal only with physical causes or to become dogmatically committed to a monolithic theory. Many psychotherapists have recognized with many neurotic patients that it was not hard to get rid of symptoms – what was difficult was dealing with the causes of the symptoms. Although this is often the case with neurotic patients, in a larger number of instances patients with physical symptoms are not strikingly more neurotic than average, and when a symptom is relieved another is not substituted. These make up the mass of medical practices. In addition, the recent experience of behavioral therapists has shown that symptom substitution is not as widespread even with neurotics as previously believed. There is no way of telling for certain if this is due to faulty observation by early or recent investigators, to a different population pool of patients under study, to a change of patients over the years, to characteristics of the different techniques of treatment leading to different results, or to some combination of these factors.

When patients present themselves for biofeedback treatment, their symptoms will have certain characteristics. These include the duration of the symptom, its intensity, the patient's attitude toward it, the role it plays in their lives, the probable structure of their lives if the symptom is removed, and other attributes. These all need to be assessed, either explicitly or implicitly, in deciding whether to treat a patient and deciding upon the course of treatment. Each attribute has its own effect upon the treatment, which we will briefly examine.

Duration of symptom. Long standing symptoms usually reflect a condition which is thoroughly integrated into the patient's life, and we must, therefore, expect treatment to be more difficult and prolonged. On the other hand, a new and acute symptom, even though severe, should be approached optimistically and with vigor, with considerable expectation of being able to provide relief. We still need an intelligent treatment plan, however, and must be aware that all chronic symptoms were once acute and that many times they have become chronic through a chain of circumstances in which inadequate treatment played a role in reinforcing the symptom.

Symptom intensity. Severe symptoms, especially if incapacitating, will often motivate a patient more for their treatment, as long as the patient is not too discouraged about possible improvement and can see progress. Sometimes mild symptoms are not bothersome enough to motivate a patient. Some conditions, such as hypertension, may not even have major symptoms so that the patient lacks the motivation derived from discomfort and must be encouraged to do the work for other reasons.

Attitude toward symptoms. Like any other life experience, the symptom will generate an attitude in the person who must bear it. Some people nurture their symptoms, while others hate them. Some bear them, while others protest loudly. Some see them as someone else's responsibility, while others stoically are reluctant to communicate about them. Some accept their symptoms as they are, while others refuse to accept and accommodate themselves to the symptom even when nothing can change it.

Role of the symptom. Some symptoms in some people take over the patient's life so that all of his emotional energy revolves around the symptom, and it replaces other issues as a focus for meaningfulness. In other people, there will be a successful effort at going on in spite of the symptom and keeping it in its place.

Effect of removing the symptom. For many people, it is easy to see that removing a symptom would merely be excising an impediment. For others, it is equally obvious that the symptom is so fully integrated into the fabric of their lives that removing it would completely change the balance of forces of their lives.

There are other aspects of symptoms discussed elsewhere, including consideration of the nature of the process which the symptom represents (Sec. 3.13), and the relationship between the symptom and the measurable biofeedback parameters (Secs. 3.10–3.11).

§3.8 **Ruling Out Unsuspected Diagnoses.** Whenever a patient is considered for biofeedback treatment, the practitioner needs to consider the thoroughness of the patient's previous work-up to decide whether he has been adequately diagnosed. For instance, although the overwhelming majority of headaches encountered in medical practice are related to stress and emotional factors, there remain a substantial number of cases in which the cause is definite organic disease. Often these organic causes are readily treatable, with complete relief of the accompanying headache, as in the case of glaucoma, and often the organic disease is serious and takes precedence over the symptom, as in the case of brain tumors. Obviously, it is inexcusable to treat such patients with biofeedback when they require further medical work-up and the evaluation process must take this into account. The best way of doing this is to take a careful history of previous medical work-up and tests, to obtain the records of the work-up, to contact the physicians doing the work-up, and to consider further diagnostic work-up before treatment is started. Unless each of these steps is carried out or ruled out with sufficient reason, the undertaking of biofeedback treatment cannot be justified.

Another factor to be considered is whether other treatment needs to be used in a particular case. Some patients we encounter will already have fully utilized other methods of treatment, but in other cases, they will not be using effective medication that can be called upon. Until a longer experience accumulates with biofeedback, it is hard to justify its use in preference to a thoroughly tested method. Thus, for instance, patients with moderately severe hypertension should not be considered for treatment at this time unless they have already been established upon appropriate medication.

The particular professional background of the biofeedback practitioner will determine how these issues need to be managed. Practitioners who are not physicians or physicians who have been out of touch with the particular skills required to manage the patient's condition should consult with the appropriate physicians. On the other hand, those physicians using biofeedback who are in close touch with the appropriate skills can often carry out the complete evaluation on their own.

§3.9 **Previous Treatment.** Many patients who come to biofeedback treatment have a long history of failure with other treatments. These patients are a particular challenge and require a careful approach. Much of what is needed in the approach has to do less with biofeedback than with overcoming the psychology of failure. It is important that the patient be correctly assessed as to his attitude toward treatment and that this then be correctly managed. Some patients are openly cynical about what can be done and need to have their hope rekindled. Other patients are overtly accepting of the previous failures and need to have their skepticism reinforced so that they can be more realistic. In general, patients with previous treatment failure require an implicit or explicit acknowledgment that previous experience has conditioned their expectations, that their expectations can be decisive in the outcome of the present treatment, that both therapeutic success and therapeutic failure are possible in treatment being undertaken, and that the results of the effort at therapeutic collaboration will be important in determining the outcome of the current treatment.

A particularly difficult group of patients are those whose previous treatments have a pattern consisting of initial positive enthusiasm followed by disillusionment in the next stage when the therapeutic agent loses its efficacy. Patient histories should be carefully listened to in order to detect this pattern, and when the pattern is detected, particularly close attention should be paid to the management through the stages where this might occur. As detailed elsewhere (Secs. 1.43; 2.16; 4.10; 4.11; Chap. 5), having effective options for the therapist is crucial.

Some patients, especially those with acute symptoms, may have had no treatment when first seen. In general, this points toward the probability of an easier course of treatment with greater chance of success.

§3.10 **Previous Biofeedback and Relaxation Experience.** By now some patients are beginning to appear who have already had biofeedback experience, either in experimental situations or in clinical settings. In addition, some patients who had previously been treated are returning because of a recurrence of symptoms. Usually these patients are seeking biofeedback by choice and are familiar with what to expect. They may feel that treatment is a progressive situation and that their previous treatment had not been carried far enough to prevent a recurrence. These particular patients are often good ones to work with and do well in their treatment. Other patients with previous experience in treatment are sometimes especially difficult if post-treatment disillusionment had been severe.

Relaxation and biofeedback training is the learning of a skill, and to the extent that it is accepted as such by the patient, there is less recourse to blaming the therapist than in most treatment where the patient has little responsibility for the outcome. In addition, there is usually a recognition that the degree of proficiency achieved at the skill depends on the amount of training and practice. Therefore, a patient who accepts this frame of reference will experience the return of symptoms as due in part to not having learned enough control to prevent recurrence and will need to consider further training as a natural way of coping with the return of symptoms.

§3.11 Symptoms in Relation to Biofeedback Parameters. Here we are giving general consideration to the treatment of a wide variety of symptoms and conditions. Some of these fall into well recognized diagnostic categories where the causal pathology is also well known, while others are part of the large wastebasket of vaguely defined disorders which make up most of medical practice and referral clinic populations. We are not attempting here to catalog exhaustively the disorders for which biofeedback might be indicated or the disorders where it has already been used. Instead, we will offer another system for classifying symptoms and the treatment which may be applied. This system is based on the degree of obvious relationship which exists between the patient's disorder and the biofeedback parameters used in the treatment. In relationship to the treatment provided, disorders may be classified into four groups: (1) those where there is a direct and obvious connection between the disorder and the biofeedback parameter; (2) those where there is a hypothetical direct connection between the disorder and the biofeedback parameter; (3) those where there is a hypothetical indirect connection between the disorder and the biofeedback parameter; and (4) those where the only connection between the disorder and the biofeedback parameter is through the biofeedback parameter mediating the relaxation response.

Obvious direct connection. These are situations where it is widely recognized that the particular parameter used for biofeedback represents the deranged function of the body which is being treated. This is the most rational and logically satisfying use of biofeedback and does not require any particular therapeutic justification to be tried. This is not at all to say that the treatment will necessarily work—only that the treatment is completely rational and obvious. This category of treatment has already been used for a number of disorders. Treatment of essential hypertension by blood pressure biofeedback is a good example. The pathology of essential hypertension is felt by many to represent a simple malfunction of the blood pressure-regulating mechanism, and using blood pressure biofeedback to attempt to remedy this is direct and obvious. Engel (1975) has been in the forefront of recognizing the merit in such an approach. In addition to working with blood pressure biofeedback, he has treated cardiac arrhythmias with direct biofeedback derived from the electrocardiogram and fecal incontinence with anal sphincter pressure biofeedback. These are also examples of disorders where the treatment parameter is directly related to the disorder.

Hypothetical direct connection. In other situations, there are parameters which are hypothesized to have a direct connection with the disorder treated, but where there is not enough accumulated evidence to validate the hypothesis conclusively. Even the efficacy of the treatment does not prove the hypothesis, since the treatment could be effective for reasons other than those hypothesized. A good example of this kind of connection is provided by electromyographic feedback for tension headaches (Budzynski, et al., 1973). The hypothesis is that tension headaches are caused by spasm and contraction of muscles of the scalp and neck, so that when these muscles are relaxed the pain will abate. The electromyographic feedback presents direct information to patients about these muscles, enabling them to work on relaxing the muscles and thereby to abate the pain. Although the treatment works well in many instances, as predicted by the hypothesis, there is not extensive experimental evidence directly supporting the hypothesis.

Hypothetical indirect connection. There are other treatments based upon an indirect connection between the disorder and the feedback parameter. In these situations, since indirect psychophysiological relationships involve conjecture, the connections are hypothetical. An outstanding example of this type of situation is the use of finger temperature feedback in the treatment of migraine headache (Sargent, et al., 1972). Here it is assumed that migraine is the result of a pattern of dilation and constriction of the blood vessels of the scalp and brain, which is controlled by the sympathetic nervous system. In turn, the warmth of the hands is also controlled by the sympathetic nervous system. It is hypothesized that when patients learn to control the warmth of their hands they are indirectly causing normalization of the blood vessels of the forehead at the same time. The reason for this is that the sympathetic nervous system tends to operate as a whole, so that as the hands warm due to the opening of small arteries allowing greater blood flow, there is simultaneously a release of the vasoconstriction of the arteries of the head, which aborts the headache. In this example the connection is both hypothetical and indirect.

Connection through the general relaxation response. This is a specific instance of the hypothetical indirect connection which deserves to be considered by itself because of its central importance in the development of biofeedback approaches. In this situation, the patient has a disorder which is either the specific or non-specific manifestation of a response to stress or reflective of the existence of a self-sustained high arousal or high anxiety state. In other words, it is hypothesized that something is wrong because the patient is too highly aroused or too anxious. Assuming this situation, the obvious remedy is to lower the arousal level and anxiety level by relaxation (Benson, 1975). This leads to the use of biofeedback of a parameter such as the electromyogram as an indicator of relaxation. This approach is lent further support by the experimental fact that arousal level, which is mediated by the reticular activating system of the brain, is sustained by the homeostatic internal feedback loop provided by proprioceptive input from the muscular system. Therefore, when muscles relax they provide less arousal-sustaining input to the reticular activating system.

This rationale for biofeedback as a means to induce relaxation has been widely used by biofeedback therapists with good results. An example is in the treatment of essential hypertension by electromyographic feedback to induce relaxation. Here the assumption is that elevated blood pressure is a specific manifestation of a stress response in which the vicious cycle can be broken by teaching the patient to relax through electromyographic feedback. It is easy to see the contrast with the use of blood pressure feedback for treating the same condition – in that case, there is the direct and obvious connection between the disorder and the parameter, whereas in enhancing the relaxation response, there is the indirect and hypothetical connection. This bears directly on the question of general versus specific treatment and training approaches discussed by Engel (1975) and Schwartz (1975).

§3.12 Classification by Previous Use of Biofeedback by Others. Another means of classifying biofeedback treatments of specific disorders is to divide cases according to whether or not biofeedback has been used by other laboratories and clinics for the treatment of the particular disorder. When the treatment has already been used successfully by others, this adds considerably to the justification of considering biofeedback treatment for a patient's disorder. However, in certain cases, biofeedback treatment should be considered even though it has not been used by others.

This book is addressed to a number of different kinds of readers, among whom are trained clinical practitioners who have complete training in older treatment methods but who have not yet used biofeedback. It certainly is wise for them to become thoroughly familiar with biofeedback before using it with disorders which have not previously been treated by biofeedback. There is a long history of conservatism in clinical practice which is based upon the sound principle that known and tried methods should be used in treatment in preference to unknown and untried methods. However, this book is also addressed to clinical researchers who already have a solid understanding of their own area of competence but who plan to use biofeedback as a treatment method with disorders where it has not previously been used. Just as much as the justification of conservatism can be seen in discouraging the use of untried methods by clinical practitioners, it can be seen that no progress can be made in science unless new things are tried. There is a social consensus at the present time that the research clinic is the proper place for such work to be carried out, and elaborate institutional safeguards have been provided to protect the patient. Operating within the limits of these safeguards, it is assumed that some clinical researchers will be using biofeedback to treat conditions in which it has not yet been tried. An especially promising area for such new use of biofeedback is at the advancing edge of instrumentation technology. Every year dozens of new measurements upon the body become possible. In many instances, biofeedback may be easily provided to the person upon whom the measurement is made merely by allowing him to see the output of the instrument or by performing signal conditioning upon the output and then using a signal display as feedback.

In the next section, another classification method will be used which divides disorders treated by biofeedback according to the nature of the disorder. This will be done largely on the basis of considering disorders where biofeedback treatment has already been found useful. However, from the classification scheme it will be readily apparent that there are many disorders in the same categories where biofeedback has not yet been used but its trial would be warranted.

§3.13 Classification by Nature of the Disorder. By considering the nature of disorders in which biofeedback has been used, by logical analysis of the methods of operation of biofeedback, and by examining elementary control theory, it is possible to classify a number of types of disorders for which biofeedback might be useful. This classification includes both disorders in which it has already been used and those where it has not. The classification is not invariant since a given disorder can be classified in more than one category, partly because the causes of a particular disorder may be multiple or may not be conclusively known. The major headings into which disorders are divided include: stress syndromes, temporary trauma with loss of learning syndromes, neurological damage with loss or failure of learning syndromes, functional derangement syndromes, homeostatic imbalance syndromes, and broken control loop syndromes.

Stress syndromes. These are disorders where stress plays a major role in the cause of the disorder or where the symptoms are made worse by stress to a degree that there is functional interference in the patient's life. Examples include tension and migraine headaches, hypertension, irritable colon, and the muscle spasticity accompanying many cases of neurological damage, which is made worse by stress.

Temporary trauma with loss of learning syndrome. These are disorders which follow a trauma. In some instances, there is no residual structural damage following the trauma, but an undesired form of one-trial learning appears to take place which cannot be overcome. An example of this is fecal incontinence following successful rectal surgery. Even though there is no residual anatomical damage, a functional pattern of failure to activate normal reflexes is established. It is as if the control system were temporarily out of order but then cannot find its way back to working.

Neurological damage with loss or failure of learning syndrome. In these conditions, there is definite organic neurological damage but there remains residual capacity. A major problem in rehabilitation of these patients is that the residual capacity may be unused because it cannot be identified by the patient and because it is not mentally associated with the learned patterns from before the damage occurred. In other words, the learned patterns of moving a neurologically intact hand are no longer relevant to the use of the hand when a significant amount of the neurological control is removed and an entirely new learned pattern of control needs to be established. It is logically obvious that the information provided by electromyographic feedback from neurologically damaged muscles can be an important adjunct in retraining the muscles. The situation of the patient is in many formal ways precisely analogous to that of a pilot landing an airplane. Neurological damage deprives the patient of information in the same way fog or darkness deprives the pilot of information, and feedback is another way of getting that information just as are the pilot's instruments.

Biofeedback has already been used to treat certain neurological disorders, such as stroke and torticollis (see Chap. 10), but there are numerous diseases and post-traumatic conditions in which equivalent neurological damage exists but biofeedback has not yet been tried. There is little doubt but that equivalent results should be expected in these syndromes. In general, it is the extent of neurological damage which determines the response to treatment more than the etiological nature of the damage.

Functional derangement syndromes. In the anatomical versus functional system of classification, disorders are divided according to whether or not anatomical abnormality can be demonstrated. In the functional class, such abnormality is not demonstrated and it is assumed that the parts are intact but that they are not working together properly. In analogy to an automobile, anatomical damage would be a punctured tire or a broken fan belt, while functional abnormality might be having the spark plug wires connected to the wrong plugs. Most psychiatric conditions, including the neuroses and the myriad psychosomatic conditions which make up much of medical practice, are conceived as having no primary anatomical damage to the affected organs, but as resulting from parts not functioning together correctly. Tension headaches and migraine headaches would be classified as functional illnesses in this system since muscle spasm, vasoconstriction and vaso-dilation are the result of normal functions of the relevant organs carried to an extreme. Likewise, essential hypertension shows no evidence of anatomical abnormality until secondary effects of the elevated pressure set in.

Homeostatic imbalance and dysregulation syndromes. According to the concept of homeostasis, there are numerous measurable bodily functions whose normal values are meant to stay within normal limits and disease is the result of an imbalance which allows the values of these functions to go outside of normal limits. Essential hypertension is considered a prime example of such a disease, understandable by anal-ogy to the thermostat controlling the temperature of a house. Blood pressure is controlled by mechanisms essentially similar to those of the thermostat controlling the temperature of the house, and hypertension is analogous to a thermostat being set too high. The problem of treat-ment becomes one of resetting the thermostat at a lower level. This is largely the equivalent of a regulatory mechanism dysfunctioning.

Broken control loop syndromes. When a patient has a stroke, the motor control of his limbs is often relatively intact, but it is the sensory inflow from the affected limb that is damaged. This can be conceptual-ized as damage to the internal control loop, and biofeedback is seen as providing the information that has been made unavailable by the dam-age. Neurological syndromes will someday be more precisely analyzed in this regard. At present, analysis is rather crude and usually not operationally related to the treatment effect we hope to obtain (Chap. 10). One important exception is the method used by Brudny, et al. (1974b) based on the concept of a broken control loop.

§3.14 Indications and Contraindications for Biofeedback Treatment. The use of biofeedback treatment in any given case depends upon all of the above factors as well as upon other issues which good judgment deems relevant. After each of these factors has been considered, the composite picture may be put together to consider whether biofeedback treatment should be undertaken. The first consideration is always whether sufficient study of the case has ruled out the need to consider other diagnoses and has ruled out the use of other treatment to take precedence over biofeedback. Once this is established, there arises the question of whether the patient's condition will respond to feedback treatment. This depends upon the patient, upon the nature of the symptom, upon the nature of the disorder causing the symptom, and upon the treatment modalities available in the facility, especially biofeedback parameters available. The evaluation of these various factors can be reduced to an algorithm and presented on a flow sheet. Although this accurately portrays steps which should not be left out of a careful evaluation, it does not help in arriving at the decision which must be made at each step before proceeding.

§3.15 **Summary.** Patients in whom biofeedback treatment is being considered must be evaluated to decide whether or not the treatment is appropriate. Much of this evaluation involves consideration of the same psychological factors assessed with other treatment methods, but sometimes with a different weighting of the factors. Other parts of the evaluation concern the particular nature of the symptoms and how the symptoms relate to potential biofeedback parameters.

. . . he will manage the cure best who has foreseen what is to happen from the present state of matters.

Hippocrates

Just as time can bring rain, roses, flowers, and shape all things from their beginning to their end, and no one can stop it, so can it also make diseases break out at will. The physician must never forget that time can do this, or he will be unable to discover what is possible and what is impossible and to understand what he can nevertheless undertake to inspire people with respect for the medical art that God has created, and to prevent the disease from getting worse, for this cannot be the intention of God. Time is a brisk wind, for each hour brings something new . . . but who can understand and measure its sharp breath, its mystery, and its design? Therefore, the physician must not think himself too important, for over him there is a master – time – which plays with him as the cat with the mouse.

Paracelsus

We are aware that the intercalation of periods of change and novelty is the only means by which we can refresh our sense of time, strengthen, retard, and rejuvenate it, and therewith renew our perception of life itself. Such is the purpose of our changes of air and scene, of all our sojourns at cures and bathing resorts; it is the secret of the healing power of change and incident.

Thomas Mann
The Magic Mountain

Good advice is no better than bad advice unless it is taken at the right time.

Danish Proverb

CHAPTER 4

Structuring a treatment program

§4.1 **Introduction.** In Sections 2.24 to 2.26, concepts of time and structure were presented as representing one basis for considering the process involved in a treatment relationship. In this chapter these concepts will be elaborated into a more detailed model of the treatment process. This will be done by successively describing the structure of action cycles (Secs. 4.2–4.12), the structure of the whole treatment (Secs. 4.13–4.18), the structure of a session (Secs. 4.19–4.24), and the structure of training (Secs. 4.25–4.30). The first three considerations of structure heavily involve the intuitive psychological management of the patient as a matter of first concern, whereas the structure of training gives the psychology of learning first priority.

In each instance, the structure has been divided into five phases. The first phase takes place before the process under consideration (action cycle, treatment, treatment session, or training cycle) is undertaken. These are always designated by the prefix *pre*. The second phase always involves becoming involved in the process under consideration and in general can be considered introductory, although designated differently in each of the different processes. The third phase is the one in which the majority of the time in the process is spent and the main phase in which the process' aims are achieved. It can always be considered a middle phase. The fourth phase is the one in which the process under consideration is finished and can be designated an end phase. The final, fifth phase takes place after the process has been finished and can be designated by the prefix *post*.

The structure of treatment, the structure of a session, and the structure of training all can be conceived as specific instances of the general concept of action cycles (Spitz, 1964; Gaarder, 1966), but if this does not meet the needs of the particular reader the text has been organized so that utilizing the concept of action cycle is not essential to reading and understanding. Since there are a number of unfamiliar ideas, many readers will find that it helps to read through rapidly at first to get an overview, returning later to absorb the fuller meaning.

STRUCTURE OF ACTION CYCLES

§4.2 Introduction. Action cycles are of several different sorts. In order to understand them, various examples will be considered (see 4.3; 4.9–4.12), but it must be appreciated that certain elements of the examples cannot easily be generalized. Action cycles may last varying amounts of time and occur at various hierarchical levels. Thus, some cycles may take much of a lifetime to complete; others occur over months, days, hours or minutes; while short ones can be completed within a few seconds. Some are repeated dozens of times every hour, while others may occur only once. Although we can appreciate intuitively and from examples that action cycles represent intrinsic natural units of behavior, often we must recognize that our best intellectual efforts fail to capture this intrinsic nature and that the units which we conceptualize are not quite the ones existing in the real situation.

In addition, there are different systemic contexts within which action cycles can be defined. In treatment, for instance, they may be considered only within the patient or they may be considered within the dyadic relationship or even more widely to include other parts of the patient's environment, including the whole therapeutic team. For the most part, we will only consider them from within the patient or the dyad of patient and therapist. Also, action cycles may be classified according to whether or not they further desirable ends. Thus, patients' action cycles which do not harmoniously further their reasonable goals will be considered pathological (Sec. 4.10), while therapeutic action cycles (Sec. 4.11) can be categorized as to whether or not they contribute to the progress of treatment and training action cycles (Sec. 4.12) as to whether learning occurs.

Action cycles are a large subject, and we will only consider them here as they apply in the most obvious ways to biofeedback treatment. In the broad sense in which we use the concept, they include the action cycles representing the structure of treatment, the structure of sessions, and the structure of training although they can also exist apart from these arbitrary structures and are not restricted to them. Thus, in one instance a particular action cycle might be completed within a few minutes of a session, whereas the next time that action cycle recurs it might begin in a session and not be completed until several sessions later.

As just stated (Sec. 4.1), for our overall consideration of structure we will divide an action cycle into five phases, although naming them slightly differently. The five phases we will consider are the pre-condition, the triggering (introductory), the crisis (middle), the resolution (end), and the reprise (post) phases.

§4.3 Examples of Action Cycles. Action cycles are the warp and woof of everyday life, intuitively understood but usually invisible before our eyes. Thus, sitting down to a meal and finishing it, chewing a bite of food, smoking a cigarette, meeting a friend on the street to chat and part, or dialing a telephone number each is a lucid, specific instance of an action cycle. Although we can gain insight by our consideration of these, from the practical point of view it is most important that we understand pathological and therapeutic action cycles.

Pathological action cycles are represented by certain things which occur within and outside of the context of therapy. Usually everything which occurs within therapy will also occur outside of therapy, but on the other hand, many specific important pathological action cycles will never be seen firsthand by the therapist. Thus, the obese and alcoholic will usually not live out before our eyes the sequence of events culminating in an eating or drinking binge. On the other hand, we may expect to observe analogous processes in their treatment having to do with the moral struggle of self-indulgence and the withering of resolution.

The structure provided by the action cycle of our treatment plan can provide the context out of which a pathological action cycle emerges. This will be seen when one considers the following as beginnings of pathological action cycles: the failure to keep appointments or follow directions or carry out home practice, falling asleep during practice, or introducing large numbers of unanswerable questions. More subtle pathological action cycles which are harder to detect may involve superficial compliance after the patient has really already departed from the spirit of collaboration the therapist hopes to foster.

The action cycles of treatment can be viewed from several points of view to have several structures. Their explicit structure involves how they are planned and carried out by the therapist. Thus, so many trials, with such and such criteria will be used in a given phase of treatment before inaugurating a new treatment routine. Behind this explicit plan will be the real results which may not be appreciated and are therefore implicit. Thus, a patient may be ready for a new stage far before we introduce it, or may be already long astray on a wild goose chase because he cannot follow our directions or does not believe something we say.

§4.4 **Pre-Conditional Phase.** Particular action cycles always begin within their own particular appropriate context and will not begin in the wrong context. Thus, a meal begins at certain times of the day, in a dining room or restaurant and would not begin during the middle of a typical church service, swimming meet, or drive in the country. Likewise, after-dinner speeches hopefully are only undertaken by invitation and the composition of music undertaken only after inspiration to at least some degree. Likewise, the action cycle of seeking treatment (see Sec. 4.14) does not begin unless the cause for seeking treatment develops, and patients do not turn up for treatment sessions until they have started a treatment program. Although these examples appear obvious and trite and seem to be circularly defined, they must be understood in order to understand the more complicated instances of structure in time still to be considered. After further specific instances are given the concepts will become clearer.

§4.5 Triggering (Introductory) Phase. This is the beginning of the action cycle per se and is introductory in the sense that it is here that a functional commitment is made to enter into the rest of the action cycle. Action cycles are often entered into because of encounter with a trigger of some sort, although such is not always the case, as for the beginning of a treatment session or for a therapist's initiation of a long planned maneuver. After the triggering occurs, the cycle then begins to unfold in its predetermined way through its early steps to reach the middle phase. These predetermined introductory steps carry the cycle inevitably into the middle phase because they unfold without variation.

§4.6 Crisis (Middle) Phase. When one is attempting to influence the outcome of an action cycle, as in treatment, or when one is attempting to understand how pathology develops, it is often most appropriate to consider the middle phase of an action cycle as a crisis phase, because it is usually here that the question of outcome is decided. Another way of looking at this is in terms of flow diagrams, where branch points are frequently encountered. In treatment, two of the most common crises occur around the therapist recognizing either that a patient has introduced a pathological action cycle which can be terminated or that an action cycle of a training procedure has been successful so that the therapist should give positive reinforcement.

§4.7 Resolution (End) Phase. Once the decision points of the middle phase have been passed, and the bulk of the time in the cycle has been spent, the end of the action cycle is approached. In general, the decisions of the middle phase cause the ending to attain a particular structure which warrants the term of resolution. Thus, when a pathological action cycle is not detected, it usually ends with the patient's expected outcome, whereas if intervention succeeded, the path is different. Likewise, if a training cycle succeeded, the patient emerges ready for the next stage, whereas if not, it needs to be repeated to success or altered to allow success.

§4.8 Reprise (Post) Phase. After an action cycle is completed, the situational context has become altered by whatever the results of the cycle have been. A reprise is a return to basic melody in music. Here the reprise is the return to the context out of which the action cycle arose, as modified by the results of the action cycle.

§4.9 Everyday Action Cycles. It is hoped by now that the reader has gained a feeling for action cycles as the structural substance of everyday life. We will examine a day's activity to see the evidence of this substance and of its hierarchical organization.

We wake in the morning and go through a routine of personal toilet. Then we dress. After this we eat breakfast. Next, we may go to work. At work, a particular routine is laid out—including sub-tasks, coffee breaks, communication with superiors, peers, and subordinates, lunch, and finishing at the end of the day. We then return from work and enter into a structured routine before going back to sleep. This includes supper, communication with family, recreation, home chores, and getting ready for bed.

This series of activities taken as a whole from waking, through the day, back to sleep, and then again waking the next morning represents a particular action cycle at the highest hierarchical level we will consider for the moment—the day's activities as an action cycle. Next, at a lower hierarchical level, the day is divided into a series of activities which form the units of the day: sleep, awakening and preparation, breakfast, going to work, lunch, work, returning from work, evening meal, evening activities, return to sleep. Each of these in turn can be considered as an action cycle. Likewise, each of these activities is also divided into subunits. Thus, upon arising, personal toilet and getting dressed are accomplished together in a particular structure wherein particular activities, such as brushing teeth or putting on trousers are accomplished. Each of these activities likewise constitutes an action cycle. Furthermore, each of these activities has its own unitary structure—thus, brushing the teeth typically involves a sequence of acts such as picking up the toothbrush, turning on the faucet at the sink, wetting the toothbrush, applying toothpaste, etc. Each of these is a lower hierarchical level of action cycle, but each is an action cycle, as much as all of the previous examples.

The subdivision into still lower hierarchical levels will not be described further, except to point out that this can be done down to the level of even considering individual nerve spikes as instances of the lowest level of action cycle (Gaarder, 1975). It can be reconized, however, that the action cycles of everyday life are undertaken in such a way that the normal homeostasis of everyday life is preserved.

§4.10 Pathological Action Cycles. As an arbitrary matter, we will define pathological action cycles as any action cycles which either lead to disease or are in themselves a manifestation of disease. After our earlier recognition that stress may lead to disease (Secs. 1.36–1.37), we may now see how the myriad activities undertaken under stress may represent pathological action cycles. Thus, in someone who later develops lung cancer each smoking of a cigarette represents a pathological action cycle, as does each puff. Likewise, in a person predisposed to psychosomatic illness, each encounter with stress which takes physiological variables outside of homeostatic limits will be a pathological action cycle. Thus, the hypertensive who drives himself too hard on a particular occasion, or who becomes angry over a necessary event, or who suppresses anger, or who avoids contact until sensitized against it, will, in each instance cited, be involved in a pathological action cycle. Once the diseased condition is established, the actions undertaken will as a matter of course usually represent pathological action cycles. Thus, the hypertensive's daily encounters with stress (even if the stress is minimal) in which the blood pressure remains elevated, represents pathological action cycles.

The particular pathological action cycle of most concern to the biofeedback therapist involves the psychological and psychophysiological action cycle in which a pathological attitude is retained. Several examples will be given. The clearest examples involve situations which occur within therapy, which will be described in greater detail in the next paragraph. However, it can readily be seen that the same process went on before therapy began.

The most common situation results from the patient's chronic expectations of failure. Thus, many patients do not believe that they have control over certain aspects of their own destinies and expect to fail in the attempt to achieve such control. Self-control of drinking and eating in the alcoholic and obese have already been mentioned in this context. Very common is the belief that one cannot learn to relax. Therefore, when attempting to learn, a particular failure is taken to prove that the entire task will fail and the patient may give up. This sequence represents that most important action cycle which the therapist must learn to detect and influence.

Another common pathological action cycle in the psychological sphere involves the widespread trait of contrariness. Almost everyone is occasionally contrary; however, in patients the trait is often exaggerated, so that when asked to do one thing the patient is impelled to do the opposite. This situation involves an action cycle which is the sequence in which the contrariness unfolds. The skill of the therapist is put to test in attempting to prevent the completion of action cycles of contrariness. The trait is apt to come out in simple history taking, where one cannot get definite information because of the need for constant modification of what is said. It is also seen when a patient is asked to relax and instead will get more tense. Ways of dealing with this have been described at length in the psychotherapy literature and will not be detailed here (Haley, 1967, 1968). We do not mean to imply that "contrariness" as we have described it may not cover other things behind it or that it may not sometimes be adaptive. It was mainly given as an example of pathological action cycle, since it can derail treatment.

§4.11 Therapeutic Action Cycles. The rest of this chapter will deal in detail with the structure of treatment. Here we merely wish to clarify that all of this structure represents action cycles and that successful therapeutic action cycles have particular structures. Likewise, unsuccessful therapeutic action cycles also have particular structure and it is our task to differentiate these.

Some examples of successful therapeutic action cycles include: the process by which an attitude of expected failure is turned into the allowing of hope; the process by which apathy is turned into self-confidence; the process by which a patient learns to relax in the laboratory; the process by which a specific task becomes associated with the different, more general task required for symptom control. Since these are dealt with in detail below, we will not go further here to describe these action cycles.

§4.12 Training Action Cycles. When training is divided as described below (Secs. 4.25–4.30), the components of a procedure are structured in action cycles defined by the therapist. One main reason for separating them from therapeutic action cycles is to emphasize the dual role of the therapist as healer and teacher, even though these two roles are intertwined.

STRUCTURE OF THE WHOLE TREATMENT

§4.13 Introduction. A biofeedback treatment can be divided into five phases, each with its own special characteristics. These five phases are: (1) the pre-treatment phase (Sec. 4.14); (2) the introductory phase (Sec. 4.15); (3) the treatment phase (Sec. 4.16); (4) the termination phase (Sec. 4.17); and (5) the post-treatment phase (Sec. 4.18).

§4.14 Pre-Treatment Phase. In this phase of the treatment program, the patient's symptoms have developed and reached the extent where the patient seeks help for them. There may be other sources of help tried before reaching the biofeedback treatment facility, or it may be the first place help is sought. Sometimes the patient knows the personnel of the biofeedback treatment program and sometimes the patient is a stranger. Most of the typical pathological action cycles (see Sec. 4.10) encountered with a specific patient will have become instilled during this phase. It is in the pre-treatment phase that the homeostatic adaptive control systems (HACS of Sec. 1.9) have gone through the successive transformation of state (Sec. 1.10), partially in response to the stresses of the particular environment (Secs. 1.36–1.37), which have resulted in the particular deranged homeostasis of disease (Sec. 1.35) for which treatment is sought.

§4.15 **Introductory Phase.** It is here that the groundwork of a successful treatment is laid. The patient assessment described in Chapter 3 occurs here; and, more importantly, there are established the working rules of the therapeutic contract (Secs. 2.8–2.15). The use of questionnaires (Appendix B) and standardized tests can ensure that the major categories of information necessary are all covered and that patients are introduced to thinking of their symptoms in a constructive and exploratory manner. Baseline physiological information is collected in the second session (Secs. 8.7–8.9). The goals of treatment (Secs. 2.12–2.13) are tentatively determined at this time also, and the method of reaching the goals is developed in the goal-setting session (Sec. 8.15).

§4.16 **Treatment (Middle) Phase.** Once the patient is introduced to the therapeutic setting, the treatment begins. In this phase the patient begins to have actual treatment sessions, and the therapist evaluates the progression of treatment on the basis of the patient's performance between sessions and during sessions. It is important here to structure the training correctly to take progress and roadblocks into account (see Chap. 5). Thus, one must not go on to a new stage until the previous goal has been achieved, but, likewise, there is loss from lingering too long with a task already mastered (Secs. 8.20–8.26).

§4.17 **Termination (End) Phase.** Once the patient has reached the goals for which treatment was sought, it is time for termination. However, this must be structured in such a way that recurrence of symptoms or the onset of new symptoms is avoided (Secs. 2.19; 5.12; 8.21; 8.27). The largest issue here is a patient's dependency or need for emotional support as against his faith in his own ability to sustain himself without further help. Anything which is threatening should be avoided, and every effort should be made to prepare the patient as gradually as possible. For a skilled therapist, the question of termination is present in the first meeting with the patient, and the entire treatment is structured around the reality of this fact. It is important to make sure that termination is not abrupt. This can often be accomplished by introducing the idea explicitly as the patient is approaching his goals and suggesting that in three or four more sessions he may be able to finish. Some patients do well without "tapering off," while other patients prefer having a gradual increase in the interval between sessions near the end of treatment. For most patients, it is a good idea to leave the door open for them to return in the event symptoms recur, whereas for a few it is important to close the door. The reason for the latter is usually when there is a mutual recognition of continuing dependency needs not being met which are apt to lead to a return of symptoms if it may justify return to treatment.

§4.18 **Post-Treatment Phase.** Once treatment is over, the further experiences of our patients ensue. If the treatment was successful, they will be relieved of their symptoms to a large extent and will not have recurrence. On the other hand, to the degree that treatment does not succeed, there may be various residuals of the presenting complaints. If treatment was for the effects of neurological damage, the patient may still have major departures from normal function which can never be relieved or he may be able to continue a self-sustaining program of gradual work toward further recovery. Some patients will have been relieved of their presenting disorders, but later find that a new condition develops for which they may seek further treatment.

As professionals with a responsibility toward our colleagues and toward our profession, it is important that we keep an open and inquiring mind turned toward the results of our treatments. There are not yet many follow-up studies of biofeedback treatment available, and it is important that we obtain information on this from our patients and report our findings. Only in this way will the actual value of different methods be established (Secs. 5.13; 5.14; 8.34).

STRUCTURE OF A SESSION

§4.19 Introduction. Just as the treatment as a whole has structure at the highest hierarchical level we consider, so does the individual treatment session have structure at a lower hierarchical level (Sec. 2.27). The five phases of a treatment session are: (1) the pre-session phase (Sec. 4.20); (2) the reassessment phase (Sec. 4.21); (3) the middle or work phase (Sec. 4.22); (4) the closing phase (Sec. 4.23); and (5) the follow-through phase (Sec. 4.24). Much of Chapter 5 deals with the details of this.

§4.20 Pre-Session Phase. This phase, before a session begins, contains the residual of previous sessions and the impingement of intervening events since the last session. The residual of previous sessions is what the experience of patient and therapist has been to this point. It includes the home practice and self-observation assignments given the patient and what has been done with them, the patient's sense of success or failure with the treatment to that point, long term action cycles which are in process, the adequacy or inadequacy of the records of treatment being kept, and the therapist's ongoing between-session assessment of the patient and the treatment. The patient and therapist are almost always completely apart during this phase and the last (follow-through) phase, whereas the times they are together are during the three phases of the treatment session itself. The impingement of intervening events is a variable for which the therapist must always allow, and always keep correct perspective. Whenever other events put either patient or therapist into an unusually bad mood, they must not expect to be able to work as well. Thus, such obviously traumatic events as illness or accidents in the immediate family, serious arguments, failing examinations, being fired from a job, etc., must be expected to disrupt treatment temporarily, while lesser degrees of similar traumas may be expected to have their effect.

Keeping intervening events in perspective includes the consideration of how it is to affect the treatment session. One particular thing for which to be on the lookout is the patient who experiences and lives life in terms of exploiting others with his sad situation. These patients experience the events of their lives as requiring special allowances from others and they will frequently find something which keeps them from doing what has been expected of them. The therapist must be firm in maintaining that the treatment plan not be violated because of alleged special circumstances.

§4.21 Reassessment (Introductory) Phase. When patient and therapist meet for a session there is a period of briefly recapitulating the events of the pre-session phase and sizing up where they are to begin. Some of this may be done formally and explicitly through direct discussion, and some of it is carried out intuitively and non-verbally. Thus, it is usually important to talk with the patient in some detail about his home practice since the last session, but some of the assessment of this will be done intuitively rather than from the direct answers the patient gives. The intuitive assessment involves: noticing the patient's greeting – whether it is open or guarded, friendly or distant; noting the response to questions – whether direct or tangential; noting mood, etc. These things must be taken into account in then planning the session. A most important part of the reassessment is the awareness of the status of long term action cycles which are being worked upon with the patient.

§4.22 Work (Middle) Phase. After the reassessment, patient and therapist decide what is to be done in the session and get down to doing it. Sometimes they will proceed as previously decided and sometimes they will need to revise their plan. The work itself is naturally the most important part of treatment, but needs be considered within the context of all of the issues already brought up here.

§4.23 Closing (End) Phase. As time runs out, the day's progress is assessed and assignment of practice is made for the interim before the next session. Practice assignments take the revised assessment at closing into account. If more progress is made than expected, the practice may be accelerated; whereas if progress is slow, the steps of the home practice may be further broken down into more manageable segments.

§4.24 Follow-Through (Post-Session) Phase. Much of the results of a session will manifest themselves after the session is over. The particular gain of the session on treatment goals is either consolidated or lost; the home practice is either observed or neglected. The above are parts of the direct therapeutic action cycles which are ongoing during the treatment; other action cycles also continue to evolve during the interim. The follow-through phase of one session may be considered to merge or overlap with the pre-session phase of the next, and we separate them partly because they are distinct as experientially encountered from within a particular session. Thus, today's follow-through phase becomes the pre-session phase from tomorrow's perspective.

STRUCTURE OF TRAINING

§4.25 **Introduction.** The learning process, as arbitrarily separated from the therapeutic process, can be viewed at several different levels. Two levels would be identical with the structure of treatment and the structure of a session as already considered above. At another level, training represents an action cycle entered into in relation to some particular learning goal of the treatment. Here these would be the same five phases with which we have become familiar — the innocent (pre-learning) phase (Sec. 4.26); the introductory phase (Sec. 4.27); the work (middle) phase (Sec. 4.28); the consolidating (end) phase (Sec. 4.29); and the post-learning phase (Sec. 4.30). We will briefly examine each.

§4.26 **Innocent (Pre-Learning) Phase.** When considering a learning process, it is often appropriate to consider the state before the learning commences as innocence, because of the profound consequences which may ensue from knowledge. Sometimes the person would never imagine the possibilities which follow the acquisition of knowledge. Other times, even though the person knows of them, they are not appreciated until experienced firsthand. In biofeedback training, we are considering innocence such things as the failure to appreciate that a person has it within his power to relax at will. Adult cerebral palsy patients often express the thought that they literally do not know what relaxation means.

§4.27 **Introductory Phase.** It is at this stage that the therapist works with the patient on determining specific goals and picking a strategy for reaching the goals. The patient encounters the therapist's belief in the possibility of achieving a particular goal and accepts the partnership implied in working toward that goal.

§4.28 **Work (Middle) Phase.** Having set goals, the patient and therapist now enter upon the process of achieving the goal in training sessions. Here the task gets further divided into smaller action cycles such as a week's home practice assignment or a trial run with a certain task. The general principles of learning will apply as constraints to what can be achieved. Of particular importance will be the structuring of the task into small enough steps so as to achieve regular success and the therapist's attention to the patient's reactions to reinforcement.

§4.29 **Consolidating (End) Phase.** Once a particular goal has been reached, it becomes necessary to consolidate that goal. One method of consolidating a goal is to begin to work toward a further goal which makes use of the skills just acquired. Another is to continue to practice the skill. A third is to practice the skill until one knows it well enough so that it can be relearned more rapidly when needed later. However done, the therapist attempts to ascertain that the necessary skill will not be lost after treatment.

§4.30 **Post-Learning Phase.** After the goal has been mastered and the formal learning ended, the patient enters into the post-learning phase in which the skills are either retained or lost and have their particular impact upon the life of the patient.

§4.31 **Summary.** This chapter has explored in depth the problem of structure existing over time. We have examined the different phases of a time-defined structure and have seen how all behavior and all process can be conceived as a manifestation of action cycles. In particular, action cycles describe everyday life, the development of pathology, the process of therapy, and the learning which takes place in a training procedure.

The one mark of maturity, especially in a physician, and perhaps it is even rarer in a scientist, is the capacity to deal with uncertainty.

William B. Bean

You will remember, of course, always get the weather-gage of your patient. I mean, to place him so the light falls on his face and not on yours. It is a kind of ocular duel that is about to take place between you; you are going to look through his features into his pulmonary and hepatic and other internal machinery, and he is going to look into yours quite as sharply to see what you think about his probabilities for time and eternity.

No matter how hard he stares at your countenance, he should never be able to read his fate in it. It should be cheerful as long as there is hope, and serene in its gravity when nothing is left but resignation. The face of a physician, like that of a diplomatist, should be impenetrable.

Oliver Wendell Holmes
Medical Essays

Some shrewd old doctors have a few phrases always on hand for patients that will insist on knowing the pathology of their complaints without the slightest capacity of understanding the scientific explanation . . . I think nothing on the whole has covered so much ground, and meant so little, and given such profound satisfaction to all parties, as the magnificent phrase "congestion of the portal system."

Oliver Wendell Holmes
Medical Essays

CHAPTER 5

Assessment and modification of treatment

§5.1 **Introduction.** Assessment of all aspects of the biofeedback treatment relates in some way to the therapeutic contract described in Chapter 2. Assessment of the pre-treatment course (Secs. 5.2–5.3), the introductory phase (Secs. 5.4–5.5), and the third visit (Secs. 5.6–5.7) results in establishment of the contract. Assessment of home practice and the clinical course (Secs. 5.8–5.9) is essentially an assessment of how well the contract is being maintained by both the patient and the therapist. Assessment of the sessions (Secs. 5.10–5.11) is concerned with progress toward contract goals during the visits to the biofeedback laboratory. Assessment during termination (Sec. 5.12) is concerned with how well the contract goals are maintained as termination is considered and whether a bridge from the laboratory to the life experience has been established which can sustain the gains. Assessment after termination, or follow-up (Secs. 5.13–5.14) determines whether the patient is able to maintain contract goals after regular laboratory visits have ended.

Each section has a part which is the patient's and a part which the therapist must do. The therapist must attend to whether the patient is doing his part and guide him if necessary, always attending to cues the patient gives. Furthermore, the therapist must have carried out his between-session responsibilities.

These general concepts apply when the treatment is for any of the conditions treated with biofeedback. The descriptions contained in this chapter will adhere closely to the treatment of a stress-related problem but would apply in some measure to neuromuscular re-education and other biofeedback-treated problems.

ASSESSMENT OF THE PRE-TREATMENT COURSE

The first session is an interview denoted to assessing whether the patient and therapist can reach positions which have been reached by prior patients with successful therapeutic outcomes.

§5.2 **Patient's Part.** To suggest that the patient must come to the biofeedback setting with an attitude of wanting to get well and a willingness to assume the responsibility for his own treatment seems a statement of the obvious. However, to emphasize that these attributes must not only be apparent, but genuine, is necessary, and the patient needs an opportunity in this early phase to recognize and adjust his stance on these matters.

If the patient is there to please someone other than himself, or if he really feels that the therapy will not help, or if he has difficulty seeing himself as symptom free, then he needs to be aware that the tools he brings to the session must be improved. Likewise, if he indicates a willingness to place himself in the hands of the therapist and allow the therapist or the machine to take away his symptom, then his therapeutic tools need adjusting.

When he adopts a stance of open-mindedness about the treatment outcome and a determination to do his part without overdoing it, along with a sincere wish to be free of the symptom, then he is doing his part in this early stage.

§5.3 Therapist's Part. The therapist must have his stance clearly in mind and his powers of observation well tuned. Beginning with the first contact, the therapist must attend to all of the information the patient is giving, both verbal and non-verbal. The patient's attitude toward treatment, his expectations, his fears, and his questions must all be observed and responded to, whether or not the patient makes them obvious. The patient's readiness to use the treatment opportunity must be assessed by the therapist, and he must help the patient to understand his position on the questions describing the patient's part.

Good notes are essential. Notes must include a description of the chief complaint and all observable or measurable qualities of the symptom such as frequency, severity, duration, and conditions of onset. Whether the initiation of the symptom is linked to any life event should be noted, as well as what makes it better or worse and whether a thorough medical examination has ruled out organic considerations. In the case of headaches, it is good to consider the possibility of allergies, especially in parts of the country where they are common. Whether as a child, the patient regularly observed any adult with the same symptom should be noted, especially if the philosophy that the symptom may be a learned response to stress is to be considered.

We use a pre-treatment symptom questionnaire form (see Appendix B.3 Part I). It lists specific, measurable considerations of the symptoms which may serve as a basis for the symptom goal to be described later and it serves as a comparison with follow-up information, since it asks many of the same questions for direct comparison of pre-treatment and post-treatment symptom measures.

Having assessed the patient's stance and obtained information from him, it is good to share with him an overview of what he may expect during his treatment experience. This discussion might begin with a question as to how he learned about biofeedback and how he feels it can help him. Wide publicity of various opinions on biofeedback has influenced many potential patients. His expectations can be managed in this early contact by sharing with him information that specific goals will be set and that the biofeedback and related activities will all be in the interest of reaching these goals. He should know that he will be instrumented in the laboratory for whatever parameters are appropriate and will spend that time acquiring physiological skills, and also that the home practice will enhance his laboratory sessions. He should know that all information will be shared with him since it is he who must use it, and if his progress is other than expected, that information will also be shared. He should also know that he should expect to come to the laboratory for 1 hour a week for approximately 8 to 12 weeks and practice at home for two 20-minute periods each day. A discussion of fees is appropriate before the actual treatment sessions get under way. In our setting, we are concerned that the referring physician is informed that his patient is in biofeedback training and that good communication is maintained with the physician throughout the biofeedback treatment.

ASSESSMENT OF THE INTRODUCTORY PHASE

Baseline physiological measures are obtained in this, the second session.

§5.4 **Patient's Part.** In this phase, the patient enters the laboratory for the first time and comes face to face with unfamiliar electronic equipment. Rarely, if ever, is this experience encountered without question. The patient should be encouraged to express his feelings and ask questions until he is comfortable that he understands what will take place in this now unfamiliar setting. He must learn to return to this setting time after time without feeling anxious about any part of it. He must allow the instrumentation to be attached to his body and attend to both the explanations and instructions which the therapist will give. Furthermore, he must be able and willing to follow any procedure such as a relaxation exercise which may be used in this session and observe his own subjective responses. After the procedure, he must share his observations with the therapist and mention any questions which may be on his mind about the home practice exercise he is to use. He must make a commitment to the home practice assignment and to return for the next scheduled appointment time.

§5.5 **Therapist's Part.** The therapist should be aware of the patient's concerns as he enters the laboratory and should prepare before the session to keep confusion to a minimum by having all materials and instrumentation in readiness. As the patient enters the laboratory, the therapist should pay particular attention to whether the patient appears comfortable or anxious. He should give the patient ample time to become familiar with the laboratory setting including the sights and sounds of the various instruments. A friendly attitude with obvious willingness to answer questions may be enough to encourage the patient's inquiry. If he has no questions, the therapist should give him some basic information such as that the equipment cannot shock him, or, in the case of EEG, that it cannot read his thoughts.

He should be told what to expect in this session: what instrumentation will be applied to his body, how it will be applied, and what it will measure. He should be told how long he will be instrumented and given an opportunity to visit bathroom facilities prior to instrumentation.

Instrumentation should proceed in a calm, competent manner, and the patient's comfort should be attended to after all electrodes are in place. He should be told that recordings will be made for the period of time involved and that during that time he should remain quiet, keeping his eyes closed and attend to further instructions as they come along.

Whenever possible, recordings of multiple parameters should be made to assess the patient's resting physiological levels, as well as reactivity in as many systems as possible. This multi-parameter recording constitutes a physiological profile and the variety of physiological information can be used as the basis for selection of a biofeedback task.

If the therapeutic goal is relaxation, the therapist should expose the patient to a relaxation exercise while instrumented to determine which potential feedback parameters are the most meaningfully associated with relaxation and whether the patient is able to use the particular relaxation exercise.

During this procedure, the therapist should make careful notes on the baseline and changing levels of all of the parameters being monitored. Following the procedure, a written note concerning the patient's subjective experience should be available along with the physiological information and considered when assigning goals.

While removing the electrodes, the therapist should offer the patient ample opportunity to express any thoughts or concerns about his experience. Special attention should be paid to whether he felt able to do the procedure and whether he was aware of having relaxed.

Home practice is assigned at this time, usually the same relaxation exercise used in the first session since the patient has already used it and has had an opportunity to clarify any questions. The therapist should get a commitment from the patient to practice on the desired schedule. After scheduling the next appointment, the therapist should let the patient know that in the next session, the physiological findings will be shared with him and both physiological and symptom goals will be established. The patient should be encouraged to think about what he would consider a suitable symptom goal and be prepared to share that information at the next appointment.

Between this session and the next, the therapist should review the notes and physiological record and arrive at a probable therapeutic contract and a potential biofeedback program to be considered with the patient in the next session. The therapeutic contract as described in Chapter 2 consists of two main parts: (1) the symptom goal, and (2) the physiological goal. The chief complaint will probably provide the basis for the symptom goal. The therapist should notice the status of measurable aspects of the symptom such as frequency, severity, and duration. Some change in one of the measurable aspects may serve as the initial symptom goal, and once reached, may be revised until the symptom is manageable. One example would be a daily headache which would meet a first level goal if the patient was headache free for 3 consecutive days. Subsequent revisions might increase the number of pain-free days per week until the symptom is manageable. Any change in the measurable aspects of the symptom may serve as a symptom goal in the therapeutic contract.

The physiological goal should be based on observations during the initial recording of multiple parameters – the physiological profile. By instrumenting the patient so as to sample recordings from several physiological systems while he is experiencing a relaxation exercise, it is possible to determine which systems are: (1) functioning at a level of arousal outside of normal limits; and/or (2) labile in that they move toward lower arousal when relaxation is achieved. Both of these observations should be considered when establishing a physiological goal and thus assigning a biofeedback task. The physiological parameter which is the most labile in a relaxed direction may be the one which is the most meaningfully correlated with the patient's relaxation response and would, therefore, serve as a useful biofeedback task when the therapeutic objective is relaxation.

An example would be when the plethysmogram indicates an observable increase in peripheral vascular blood flow with relaxation, the therapist might expect finger temperature to be meaningfully associated with the patient's relaxation response.

If there is a parameter which is functioning at a higher than normal level which does not change with relaxation, it must be reduced during the course of treatment in order to assure a meaningful level of relaxation. One example might be a frontalis EMG in which the resting level is in excess of 10 μv and does not necessarily change during relaxation. It might be assumed that relaxation of the frontalis EMG is difficult to control. This parameter might be more easily controlled after initial success has been achieved in a more labile parameter. By beginning with a more labile parameter and allowing the patient to achieve initial success using it, he has: (1) gained confidence in his ability to control his physiology; and (2) achieved an initial change in his level of relaxation, facilitating further change.

GOAL-SETTING SESSION

§5.6 Enlisting the Patient. With symptom information gathered in the first visit evaluation of the patient, and physiological measurements made in the second visit, part of the third visit can be used for establishing the therapeutic contract. The contract will serve as a guide to the ongoing responsibility of both the therapist and the patient, and therefore, the patient should have maximum input into its elements. The patient may have in mind a symptom goal since he was encouraged to consider one in the second visit. He should be encouraged to share his thinking and the therapist should be open to accepting the patient's suggestion if it is at all reasonable. If the patient's suggestion needs some revision, the therapist should work with him until a suitable symptom goal is reached.

Physiological findings from the previous session should be shared openly with the patient. In sharing technical information, an effort should be made to express findings and their meanings in ways readily understandable by the patient. The physiological goal will form the basis of the patient's biofeedback efforts and should, therefore, be agreed upon by him. Examples of physiological goals are: (1) to reduce EMG levels to an average of 5 μv; (2) to vary skin temperature 2° in either direction; or (3) to increase EEG alpha production to an average of 100% over the amplitude levels observed in the baseline measurements.

A physiological goal involving two parameters seems desirable in several instances. In this case, there are actually two physiological goals combined to form this half of the therapeutic contract. An example might be reducing frontails EMG to 5 μv *and* altering finger temperature 2° in either direction. When a goal combines two parameters, the patient is instrumented for both parameters in each visit, fed back information from one while the therapist monitors activity from the other. This combined approach has the advantages of reducing boredom by offering variety, allowing the therapist to note the amount of generalization taking place as relaxation is learned, and it ultimately provides the patient with substantially more self-awareness and more than one approach to lowering his arousal. As a part of the physiological goal, some mention of the development of a subjective cue associated with the physiological skill is essential. The subjective cue is an awareness of when the physiological task is being accomplished and provides the patient with a way of using his laboratory skills when he is not receiving biofeedback. The cue tends to come into awareness as the biofeedback skills develop and will be discussed in subsequent sections of this chapter.

Once the elements of the therapeutic contract are agreed upon, they should be noted in the chart along with the patient's comments surrounding agreeing to them.

§5.7 **Beginning the Task.** The remainder of the third session should be spent with the patient familiarizing himself with the biofeedback task. He should be instrumented in accordance with the physiological goal and allowed to experiment with the information available to him through the biofeedback instrument. Ten or 15 minutes of experimentation is usually enough to allow the patient some initial awareness of the sorts of tactics which are likely to aid in the task accomplishment.

The session should end on an optimistic anticipatory note with the patient looking forward to returning and with a reminder to him to enjoy his home practice.

ASSESSMENT OF THE HOME PRACTICE AND CLINICAL COURSE

§5.8 **Patient's Part.** The patient's part is crucial to the treatment outcome. Our experience has shown that the degree to which the patient adheres to the contract is the single most important factor in whether the treatment is successful. Home practice must be carried out according to schedule and any observations about how the home practice is progressing should be shared with the therapist on each visit. If the home practice is not being done or if it is unpleasant or ineffective, the patient must be quite frank about these things in his discussion with the therapist. The patient is the only one who knows how things are progressing and his self-observations must be shared. The patient is responsible for keeping his appointments and arriving on time. A chronically late arrival might have clinical significance.

Whatever is agreed upon between patient and therapist becomes a part of the contract and the patient becomes responsible for carrying out his portion or discussing with the therapist the need to revise the contract.

§5.9 **Therapist's Part.** It is important that the therapist be prepared for the session. Any lack of preparation results in disorderly progression during the session and is a potential detriment to the establishment and/or maintenance of a good therapeutic relationship. Looking through records, setting up instruments, or looking for supplies that should be at hand are examples. Before the session begins, the therapist should refresh his memory by reviewing the patient's progress, making mental notes of the plan for the session, details of the home assignment, information to be shared or decisions to be reached, and any problems or success that may need to be addressed. The therapist should be ready on time with his plan in mind and his equipment in readiness, having adjusted his attitude to one appropriate to benefit the expected patient.

Pre-session observations of the patient should include whether he is on time, his general appearance and affect, and whether he appears anxious or reluctant to get started. Often whether he arrives on time is a good clue as to his general developing attitude about the treatment. A patient who is chronically late or who misses two appointments in a row may need to be viewed as one in whom these behaviors have therapeutic implications. When the patient's attitude is one of "let's get started," the therapist may need to be especially alert to opportunities to praise the patient for some progress he may be anxious to share.

By the same token, patients who are either reluctant to get started (as shown by their slow movements getting into the treatment room or silence once there) or who are anxious to be finished with a session may be having some difficulty with the treatment. They may not want to have to tell the therapist that they have not been doing their part, or that their expectations are not being met, or that there is some other problem keeping them from making the best use of the sessions. The therapist must notice these cues and respond to them by setting an atmosphere in which the patient may express difficulties with ease. By the same token, the therapist needs to maintain the session's structure and if the problem is either not related to the treatment, or lengthy discussion is likely to derail the treatment, a decision should be made about the use of the session. If the problem can be managed by allocating the session to a clarification of goals or other elements of the contract, then that use of the time should be agreed upon by both patient and therapist and the previous treatment plan for the session postponed. If managing it in this way is not possible or desirable, the practitioner should be consulted following the session to determine whether a meeting with him is in order, and the patient should be encouraged to carry out the planned program for the session.

In most sessions, patients will not present the aforementioned special problems and will arrive on time with a good attitude. In these cases, the therapist may start the conversation by asking about the patient's week or time since the last appointment. Usually, patients have in mind things they want to say or ask. Here is where the therapist's experience plays an important role. There are some comments that seem to surface at expected times in the patient's progress, and the therapist is well advised to have a repertoire of responses developed to deal with these things. An example is when the patient reports falling asleep during the home practice sessions; the therapist needs to be ready with suggestions that will help the patient avoid falling asleep and observe the spirit in which the patient accepts or rejects those suggestions. When the patient indicates a willingness to try the suggestions and expresses an attitude that they will help, the therapist should reinforce this thinking and add a measure of support to the notion that the patient will control this. Any less desirable acceptance of the suggestions should be met with comments designed to encourage and support the patient in his development of self-management. Tables 5.1, 5.2, and 5.3 list additional examples, along with suggestions as to how they might be viewed and managed.

TABLE 5.1

Management of Problems with Relaxation Exercises

Problem	Management
Falling asleep.	1. Don't schedule exercise just after meals or before bedtime. 2. Sit up in a chair.
"No change" (translated: "What I expected didn't happen").	1. Question for more details. 2. Identify with disappointment. 3. If "no change" is intransigent, terminate treatment.
Mind wanders.	1. Suggest this will lessen with practice. 2. Use "Peaceful . . . 1, etc." exercise as adjunct just prior to relaxation.
No carry-over after exercise.	1. Suggest this will improve with practice. 2. Consider whether exercise is "recited" or internalized.
Wonders whether is doing details correctly (overly concerned).	1. Consider that the patient is trying too hard and suggest an attitude of allowing relaxation to happen and observing changes.
Negative comments in conversation (I can't).	1. Encourage awareness of negative comments and change to positive.
No subjective cue.	1. Encourage patience and remind that it will be subtle. 2. Encourage attention to changing sensations.
Gets better and then worse.	1. Suggest that learning takes place in increments with some plateaus. 2. Suggest that the symptom may be present at times but the important thing is that the patient can control it when he wants to.

TABLE 5.2

Management of Positive Responses to Relaxation Exercises

Response	Management
Feels better.	Show encouragement and pleasure.
Relies on exercise.	Reinforce and praise for patient's part in developing skills.
Aborted or stopped anxiety symptom.	Praise.
Aware of subjective cue.	Praise, note cue, and refer to it in subsequent sessions. Suggest awareness in daily situations.
Others notice difference or respond differently to patient.	Relate any differences you have noted by way of reinforcement.
Sleeps better.	Suggest this shows progress, often sleep improves first, then other symptoms change.
Dreams more.	Suggest this often happens, encourage him to enjoy dreams, and know that this phase will pass, but shows progress.
Aching muscles.	Suggest relaxing, that aching will pass.

TABLE 5.3

Management of Problems in the Biofeedback Setting

Problem	Management
No change in physiological parameter.	Reduce threshold to make task easier. If no change across two sessions, consider new task.
Patient does not understand feedback signal.	Demonstrate changes in the signal.
Patient doesn't think he is changing the signal.	Encourage patient to experiment.
Parameter moves in wrong direction.	Encourage more passive stance—may be trying too hard.
Is bored with task.	Consider alternate task.
Performs for therapist.	Leave the room for short periods while the patient works on the task.
Cannot recognize when doing task, except feedback signal says so.	Encourage awareness of subjective cue.

With continued experience, the therapist is likely to develop his own list, and each new topic adds to his repertoire of responses, making him a more comfortable and thus more effective therapist. Generally, unless the patient is absolutely negative about the outcome of treatment, his mention of problems may be considered an appeal for help with them and an indication that he hopes to work them through. The therapist should view the patient's mention of problems in this way and use the opportunity to guide the patient toward a solution, being careful not to consider mention of problems as a threat to his (the therapist's) effectiveness or the potential effectiveness of the treatment he has to offer. To do otherwise may result in the therapist's developing a defensive attitude toward the patient and thus affecting the rapport.

Any problems that the patient mentions should be met with considerable concern and support on the part of the therapist while expressing a confidence that the patient can overcome the obstacle. Any mention of progress on the part of the patient should be met with praise from the therapist and a reminder that it is he, the patient, who has done the work and made the progress possible, and that he can continue to improve on the skills he is developing so that they become a permanent part of his life.

The therapist should use every opportunity to remind the patient that he is responsible for any progress that is being made because it is he who is doing the work and learning the skills. Remember, most therapeutic settings which the patient has experienced thus far have been very different from this one in which his role is as a responsible part of the therapeutic team and the patient may require several reminders before he realizes how important his role actually is.

ASSESSMENT OF THE SESSIONS

§5.10 Patient's Part. In the session itself, the patient's responsibility lies in making the very best use of the time. He should pay attention to the feedback signal and use it both to learn the physiological task and to validate his subjective cue. This is not a time to discover what other than the physiological task will cause the feedback signal to change and the patient's use of such artifacts should be discouraged in that they stand in the way of valid learning.

Sometimes the patient needs to learn to give himself permission to turn off his daily pressure so that he can best use the therapeutic session. This must be learned and it is up to the patient to acquire this ability. He should turn inward and discover the "passive volition" essential to accomplishing of physiological task. Furthermore, he should keep an open-minded alertness to the development of his subjective cue. The subjective cue is whatever the patient is aware of that is present when relaxation occurs. It is usually a subtle sensation somewhere in the body that the patient realizes is present when he is meeting his physiological goals, and which he can use as a built-in feedback device when he is not instrumented.

If he has difficulty with the feedback task, he should share those feelings with the therapist and be ready to allow the therapist to coach him to a successful outcome. He should always view the therapist as a sort of coach and avoid both performing for the therapist and expecting the therapist to make the task easier or do it for him.

§5.11 **Therapist's Part.** In each session, the therapist must provide the best possible environment in which the patient can learn the tasks. The feedback must always be relevant, understandable, and consistent from one visit to the next. Electrodes must be applied in a careful, consistent manner and the feedback machine must be in readiness. The therapist must observe the patient's progress while avoiding encouraging the patient to perform for him. Whether the therapist remains with the patient throughout each session or allows the patient to work alone for short periods is a decision that the therapist needs to consider. If the patient is distracted by the therapist or is very concerned about his performance in his presence, a few short periods of working alone might be in order with the therapist appearing after 10 minutes or so in order for the patient to report his observations. The therapist must be alert to the influence of artifacts on the feedback signal and help the patient avoid them.

Good notes are still essential and the therapist must keep ongoing notes about the treatment including changes in values of the physiological parameters as they move toward the goal. If the physiological levels are not moving toward the goal, the therapist must size up the situation and make changes or suggestions that will help the patient make the desired progress. Table 5.3 suggests ways to manage some of these problems. When progress is achieved, the therapist should use the opportunity to let the patient know that he is responsible for the progress and to support continued movement toward the goal.

At the end of the session, the therapist should share his observations with the patient and allow time to discuss with him plans for the next session. Home assignments should be mentioned as well as a reminder of the next scheduled appointment.

ASSESSMENT FOR TERMINATION

§5.12 **Conditions of Termination.** As with all forms of therapy, termination may occur as a result of treatment failure or treatment success. In the former, termination should best occur by mutual consent of both the patient and therapist if it becomes apparent in the treatment that no progress is likely to occur. The therapist should discuss the situation with the patient and give him an opportunity to participate in the decision to terminate. The newness of biofeedback as a treatment modality means that there are not yet well developed ways of predicting whether any particular patient might be able to use this technique. The patient selection process (Chap. 3) attempts to reduce the likelihood of failure, but the elements are based on clinical experience. Until there are tried and tested measures for patient selection there will be errors. When no progress toward the agreed-upon therapeutic goals is made over a period of two or more sessions, this observation should be discussed with the patient. If it appears that no further progress is likely to occur, termination should be carried out. It is very important to leave the patient with an opportunity to return if he should wish and to be sure that he feels able to do so with ease. The therapist must recognize that treatment failure is not a personal affront and should not convey a personal disappointment to the patient who may then be reluctant to return in the future if he should feel better able to use biofeedback techniques. Rather, the patient should be encouraged to recognize that although he may feel unable to progress at this time, there may be a time in the future when he would like to try again and that you, the therapist, will be happy to work with him then. Treatment failure is likely to occur when the therapeutic contract is broken by either the patient or the therapist. When appointments are not kept, when home practice is not done, when attention is not given to the development of physiological skills on the part of the patient, he is, in fact, breaking the therapeutic contract and making the outcome of success very unlikely. When the therapist is not ready for the appointments, when he does not maintain good rapport, and when he does not provide a good learning environment for the patient, the therapist is breaking the contract and the outcome is likely to be similarly bleak.

When the therapeutic goals, both symptomatic and physiological, are reached, the contract is fulfilled and termination by mutual consent should be considered. The therapist should set aside time to discuss the status of the therapy with the patient, making sure that the patient is aware that the goals have been reached. The patient should again be reminded that it is he who has achieved the goals and it is he who can maintain them when he is no longer coming to regular appointments. Appointments should be spread further apart for a short period before final termination to allow for the possibility of recurring problems as termination approaches. Sometimes, patients are seen on an every 2 weeks schedule for two or three appointments, and then on a once a month basis, each one leading to the final regular appointment. During this time, very careful assessment of the patient's symptoms and attitude is made. As long as the patient is able to maintain control of both the symptom and the physiological skill while developing increased reliance on his subjective cue and his control skills, movement is made toward the final appointment. When termination is carried out, it is done so leaving the door open. The patient is encouraged to return if he feels the need or desire and assured that he may do so without risk of disappointment to the therapist. He is informed that follow-up question-naires will be sent to him at 3-, 6-, and 12-month intervals.

FOLLOW-UP: ASSESSMENT AFTER TERMINATION

§5.13 **Patient's Part.** Discussion with a variety of biofeedback clincians and our own experience combine to suggest that follow-up is necessary and desirable, but that the time intervals and methods of follow-up vary considerably. Some clinicians telephone patients fairly soon after the last appointment and continue to do so on a rather frequent schedule for several months. Others send follow-up letters or questionnaires every 3 months or so both to assess the maintenance of symptom control and to remind the patient that he is welcome to return to the laboratory if he feels he needs to. We follow the latter course and find that the ability of the patient to remain symptom free is closely associated with how well developed the subjective cue was prior to termination and the extent to which the patient integrated his skills in his daily life, and that this is more important than how often he is contacted in the follow-up phase.

The patient's part then is to maintain both his skills and the aware-ness of those skills. This sometimes requires that he continue to practice a relaxation exercise on a once or twice a week schedule. More often it requires that the patient continue to use his subjective awareness of relaxation and take time to relax when he feels a growing tension. Patients who are able to incorporate this activity into their way of life are able to maintain symptom relief for long periods of time. Follow-up after 3 years has shown that most of those patients are still symptom free. If tensions do begin to cause some discomfort, it is up to the patient to come back to the therapist and request more treatment and to overcome any latent embarrassment or sense of failure.

§5.14 **Therapist's Part.** Depending upon the follow-up policy of the treatment facility, it is up to the therapist to keep track of when follow-up is due and to make contact with the patient on the correct schedule. Contact should be in a manner that encourages the patient to respond freely and openly and to state his difficulties if any are present. The patient should be made to feel free to return to the treatment facility without fear of having failed or of disappointing the therapist. In general, a practical schedule is to have follow-up every 3 months for the first year, every 6 months for the next year, and then once a year for as many as are possible.

Here's good advice for practice: go into partnership with nature; she does more than half the work and asks none of the fee.

Martin H. Fischer

As Matthew Arnold said of religion, that it is morality touched with emotion, so practice is science touched with emotion.

Stephen Paget
Confessio Medici

It is always best to do a thing wrong the first time.

Sir William Osler

CHAPTER 6

Establishing a biofeedback program and learning the practice of biofeedback

§6.1 Introduction. This chapter will take up two similar issues — the establishment of a program (Secs. 6.2–6.7), and the learning of practice (Secs. 6.8–6.13). These issues can be viewed from the same frame of reference we have used to describe the course of illness and the course of treatment — i.e., the frame of reference of structure in time (see Secs. 1.43; 2.24; 2.27; Chap. 4). Thus, to establish a program or to learn to practice biofeedback, certain steps need to be followed. In both instances, it is possible to follow either a strategy of immersion or a strategy of incremental progression. In the strategy of immersion, one attempts to "do everything at once," with the order of learning dictated by the needs of the moment, whereas in the strategy of incremental progression it is ascertained that one task is completed before the next is begun. For practical purposes, we have chosen to describe the strategy of incremental progression to illustrate both issues covered in this chapter. However, we wish to stress that it is fully as likely that circumstances or choice might make it desirable in a particular instance to follow the strategy of immersion. For instance, if a fully operational, busy biofeedback clinic hires a new technician, it may be more practical for the technician to be fully immersed as an observer of a trained therapist than to follow sequentially the steps we outline.

ESTABLISHING A BIOFEEDBACK TREATMENT PROGRAM

§6.2 Coordination with Existing Programs. In many instances, a biofeedback program will be added into existing programs carried out by the same personnel. Thus, a privately practicing physician may have an office alone or with partners, already staffed with nurses and other personnel, treating patients by other means. It then is most practical for the physician and the other personnel involved to begin to use relaxation training as outlined below (Secs. 6.9–6.13) until it is mastered. While this is being done they can also examine potential equipment and make purchases, begin to screen potential patients from the current clientele, and then start biofeedback treatment with selected patients. In those situations, it will be possible to use the foundation provided by the existing practice to support the new venture. The progressive use of more complex techniques outlined below allows one set of skills to be thoroughly mastered before going on to the next.

The same strategy of adding a new function into an existing program can be used in certain institutional settings when biofeedback is added to existing programs. Here it must be determined by the program director who is to be assigned to learn the new skills. It cannot be too strongly emphasized that the bulk of treatment can be carried out by someone other than the holder of an advanced degree and that it is wasteful of resources to use highly paid personnel for the treatment methods we have outlined. On the other hand, it is highly desirable for the entire professional staff to understand the treatment procedures thoroughly through their own experience in using them. Once it is determined that a biofeedback program is to be started, the implementation plan needs to be made. Again, there is a natural good use of time to be found in learning relaxation procedures at the same time that equipment is being evaluated and ordered.

In large institutional programs, it will be possible to learn biofeedback techniques through a training seminar. Such a venture would best be served by having professional and technical personnel work together, so that each is as familiar as possible with the other's special areas of competence, particularly for understanding the therapeutic relationship and the evaluation of patients. A working seminar could have as few as two or as many as about a dozen people and still be expected to function well.

When a biofeedback program is added onto an existing program, it is the responsibility of the program director to ensure that the personnel assigned are relieved of enough of their regular duties so that they can devote proper attention to learning the new skills. The program director also needs to anticipate the further shift of their duties as the biofeedback work requires more of their time. Sometimes the biofeedback patients will be part of a stable-sized pool who would otherwise have been treated by other methods. On the other hand, there are times when the existing patient pool will have the biofeedback patients added on and further staffing to manage the increased load will be required.

In some institutional settings and in a few practices it may be desired to set up a biofeedback treatment program which is clearly demarcated from the existing programs. This assumes that there will be separate staffing and separate office space. Either new staff will be brought in or old staff will be relieved of other duties. Sometimes some of the responsible staff will have biofeedback experience and sometimes not. Most often some training will need to be done. Here much will depend on the scheduling of hiring, the existing patient load toward whom the facility is responsible, the availability of equipment, the relationship with referral sources and other such administrative questions. Obviously administrative coordination is required.

§6.3 **Pacing the Process.** From the above it is obvious that any particular program requires careful planning to ensure its success. This includes establishing and maintaining adequate financing, hiring of staff, training of staff, selection and purchase of equipment, establishing contact with adequate referral sources of patients, regulating the flow of patients through the facility, establishing a reasonable basis for patient billing and so forth. Each of these issues must be dealt with in turn at the appropriate time and certain of them must be resolved before others can be undertaken. The recognition that there are many action cycles (Secs. 4.2–4.12) involved in this process can provide some guide to the practitioner and program director.

§6.4 **Selection of Personnel.** Since biofeedback programs are usually small programs, it is possible for personnel to be cross-trained. Thus, receptionists and secretaries can often have the training to take over for the primary therapist during illness or vacation. Likewise, if there is a business manager or other administrator in the program it is good for them to be cross-trained so that they have a full appreciation of what is done.

The chapter on the therapeutic relationship went into some of the qualities needed in a therapist (see Secs. 2.4; 2.5; 2.15) and these should be reviewed in considering the selection of personnel. In general, the needed qualities have to do with the ability to establish a good therapeutic relationship—requiring empathy, stability, a good disposition, intelligence, and tactfulness. It is hard to justify exposing patients to staff who might be uncouth, indiscrete, too familiar, unsympathetic, self-indulgent, unreliable, or untrustworthy. The evaluation of these qualities is subjective and individual, yet there is nothing more crucial to the success of a treatment program than the selection of appropriate personnel.

§6.5 **Staff Working Relationships.** After appropriate personnel are selected, there remains the problem of their learning to work well together. Sometimes institutional policies dictate part of the working relationship, but there is always the opportunity to optimize what can be done within the constraint of those policies. We must take for granted that, other things being equal, the well coordinated, contented staff will do a better job than a staff who feels unhappy. Everything possible needs to be done to minimize interdisciplinary disputes, personal rivalries, power grabbing, passive non-compliance, clique formation, rigid hierarchical stratification, and other disruptions of a well functioning group. Likewise, the encouragement of a sense of personal fulfillment of all of the staff and of pleasure in working together will enhance treatment efforts. When personnel problems arise they must be given high priority by the person in charge.

§6.6 **Patient Flow.** The number of patients to be drawn upon will depend upon the individual situation of the treatment facility, but obviously must be coordinated with the size of staff available. When only small numbers of patients are available it is important to maintain other activities until the number picks up. It will also be important to make the service offered known to referral sources. This should be done ethically and in the particular way required by the setting. Sometimes in institutional settings it is necessary to supplement announcements with personal contact with referral sources. Introductory training lectures, talks before professional organizations, and other such contact also make the availability of the service known. Once a facility is established the flow of patients sometimes becomes too great. In such circumstances it is important either to enlarge the staff to manage the increased flow, or to ensure that the time taken in turning away patients does not interfere with the treatment to be done.

§6.7 **Clinic Procedures.** During the establishment of a treatment facility various methods of operation can be experimentally tried. Once the program is operational there should be routine procedures which ensure that things go smoothly and efficiently. This includes a variety of routines such as making sure that equipment is operational, relaxation tape cassettes are ready, electrodes are clean, the treatment area is orderly. It also means that the practitioner must efficiently cover the needed screening to select patients and that the therapists keep adequate records to document progress in treatment. One way of ensuring such coverage is to use standardized flow sheets and questionnaires to assemble the needed information. Some examples are provided in Appendix B for guidance, but any particular facility should be encouraged to take the time to arrive at procedures best suited to their particular situation.

LEARNING THE PRACTICE OF BIOFEEDBACK

§6.8 **Alternative Methods.** We assume that anyone learning biofeedback practice must arrive at a learning strategy. In the past almost everyone was self-taught with minimal peer contact to assist. As the practice has grown, it is now possible to describe the process systematically as we do here. The self-taught individual most often learned by a great deal of trial and error. In particular, the clinical situation most often involved a patient presenting a condition which the therapist may never before have encountered. A diffident therapeutic contract was likely to be struck, with great caution about expectations. There was unlikely to be home practice assignments and it was almost taken for granted that the biofeedback sessions might be of value by themselves in some way that was not understood very clearly.

The current situation has evolved a great deal. Now there are a number of reasonably well established clinical indications for biofeedback treatment. Home practice of relaxation has been widely assimilated into most practitioners' methods and the delegation of the treatment task to a trained biofeedback therapist or biofeedback technician is widely accepted.

The next step after the evolution of methods is to develop means of teaching these methods. When the attempt is made through a manual, such as this one, it is best if the process is broken into steps that can be readily assimilated. Our effort has been to do this in the plan which follows. We first recommend that the learner give a single relaxation session to a patient or a friend using a simple method (Secs. 6.9; 7.2; 7.6). This can be learned rapidly after a few trials, but it is an essential part of being able to carry a more extensive relaxation training to conclusion (Secs. 6.10; 7.7–7.13). After the use of the relaxation method has been mastered, biofeedback parameters may be added into the treatment (Secs. 6.11; Chap. 8). In addition, at any time during the learning process the therapists in training can themselves experiment with particular biofeedback and relaxation methods. We will make particular recommendations as to how this be done (Sec. 6.12). Finally, after the elementary techniques have been mastered, the therapist will go on to advanced methods (Sec. 6.13; Chap. 9). The remainder of this chapter will outline the above steps of training which will then be explained in detail in Chapters 7 through 9.

§6.9 **Learning Relaxation Training—Step One.** Before carrying to completion an entire relaxation training, it is desirable to learn to do a single relaxation session where it is not necessarily intended that further sessions be given. A friend, working associate, spouse, or relative can assist in this learning by taking the role of learning to relax while you read the relaxation script to them. It can also be done with a patient when appropriate (see Sec. 7.3). This should be mastered to the point where the trainer feels comfortable carrying it out before he goes on to carrying out a complete relaxation training. One reason this is a desirable first step is that a trainer can learn more easily in a situation where he is not asking a longer term commitment from the person being trained.

§6.10 Learning Relaxation Training – Step Two. In order to carry an entire relaxation training to completion, the trainee must have sufficient reason for being willing to make the commitment to practice, such as a wish to overcome symptoms, a desire to learn the procedure, intellectual curiosity, a wish to achieve self-mastery for its own sake, or a wish to achieve peace of mind. This excludes many potential trainees to whom the method might be taught. It leaves mainly patients, exceptional friends or relatives, and oneself. As we explain elsewhere (Sec. 7.8), the motivations of the casually curious are apt to be insufficient to provide a completed experience and it is probably better to seek someone who will complete the training. When this person is found, a complete relaxation procedure can then be taught to them to the point where they achieve mastery. Depending upon the needs of the training therapist, one or more such complete procedures may be carried out before going on to the next step.

§6.11 Learning Use of Biofeedback Parameters. As with relaxation training, the simple use of a particular biofeedback parameter with no particular goals in mind can be learned by patients, friends, co-workers, relatives or oneself in order to master the technical rudiments. However, this does not constitute an actual treatment, for which a schedule of practice with goals, session length, session frequency, staging of goals and other dimensions must be specified. The learning of how to use biofeedback parameters is covered in Chapter 11, where instrumentation techniques are discussed, whereas the details of carrying out a biofeedback treatment are given in Chapters 8 and 9.

§6.12 Therapist's Self-Experience with Biofeedback Parameters and Relaxation Methods. One of the best ways to learn to teach a skill is to practice the skill oneself. At all levels of the training it is possible for therapists themselves to practice. There is a great deal of individual preference involved, as well as variations in the personal motivations which might lead one therapist to go further than another in the learning. Therefore, we have not described in detail a particular path of self-learning, but merely endorse self-experience insofar as it is kept within the limits common sense would dictate.

§6.13 Advanced Techniques. Once the basic element of biofeedback treatment has been mastered, therapists will go on to refine what they do. We will describe some of these advanced techniques in Chapter 9, but will not prescribe a method of learning them because individual variations in different therapist's practices make that difficult. In addition, there are sure to be improvements to be incorporated which we have not anticipated.

What you should put first in all the practice of your art is how to make the patient well; and if he can be made well in many ways, one should choose the least troublesome.

Hippocrates

There is nothing men will not do, there is nothing they have not done, to recover their health and save their lives. They have submitted to be half-drowned in water, and half-choked with gases, to be buried up to their chins in earth, to be seared with hot irons like galley-slaves, to be crimped with knives, like codfish, to have needles thrust into their flesh, and bonfires kindled on their skin, to swallow all sorts of abominations, and to pay for all this, as though blisters were a blessing, and leeches were a luxury. What more can be asked to prove their honesty and sincerity?

Oliver W. Holmes
"The Young Practitioner," Medical Essays

CHAPTER 7

Basic elements of treatment: relaxation training

§7.1 Introduction. This chapter and the next will cover the basic elements of biofeedback treatment. In this chapter we will describe simple relaxation training. It may be used with or without biofeedback. Here we will describe its use alone, without biofeedback. Then Chapter 8 will cover the use of simple biofeedback parameters along with the relaxation training. The first part (Secs. 7.2–7.6) will cover the routine of a single self-limited relaxation session with no contract to repeat the experience. The last part (Secs. 7.7–7.13) will cover relaxation training as it would be given from start to finish with a patient or other training subject.

RELAXATION SESSION

§7.2 Introduction. Our purpose here is to give the complete details of how to carry out a single self-limited relaxation training session so as to allow the therapist in training to acquire a sense of confidence and skill. The subject for training may either be a patient or a friend, relative, co-worker, or other trainee (see Sec. 7.3). When the learning is taking place in a seminar the students can take turns as coach, with the entire class – including the seminar leader – being subjects to practice learning relaxation. Whether or not the subjects are patients, it is important that they understand fully in what they are participating. If they are not in treatment it is important that they be reasonably stable and not currently going through unusually traumatic life experiences. What could be considered a mild transient transference reaction is to be anticipated from the practice and it is desirable that this be kept within easily manageable limits. This reaction is not different from the usual spectrum of reactions to any teaching situation and the same common sense rules used would apply to ensure the stability of the situation. These rules have mainly to do with not coercing subjects, fully informing them of what to expect and properly finishing the exercise; they are covered in consideration of the contract (Sec. 7.4). Carrying out the exercise is then covered in Section 7.5 and the termination and debriefing of the subject in Section 7.6.

§7.3 Selection of Subjects. When a patient is given a relaxation training session it is important that there be an ongoing therapeutic relationship—either with the therapist presenting the exercise or with a physician or other therapist who knows that the training is being given. The general therapeutic principles guiding treatment demand that nothing be done without there being other avenues open for dealing with any negative reactions. Likewise, patients selected for treatment where the therapist is learning (Sec. 7.8) should be especially suited to tolerate the procedure well. This mainly means that the patient should easily meet the criteria mentioned in Chapter 3—particularly having good ego strength (Sec. 3.4). Depending upon whether the learning therapist is already a trained practitioner with experience in managing the therapeutic relationship or a biofeedback technician in training, this may involve choosing patients seen in one's own practice, asking a colleague in an institutional setting to inform one of a prospective patient, or having a supervisor choose a case with which one works.

Similar considerations apply to the therapist learning to give a relaxation session in a non-therapeutic setting to a non-patient. As mentioned before, such a person might be a relative, friend, co-worker, or classmate. It is desirable that the subject should be reasonably stable in a stable period of his life and have a positive relationship with the learning therapist. If the subject himself is also learning to give the treatment, so much the better, because he will be more tuned to present good observations about the procedure. If the subject has considerable ambivalence toward the learning therapist the session might not go as well.

§7.4 Setting a Contract. Even in giving a simple single relaxation session it is necessary to have at least an informal and implicit contract with the patient or subject. We will discuss the details of this for three different situations—a patient with whom the learning practitioner is already working, a patient assigned to a learning biofeedback technician, and a subject who is not a patient. The main details of the contract have to do with agreement between learning therapist and patient (or subject) that there is a reason for going through the procedure, that the patient (or subject) has the opportunity to experience the pleasurable feelings of relaxation, that no particular long range positive results are implied, that no serious complications are expected, and that this is a single experience, with no commitment from either party to repeat it.

When dealing with a patient whom the learning practitioner already knows, the practitioner should place the relaxation within the context of the patient's need to learn to relax. There are, of course, large numbers of patients who have an awareness of the need to relax or who could profit from an awakening of such awareness. In the course of working with such a patient it is appropriate to say, within the context of considering this need, words like *"How about trying a little experiment? You feel it would help you to learn to relax better, and I tend to agree. Let's see if you can allow yourself to relax and let's see how you feel after you do. If you are willing to try, I will give you some simple instructions about letting go of tension within your body and you follow the instructions and we will see what happens. Do you have any questions before we start?"* What is offered the patient is a short period of self-observation of a pleasurable experience. This can have a positive effect upon the patient and his overall treatment and will do no harm as long as the patient has been properly selected and this single experience is properly assimilated within the wider context of the rest of his treatment according to the general principles of treatment of the practitioner.

When a learning biofeedback technician has a patient assigned by his supervisor for a single relaxation session, the supervisor will present a brief description of the patient and how he has been prepared for the experience. The technician then may approach the patient with such words as: *"Doctor A has talked with me about my teaching you a little bit of how to relax. Could you tell me something of what you feel about this?"* (After dealing with the patient's response satisfactorily the technician can go on.) *"Since we all tend to agree it would help you to learn about relaxing let's go ahead and get started. I'll give you some simple instructions, mainly about paying attention to different parts of your body, and you follow them as best you can and then we'll talk about what you noticed."* Here, instead of the technician being solely responsible for managing any problems arising, the prescribing practitioner will be available to deal with the problems.

It should be kept in mind that the chances of any problems are slight, that the problems are certain to be of a sort which the patient has already experienced innumerable times as a result of the particular pattern he is locked into, that the re-experiencing of the problem probably has an appropriate place within the treatment, and that it is exactly toward the management of such problems that most of the practitioner's previous training in his therapeutic discipline has been directed. When the patient has been properly chosen, the contract properly handled and the relaxation exercise properly given, the reactions to be expected might be of the sort described in Section 5.5, but milder, since the patient will not have as severe symptoms as those with whom an experienced therapist is working and the single experience is less intense than the long term relationship.

In arriving at a contract with a non-patient subject, the learning therapist needs to consider the wider context of their relationship and should work toward making the relaxation session an encapsulated episode separate from the rest of their relationship. This can be done by implicitly emphasizing the impersonal aspects of the relationship – that the learning therapist could learn by working with any subject and that the learning subject could learn to relax with any teacher. Likewise, it should be implicit that responses to learning situations are ubiquitous, that the responses are unique to the individual, but that the range of responses may be anticipated from experience. Thus, the learning therapist might say to the subject: *"I would like to work with you for you to have the experience of relaxing as deeply as you can. It is a quite simple thing, all you have to do is to let yourself follow my directions. It will not take very long, and if you are able to let yourself go you will get the good feelings accompanying relaxation. Anyone who is trained can teach this and anyone who is willing can learn it. You may have some particular reactions which I want to talk over with you when we are through. There are different things which happen to different people that can tell you a bit about yourself."*

Contracts are discussed in detail in Sections 2.8 through 2.19, which should be consulted for questions concerning the limited contract dealt with here. What has been presented here has been an informal and implicit contract, which is usually more than adequate for this kind of situation and it is recommended that the learning therapist learn to use such a technique. On the other hand, there may be some situations in which it is desirable to be more formal and explicit and in such the contract may be appropriately modified.

§7.5 Presenting the Exercise. Once the learning therapist and the patient or subject have arrived at an implicit and informal contract concerning their practice of the single exercise, they can usually begin. There is rarely a need for arriving at a contract on one occasion and carrying out the exercise on another and this should be avoided when possible. In giving instructions for a single exercise the therapist will not cover home practice and the details of different practicing positions, so the overall attitude conveys more of teaching the immediate session and less of teaching a procedure to be done repeatedly, since there is no expectation of the patient learning how to do the exercise again.

The first thing to do is for the patient to get himself comfortable – preferably in a comfortable chair or lying on a couch or soft rug. Some attention should be paid to being sure the assumed posture is reasonably comfortable, with the feet both firmly on the floor, the arms and hands in a position where they will not cramp and the head and neck at rest or equilibrium. The two major principles to follow are that the body parts be as comfortable as possible and in a position where further relaxation will not cause them to fall from the force of gravity. To achieve comfort the hands should be loosely open, the legs uncrossed and the clothing not binding. To prevent falling, the hands and forearms should rest on the lap, floor, or chair arms. The head and neck present particular problems because they are positioned by the unconscious and almost involuntary gravitational neck muscle reflexes and because they are often involved in the pathophysiology of stress-related syndromes. When a high chair back or the lying down posture allows the head and neck to be supported there is less of a problem, but even then many persons will be surprised to find that they continue to hold their head and neck rigid. When support is not available the subject can either let the head hang forward or can keep it held balanced neutrally upright with minimal exertion.

If the exercise is part of a series, the instruction regarding posture needs to be more detailed (see Sec. 7.11); for a single session it is desirable that the instructions be brief and related to the immediate circumstance. We have gone into detail here not for the sake of ritualizing the exercise but because of the variety of situations to which learning therapists must adapt. The therapist always has a choice between easily passing over the details of such instructions, especially when the subject has already done what is wished without being asked, versus ritualistically going into minute detail. Being able to do either as the situation requires is desirable. In what might be called the simple and uncomplicated situation, things may be easily passed over. On the other hand, when dealing with more difficult situations, it is possible to gain therapeutic advantage by going into detail.

Once the subject has gotten comfortable, he may be asked to close his eyes, listen to your voice, and let his mind go to the parts of the body to which you refer. Then you may read the exercise (Table 7.1) in a clear, calm, slow voice, while at the same time observing how the subject is progressing. The particular exercise presented has been chosen for simplicity; later (Secs. 7.13; 9.2–9.4), details will be given on how complexity and variety may be added to the exercises. While the exercise is being read the therapist should carefully observe the subject to notice particular reactions to the exercise. Table 7.2 lists some of the signs to be evaluated.

§7.6 **Debriefing.** After the exercise has been completed, the subject should be implicitly encouraged and observed to stir about a bit so as to be sure that he does not remain in a state which is too relaxed for him to get up and walk when the time arrives to do so. If necessary this may be

TABLE 7.1

*Simple Relaxation Exercise**

I. (To be read in a slow soothing voice) Lie back – arms to your sides. Get yourself in as comfortable a position as you easily find. It helps if you close your eyes. (That's good.) Just try to feel yourself relaxed and comfortable. All right . . . (Good.) Now, let yourself follow my directions to the best of your ability.

II. We start out by taking a very deep breath. Breathe deeply – now hold it an instant – and slowly let the air out. (That's good.) Now do it again when you're ready – a very deep breath – hold it – and slowly let the air out. Try to feel yourself relaxing. Once again, very deep – hold it – then slowly exhale and relax. Feel yourself relaxing as you exhale. Feel the muscles of your body letting go – relaxing. (These instructions are continued for five deep breaths.)

III. Now continue breathing deeply and regularly and try your best to follow my directions. Imagine a kind of relaxation that starts in your toes – that very gradually spreads throughout the muscles of your feet. Slowly, begin to feel relaxation spreading. Try to feel the muscles of your feet loosening up. Feel them getting more and more relaxed – getting limp. Now imagine that relaxation spreading – slowly spreading upward – over your ankles to the muscles of your legs. Feel your leg muscles begin to loosen up – getting relaxed. Feel it spreading. Your muscles getting more and more relaxed. Very gradually, very slowly, feel that relaxation spread over your knees – to the muscles of your thighs and hips – loosening your muscles – making them feel relaxed and limp. Try to feel all the muscles of your lower extremities completely relaxed – all the muscles loose and limp. (That's fine . . . .)

IV. Now try to imagine the same process starting in your finger tips. Try to feel the relaxation spreading throughout all the muscles of your hands. Try to feel the muscles of your hands loosening up. Feel the muscles relax so that your hands feel limp. Now imagine that relaxation spreading upward – slowly – over your wrist – slowly spreading upward – relaxing the muscles of your forearm – making them feel limp and relaxed. Feel it spreading – up over your elbows – slowly spreading – relaxing the muscles of your upper arms and shoulders. Try to feel all the muscles of your arms loose and limp – completely relaxed.

V. Now imagine that relaxation spreading upward to the muscles of your neck. Feel the tension begin to leave your neck muscles. Feel them gradually beginning to relax. Feel it spreading – more and more – until you feel the muscles of your neck completely loose – limp and relaxed. Now feel that relaxation spreading upward – over your face. Feel your face muscles let go – your jaw muscles relax. Feel it spreading – more and more – upward – over your temples – relaxing the muscles of your forehead – your eyebrows – your eyelids – making those muscles loose and limp and relaxed – heavy.

VI. Try to feel yourself just relaxed and comfortable, and resting quietly.

---

* Adapted from Pascal (1949).

TABLE 7.1 – *Continued*

(Good.) Now let's take another very deep breath – hold it – slowly exhale – feel yourself getting more and more relaxed. Once again – very deep – hold it – slowly relax. One more, a very deep breath – hold it – slowly relax.

VII. (Fine.) Now listen carefully and try to follow directions. I'm going to count to seven. As I count you will feel yourself getting more and more relaxed . . . One – two – three – four – five – six – seven. Feel yourself just very comfortable, very relaxed.

VIII. You've now let go of a good deal of your tension, but you can let yourself relax still further. We'll return now and repeat some of the earlier parts of the relaxation exercise before we finish. We're now (a third of the way; halfway; two-thirds; almost) through.

IX. (Now repeat enough of the previous parts so that the exercise is of the desired length. Use Parts VI and VII for a short exercise. Use Parts III, IV, and V for a longer exercise. Repeat the entire script from Part II for a still longer exercise. Then, when ready to stop, go to Part X.)

X. Okay, now stay relaxed but open your eyes and move a little bit before you go back to the rest of your day's activities. Don't get up very rapidly at first, but move more slowly for a few minutes.

TABLE 7.2

Indices of Relaxation

Signs of Relaxation	Signs of Failure to Relax
Face relaxing; muscles loosening; slow letting go of tension in limbs and neck; toes turning out; slower breathing; more audible breathing.	Rigid face; fidgeting or rigid immobility; closed eyelids twitching; inability to close eyes.

explicitly mentioned, but usually there is no need. The patient should be asked to describe what happened and how he felt about what happened and should be given appropriate reassurances about any concerns he shows. How to do this is described in more detail in Sections 5.8 and 5.9; 7.11 (also see Tables 5.1 and 5.2). When the subject is seen again he can be asked for further reflections upon the experience.

One of the most common reactions is for subjects to enjoy and wish to re-experience the relaxation exercise. They then may attempt to do the exercise on their own, without help and will quite likely find they are unable to repeat it. It is therapeutically appropriate in this situation to emphasize the value of what was experienced and to play down that the subject is not able to do the exercise on his own.

If the therapist will not see the patient again it is appropriate to end the session by saying goodbye, wishing him well, and hoping that he had a good experience in relaxing. This is the completion of an action cycle (see Secs. 4.8; 4.17; 4.23; 4.29) and this fact should not be overlooked in the learning therapist's self-education.

RELAXATION TRAINING

§7.7 Introduction. Relaxation training differs from giving a single relaxation session mainly in the acceptance of responsibility by both therapist and patient for bringing the treatment to closure at some agreed-upon end point of achievement. In order to accomplish this, each of the procedures described above in the preceding sections (7.2–7.6) must be appropriately modified. Thus, selecting a subject (Sec. 7.8) must be more rigorous, arriving at a therapeutic contract (Sec. 7.9) asks more of the participants, home practice (Sec. 7.10) is essential, there are now multiple practice sessions (Sec. 7.11) instead of just one, the termination of treatment requires attention (Sec. 7.12), and finally we will mention variations possible in the training (Sec. 7.13).

Relaxation training has diverse roots. It is certainly similar to various forms of meditation, such as transcendental meditation, Zen meditation, yogic meditation, and other types (Tart, 1969). However, these practices were originally designed for purposes having to do with attitude toward life and philosophy of life, rather than for therapeutic intent, and their connection with relaxation training per se has been strengthened only recently during the flowering of esoteric interests of the 1960's. Jacobson (1938), working to a large extent singlehandedly, developed relaxation training in this country during the last half-century. Schultz and Luthe's (1959) autogenic training was another form of relaxation training with its own special characteristics. Also, it is not hard to recognize the similarity of all of these techniques to mild, self-limited hypnosis.

The major differences between these techniques and the one offered here is that ours has been especially tailored for ease of learning both for the therapist and for the widest variety of patients. This is accomplished by use of a tape recorder and by elimination of all but the simplest instructions. Once this technique has been learned by the therapist, it may by choice be elaborated (see Secs. 9.2–9.4).

§7.8 Selection of Subjects. To participate in a relaxation session is but an interesting interlude, while to learn relaxation thoroughly is a definite task requiring mainly persistence and repetitive practice. This means that the learning subject must be motivated, and this motivation can be expected only in particular circumstances, such as when the subject is a patient whose symptoms are bothersome enough to give the reason to work on treatment, or when there is a positive relational bond between the learning subject and the teacher, as sometimes between relatives, classmates, or friends. We by no means advocate pressing this upon a relative or friend, however, and do not feel that there is any reason to assume that reluctance on their part is a sign that there is anything wrong with a relationship. In fact, it would seem to be the exception rather than the rule for relatives and friends to be willing to commit themselves to diligent practice when manifest need of the training was not present. We do not yet have the specific experience to recommend whether or not the treatment of symptomatic relatives and friends, who therefore become patients, is to be undertaken. One of the hardest parts of such a treatment is the mutual management of non-compliance. If the patient does not practice there are implications for all of the rest of the relationship with the therapist which should not be taken lightly. The other major group who might commit themselves to training would be members of a learning seminar, where consideration of individual commitment and group process must dictate whether this should be attempted.

All of the above issues tend toward the subject of relaxation training being a patient rather than a non-patient. For the learning therapist it is best that the patient be relatively easy to work with. We therefore recommend that the criteria of Chapter 3 be reviewed in selecting a case and that the patient be one who easily meets the criteria rather than falling close to the borders of them. It may be someone with whom the therapist is already working in other treatment, but it is preferable if the learning therapist have only the training relationship with the patient and that the overall therapeutic responsibility belong to some-one else. The main reason for this is so that the learning therapist not have the confusion of playing several roles in relation to the patient, as when combining the open-endedness and verbal permissiveness of con-ventional psychotherapy with the structured task orientation of relaxa-tion training.

In choosing a patient for relaxation training by a learning therapist, it is important that relaxation be the best available treatment for the patient at the time. Therefore, it is usually best not to so treat patients for whom biofeedback training is indicated and available. Thus, tension headache or migraine headache patients should only be treated with relaxation training alone by a learning therapist if biofeedback treat-ment is not available. Probably the main group for whom relaxation training alone is warranted are patients with chronic anxiety and high levels of physiological arousal with such somatic symptoms as insomnia and restlessness. The patients must have enough discomfort with their symptoms to motivate them in treatment and must be in an ongoing treatment relationship with someone.

Choosing a particular patient for the learning therapist is contra-indicated when the patient lacks ego strength or motivation, is exces-sively and complexly involved interpersonally, has excessive depend-ency or secondary gain from his symptoms, shows superficial compli-ance without real involvement, is excessively contrary, or is unable to experience hope. Once a patient has been tentatively chosen for treatment, the next task is arriving at a therapeutic contract.

§7.9 Therapeutic Contract. Earlier (Sec. 7.4), we gave details for a therapeutic contract for a single session in a variety of circumstances, including work with non-patients. Here we will not give as many examples, but will assume that the contract is between a learning therapist who is not responsible for the patient's overall treatment and a patient who wishes to learn to be able to relax better.

Presumably the patient has come from a colleague or supervisor and the need of the patient to learn to relax is mutually agreed upon by all parties, given the patient's circumstances. The learning relaxation therapist then has the task of conveying to the patient what is required of him to carry out his learning to relax and assuring that therapist and patient agree to accept the task.

The major items in a standard therapeutic contract for relaxation training have to do with: the patient agreeing to keep appointments, usually once a week; the patient understanding the likely length of the training; the patient having available a cassette tape recorder and acquiring from the therapist a cassette tape of the relaxation exercise; the patient agreeing to practice relaxation, while listening to the tape twice a day; the patient and therapist agreeing upon times to practice the exercise; the patient agreeing to report the effects of the practice and any difficulty carrying out the practice; and both patient and therapist agreeing to work for the success of the treatment. Each of these items will be discussed briefly next.

Weekly appointments. By experience it has been found that weekly appointments work out well for relaxation training. More frequent sessions are not usually necessary and consistently less frequent appointments do not offer enough contact between patient and therapist for the learning to take place well. On the other hand, the weekly schedule need not be rigidly adhered to and occasional missed appointments for brief vacations or practical reasons do not usually interfere with treatment.

Length of treatment. Experience has again shown that reasonable gain in learning to relax by use of cassette tape recorder can be expected to progress for 2 to 4 months and that it is better for treatment not to go beyond that length of time. When the therapist is inexperienced it is even more important that the length of treatment not be open-ended to avoid the risk of entering into progressively less effective encounter with the patient. Depending upon the learning therapist's situation and the needs of the patient, the patient can either be told that he and the therapist will work together for a certain number of sessions—such as six or 10—or that there are likely limits to the treatment of 2 to 4 months and that it is very unlikely that treatment will be longer than that.

Tape recording. The standard inexpensive cassette tape recorder is essential for the patient's home practice. Since they are available for about $30.00, most patients can acquire them; however, in institutional practice or with low income patients, it is sometimes essential for the facility to make the tape recorder available on loan to the patient and to have a system for keeping track of the whereabouts of the recorder. The facility should also have available better quality tape recorders for making duplicate tape recordings and different tape recordings as needed. The therapist must make available to the patient a cassette recording of the exercise to be used. This can either be in the therapist's voice or someone else's. If the recordings by someone else are already available there is no reason not to use them; if they are not already available the therapist should prepare a recording for the patient in the therapist's voice. This should be done before the treatment session until the therapist has become thoroughly acquainted with the procedure. If a skilled and trained therapist wishes to make the recording during a treatment session this can work well, but the inexperienced therapist merely adds another element of which to try to keep track and this should not be attempted. It must be emphasized that the learning therapist should be thoroughly familiar with the relaxation exercise on the tape. There is no surer way to deservedly lose the patient's confidence than to talk with him about one procedure when his tape recording presents a different procedure.

Home practice. The patient must agree to practice the relaxation procedure twice a day. Many people resist making this commitment, especially those who are very busy. If there is a problem it must be clarified before treatment is undertaken. Most often it is not necessary to ask the patient to record his practice or to verify rigorously the frequency of practice, and there is usually no reason to be rigid about patients occasionally missing home practice sessions. The patient's manner in response to questions about home practice will usually inform the therapist and if sessions are consistently missed it must be dealt with (see Secs. 5.8; 5.9).

Home practice times. The therapist can learn a great deal about how the patient will carry out his training by conducting a brief negotiation concerning the times of day the patient should practice. This is also an opportunity to heighten the effectiveness of treatment by building a sense of anticipation in the patient. Usually one asks if there are two fairly regular and convenient times in the day that the patient can practice. If the patient's busy schedule does not make this convenient one can concede a bit on regularity of time of practice while pointing out that this very overactivity is a likely causal factor in the patient's problems and is something he needs to re-evaluate. If the patient proposes to practice just before going to bed or to practice in bed before going to sleep, this should be countered by recommending that for the time being we wish to separate practice from going to sleep so as to avoid interference with practice by falling asleep. If the patient asks to be able to use the relaxation exercise to help go to sleep one can build expectancy by advising him not to do so until the therapist has found the treatment beginning to work and will advise him later to do so.

Report of practice. The patient should be instructed to tell the therapist about the home practice in as much detail as necessary. Thus, if it goes well, detail may be spared, whereas if there is difficulty the option of exploration in depth is open. The patient will usually acquiesce to this part of the contract. Occasionally someone will present an objection which may be dealt with at the time. The more usual problem is for the patient to agree to report home practice and then fail to be prepared to do so. The management of this is described below (Sec. 7.11).

Collaboration for success. Depending upon the particular characteristics of the patient with whom one is working, the therapist should either explicitly or implicitly assure that there is good collaboration between them. A patient with long standing chronic symptoms may need hope rekindled, whereas a patient who has some secondary gain may need a trace of skepticism from the therapist to mobilize his need to have approval. The competent patient who has symptoms in only one area of his life needs less concern than the neurotic patient who has a delicate balance between physical symptoms, mental concerns, and interpersonal relations. The patient with an unusual degree of contrariness will require that the therapist not ask too loudly and strongly of the patient for his collaboration because of the patient's innate need to do the opposite of what is expected. Here an implicit understanding of working together is better than too vigorous attempts to nail down agreement.

The details of practice and sessions have been the material out of which the essential element of the therapeutic contract is built. It is the agreement between patient and therapist to collaborate for the success of the treatment which is the essence. More important than any other element of the treatment is the learning therapist becoming able to tell when he and his patient are working together and when they are failing to do so.

§7.10 Treatment Sessions. The therapeutic contract contains agreement upon the patient practicing the relaxation exercise at home and then having weekly treatment sessions. The **first session** is initially directed to the therapist satisfying himself that the patient is suitable for treatment and arriving at a therapeutic contract with the patient. Also, when time allows, it is a good idea to give the first relaxation training session with the therapist either reading from the script or reciting the exercise from memory (Table 7.1). Until the therapist has learned it well enough to recite without faltering or hesitancy, it is better to read the exercise to the patient from a script. After the therapist has carried the patient through the exercise, the patient is questioned about his experience with the exercise and suitable comments are made to his reactions (see Tables 5.1; 5.2; 7.2). Usually the patient will also be given the needed cassette tape recording gear and instructed in how to use the tape during the time until the next session. The first session may need to be longer than subsequent ones because of all that has to be done. Usually an hour is more than enough time for even the first session and subsequent sessions can often be completed in less than half an hour.

The **second session** is the first session in which it is possible to debrief the patient concerning home practice and this is usually the first thing done after the initial greetings and inquiry as to the patient's general well-being. When the therapist has heard how the home practice has gone it is possible either to respond immediately to the information with management suggestions or to defer comment until after the exercise is practiced. If things are going well it is all right to comment immediately, whereas if the therapist does not have a clear idea as to the best way to respond he may ponder the problem for a while longer before having to do so. The practice of the relaxation exercise during the session may either be done by playing a tape recording or by the therapist speaking the exercise to the patient. The latter is preferable while the therapist is learning because it leads to greater familiarity with the material used. Once the therapist has acquired experience there is no reason not to use the tape recorder. After the patient has practiced the exercise the therapist asks for reactions and then can close the session by making or reviewing recommendations for any changes in the routine to be carried out in home practice.

In **subsequent sessions** the same routine may be carried out by beginning with review of home practice, practicing the relaxation exercise, asking questions about reactions, and reviewing any recommended changes. As treatment progresses termination becomes an issue (see Sec. 7.12).

§7.11 **Home Training.** In the preceding sections (7.9; 7.10), some of the details of home practice were given — that a cassette tape recorder with a cassette tape of a relaxation exercise is available, that the patient decides upon two fairly regular times per day to practice and reports on the results of this practice, that the patient accepts the responsibility to report on practice and the therapist will then advise on modifications as needed. Here we will deal in more detail with home practice and the handling of the problems that arise.

The most serious problem in home practice is when the patient fails to practice. Sometimes the patient will admit this, but occasionally a patient will say he is practicing when he really is not. Usually reason for further questioning can be gleaned from the patient's manner — vagueness about practice, lowering the eyes when answering questions about practice, or blustering complaint about not getting better. When the patient is not practicing or the therapist strongly suspects so, this requires reclarification of the therapeutic contract. If the patient's collaboration cannot be obtained, treatment should be discontinued.

Other common negative reactions include falling asleep, experiencing no change, feeling more nervous, having the mind wander, feeling no better afterward, obsessive ruminations about the details of the exercise, fear of failure, not developing a subjective cue, and having initial improvement followed by getting worse. These reactions are dealt with in more detail in Chapter 5.

Responses indicating progress include feeling better, using the exercise to cope with stress, aborting or preventing anxiety, awareness of the subjective cue, being seen better by other people, sleeping better, dreaming more, and noticing the ache of relaxing muscles. Generally these are to be given encouragement and praise. Assuming that treatment progresses well, the patient will gradually work out the obstacles to relaxation, will become more adept at the exercise, and will have symptomatic improvement. It is important for the therapist to respond positively and let the patient know that progress is being made.

One of the major signs of progress and the ability to terminate is the development of the subjective cue (Secs. 5.6; 5.10; 5.12; 5.13). In learning to use the relaxation exercise the therapist should introduce the idea of the cue to the patient and begin to inquire about its being noticed by the patient in practice. After the therapist is more experienced he will be able to search for evidence of the development of a subjective cue without explicitly asking, but initially it is better to ask explicitly than to leave the issue unexplored. Failure to develop a subjective cue is a sign that the treatment was not fully successful. However, for a beginning therapist it is probably best not to extend the treatment of the patient who does not develop the subjective cue, since it will probably not come later.

§7.12 Termination of Treatment. The major purposes of the use of relaxation exercises as we have just detailed are to enable the patient to have enough mastery of the technique to be able to continue using it on his own, to have enough experience with the exercise to have worked through the major obstacles, to being able to gain benefit from it, and to have acquired the necessary determination to continue making use of the exercises to cope with the particular symptoms for which treatment was begun. When those goals have been met there is no further reason to continue the training. If the patient and therapist have been working together well, the patient will have been made aware of the progress and of the achievement of the goals for which treatment was undertaken. Implicit in that is the idea that treatment is soon to end. Another issue at this time is how well the patient has learned to do the exercise without the tape recorder. The therapist may either teach the patient to do the exercise without the recorder playing, i.e., by being able to use his own mind to control the entire relaxation exercise, or the patient may be permitted to retain the tape and continue to use it after termination. The major determinant here is how autonomous the patient is. Patients who are very independent minded will wish to be able to do the exercise on their own without external assistance, while those who are more dependent will prefer to retain the external support of the recording. For our purposes, either result is acceptable.

When the patient chooses to learn the relaxation exercise without the tape recording, this may be facilitated and begun by his initially turning off the recorder about halfway through the exercise half of the time, then going to practice without the tape recorder half of the time, and finally to practicing without the tape recorder all of the time. While this is going on, the patient and therapist can begin to discuss what sort of mental content the patient will have while relaxing. Generally, the patient should be encouraged to keep his mind focused on the body and the pleasant body sensations of relaxation and not to get too involved in thought processes. To do otherwise is to begin to use a special meditative technique which it is not our purpose to describe.

Depending upon the achievement of the relaxation exercise in relation to the patient's symptoms, the patient should be encouraged to continue to practice relaxation twice a day or merely to retain the skill to use again as needed.

At least two sessions before treatment is to be finished, the topic should be thoroughly discussed with the patient. If a joint decision to terminate can be made this is best. When circumstances do not allow this, the therapist should make the decision, but inform the patient as soon as possible. The decision to terminate should almost never be made during the last session and usually earlier than the next to the last session.

The major problem in termination is with the overly dependent patient who either does not believe he can tolerate termination or whose symptoms return in the face of termination. Sometimes this problem can be skillfully managed by a sensitive therapist, but it usually means that the patient should be expected to continue in another form of therapy with another therapist. Depending upon circumstances, this may mean medical management with a primary care physician, psychotherapy, or use of some other treatment modality.

§7.13 **Variations of Relaxation Exercises.** The particular relaxation exercise chosen here has been carefully chosen to have certain characteristics for particular reasons. These characteristics are being tape recorded, dealing only with the experience of relaxation, focusing upon the parts of the body in a systematic way, and being about 20 minutes in length. It is easier for both patient and learning therapist for the exercise to be tape recorded. In a heterogeneous pool of patients there will be a fairly large proportion who would not be able to do the home practice of relaxation without the external aid of a tape recorded voice to guide them. Likewise, the learning therapist would be overwhelmed by the task of differentiating such patients and of dealing with the greater difficulties with the exercise which other patients would have.

Other methods, such as Jacobson's (1938), Schultz and Luthe's (1959), Lazarus' (1970), and Benson's (1975), use a narrower or wider verbal content to the mental script of the exercise. Thus, Jacobson and Lazarus have the patient alternately tense and relax muscles, Schultz and Luthe elaborately develop specific sensations of heaviness and warmth, and Benson has the patient focus upon the phrase "one." Each of these methods requires more of the learning therapist than does ours, and although they may be learned later if desired, we believe that we will have provided the therapist with a solid foundation upon which to build.

We have used an exercise of about 20 minutes length because that is a practical compromise for the patient with enough symptoms to give motivation to work. A shorter practice period will give less likelihood of reaching a very relaxed state and a longer period will impose upon what time the patient is able to provide for the treatment. It is possible to shorten the exercise to about 10 minutes for asymptomatic non-patient subjects, for patients with mild symptoms, or for patients who are unusually busy but who can remain in training over a longer period of time.

In a later chapter (Secs. 9.2-9.4), we will explore how the tape recorded relaxation exercise can be suitably modified to meet the special needs of particular patients. This includes the addition of focusing upon particular parts of the body and noticing the particular contents of perception and the mind. Also we will describe an exercise which may be used by the patient who is too tense or distractible to use the usual simple relaxation exercise (Sec. 9.5).

§7.14 **Summary.** The foundation of a biofeedback treatment is the training of the patient in relaxation. This is usually done by teaching home practice of relaxation with a cassette tape recording of the relaxation exercise. The learning therapist can best learn to teach a relaxation exercise by first giving a single relaxation session, and after this is mastered, learning to teach an entire course of the relaxation exercise. These steps are described in detail.

People rather admire what is new, although they do not know whether it be proper or not, than what they are accustomed to, and know already to be proper; and what is strange, they prefer it to what is obvious.

Hippocrates

CHAPTER 8

Basic elements of treatment: biofeedback

§8.1 **Introduction.** In the last chapter the reader was provided detailed instructions in giving relaxation training, which is always an integral part of simple biofeedback treatment. Next we will describe a complete biofeedback treatment from start to finish. This will be done by going into detail about the entire course of treatment in the order of occurrence of the sessions. First we will describe the initial interview (Secs. 8.2–8.5). The second session – the baseline session – will be described next (Secs. 8.6–8.10). The third session, the goal-setting session, will follow (Secs. 8.11–8.15). These are all of the specially structured sessions undertaken before the beginning of the biofeedback training per se, which will then be described for electromyographic (EMG) feedback (Secs. 8.16–8.21) and skin temperature feedback (Secs. 8.22–8.27). Finally, the chapter will end with a brief review of all of the elements of a typical treatment (Secs. 8.28–8.34) accompanied by a block diagram of the flow of treatment (Fig. 8.1). Notice that all of the methods described enhance the relaxation response (Benson, 1975).

INITIAL INTERVIEW

§8.2 **Introduction.** This is the first occasion upon which practitioner and patient meet. With rare exceptions, both would be present at the initial interview. Occasionally, in an extremely busy practice or during a short absence, the initial interview might be with the senior biofeedback therapist, who would then completely brief the practitioner before his meeting the patient at the second or third session. Likewise, in an institutional setting the senior biofeedback therapist might, under the supervision of the practitioner in charge of the biofeedback clinic, accept patients who had been screened and referred for treatment by colleagues from the practitioner's own department. In most circumstances, though, the practitioner will meet the patient at this time. The three major tasks of the initial interview are establishing the therapeutic relationship

(Sec. 8.3), conducting initial assessment (Sec. 8.4) and giving first information about biofeedback to the patient (Sec. 8.5).

§8.3 **Establishing the Therapeutic Relationship.** In Chapter 2 we went to great lengths to emphasize the importance of the therapeutic relationship. Implicit in that discussion is the idea that the relationship's tone is set by the first meeting between patient and therapist. The circumstance of the initial contacts—probably by telephone, the attitude in making the initial appointment, the manner in which office personnel greet the patient, the decor of the office and waiting room, the promptness of keeping the appointment, and the attitude of the practitioner will all be assessed by the patient with a rapid scan which may affect the rest of treatment. Those failings for which modern practitioners have been criticized (Lain Entralgo, 1969) may not be forgiven and treatment jeopardized if personal concern is lacking, if details are neglected, if tact is not forthcoming, or if scientific preoccupations prevail. The treatment will do best if the patient feels from the practitioner and his staff a sense of concern, compassion, competence, comprehension, and coherence which is conveyed in the manner of the initial contact. These elements do not in themselves completely constitute the structure of treatment but are crucial as a framework upon which to build our influence upon the patient.

§8.4 **Initial Assessment.** Both in Chapter 3 and in later sections (Secs. 4.14–4.15; 5.2) the criteria for choice of patients and for patient evaluation have been discussed at length. Most of this evaluation is carried out in the initial interview when the history of the presenting complaint and the rest of the patient's pertinent medical and psychological history are taken. Also, permission is obtained to talk with the patient's other physicians and psychotherapists and to request his concurrence in proceeding with treatment. Usually a tentative decision can be made and conveyed as to whether or not to undertake treatment.

§8.5 **Initial Briefing.** An important part of the initial interview is concerned with informing the patient about biofeedback and the treatment plan. Two reasons for this are that it gives the practitioner another opportunity to assess the patient's attitude toward treatment, and that it reassures the patient about possible fears he has of treatment. The amount of information to be provided depends upon circumstance of the individual situation and cannot be generalized. However, at a minimum it is desirable to inform the patient of the probable length of treatment, the frequency of appointments, the need of home practice, the fee and possible insurance coverage, the scope of possible outcomes, any complications that may arise, the rationale of the treatment, the options of biofeedback parameters, the nature of the next (baseline) session, and the nature of most treatment sessions. Elaboration of some of these issues has been given for the specific instance of relaxation training (see Sec. 7.9).

BASELINE SESSION

§8.6 Introduction. This heading describes a particular part of biofeedback treatment—the baseline session—which needs to be considered before the actual biofeedback treatment sessions because it precedes them and is used in selecting the feedback parameter. The heading is organized into four parts. The first describes the psychophysiological profile (Sec. 8.7), which is the foundation of the baseline session. The second part describes alternatives available for the clinical assessment of the physiological profile (Sec. 8.8). Then the actual procedure of a baseline session is described (Sec. 8.9), and finally, the method of selecting a biofeedback parameter based on the physiological profile of the baseline session is described (Sec. 8.10).

§8.7 Psychophysiological Profile. In most branches of medicine, psychiatry, and psychology, there are standardized laboratory procedures widely or universally used for the clinical assessment of the patient—both for diagnosis and for following treatment. Thus, for example, the electrocardiogram tells the cardiologist a great deal about the heart and the profile of blood chemistries helps in the diagnosis and treatment of electrolyte imbalance. By the same token, the Minnesota Multiphasic Personality Inventory and the Rorschach Test provide data which closely match and supplement clinical observations. It is strange, then, that so little use is made clinically of the considerable information available about an individual's psychophysiological functioning. Upon pondering the issue, it is apparent that psychophysiological functioning is complex, multi-dimensional, and not easy to comprehend. Also, the area of concern is divided among different disciplines where often those in one field are unaware of what goes on in another. Finally, until recently there have been no readily available therapeutic techniques for intervening upon the measured variables.

The advent of biofeedback would have appeared to have drastically changed this picture now, since the therapeutic technique directly affects psychophysiological variables and provides strong incentive for correctly characterizing the variables. The development of a psychophysiological profile may begin by considering past attempts at establishing profiles and by considering the nature of the psychophysiological system it is desired to characterize. Major past attempts have been those of Wenger (1966) and Lacey (1967), both based on solid and thoughtful work, but neither achieving wide usage.

The system to be characterized consists of the major dimensions of arousal levels, muscular activity, autonomic nervous system balance, and central nervous activity. However, each of these major components may be divided into subunits according to several different plans. In addition, each of these major dimensions has characteristic patterns which may be different in different steady states, in transient responses to various stresses, and in progression into relaxation. It is out of this particular kaleidoscopic picture that the biofeedback clinician seeks useful information about his patient. So far there are no standardized profiles such as used for blood chemistry or psychological assessments. However, a combination of common sense observation and laboratory data is beginning to be combined by a number of workers to reach some tentative conclusions (Gellhorn and Kiely, 1973; Pelletier, 1975; Budzynski, 1976; G. Schwartz, personal communication).

We will now describe an idealized psychophysiological profile which does not yet exist. This will then be used as a map for a much more restricted profile, with only a few of the dimensions covered, yet still giving some useful information. The idealized psychophysiological profile is based on information obtained from the three sources of *historical information* obtained from the patient, *physical observation* of the patient, and *psychophysiological testing* of him. This information is then organized into the major system dimensions previously mentioned – arousal levels, muscular activity, autonomic balance, and central nervous activity, and categorized in the different state dimensions of steady state, transient stress responses, and progression into relaxation.

§8.8 Alternatives for Clinical Profiles. Because the average clinical biofeedback facility is now able to work with several parameters and because the average patient seen is most apt to have a hyperarousal stress reactivity syndrome, it is of practical value in most clinical settings to collect as much of a psychophysiological profile as can be conveniently obtained. Apart from the information of history and physical observation, there will be a limited amount of testing which is practical. This may consist of measurements made with the clinical instruments used in treatment. Most often this will especially include the EMG level and absolute digit temperature. Occasionally it will include continuous measurement of GSR, digital pulse plethysmogram, EEG, and a variety of other parameters. Almost always it can include pre- and post-test measurement of pulse rate, respiration, and blood pressure. Depending upon the past experience and treatment philosophy of the clinician, it is almost certain to either employ mild stress testing or testing during progression into relaxation. Steady state baseline testing is not likely to be used since the definition of an appropriate steady state task is hard to agree upon. It is obvious that merely sitting during measurement for a period of time is far from a steady state and is almost certain to lead to state change — either of increased anxiety and tension or of relaxation, depending upon the individual and the setting.

We favor taking the profile during progression into relaxation and will describe the method for doing so in the next section. One reason we favor this is that we wish to strengthen the patient's association of the following elements: the treatment setting, the need to relax, the therapist as a helping person, the possibility of improvement, a respite from stress, and a new venture. However, we also recognize the desirability of testing reactivity to stress and of teaching the modulation of reactivity to stress and expect that when appropriate procedures are well developed, we may change our practice on this point.

§8.9 **Conducting a Baseline Session.** Bearing in mind the technical issues just raised, we would now like to shift the scene. We are attempting to establish the way that a patient is introduced into biofeedback treatment. In the earlier parts of this chapter we dealt with the patient who received relaxation training in which only clinical judgment and intuition were used to assess the dimensions of a psychophysiological profile and where no instruments for testing might be available. However, in the biofeedback treatment setting as usually used and as we will describe in detail, the progression into treatment usually follows a different course. Usually the patient has an initial evaluation and intake session in which no treatment is given or at most he is instructed in the use of relaxation tapes. Then the patient leaves and comes back in a few days or a week or so for his baseline session which we will now describe.

During the intake session the patient is told that he will return for the baseline session in which we will measure a number of variables as they are upon arrival into the lab and after relaxation. We explain that the measurement techniques cannot harm him in any way nor do anything *to* him, merely measuring *from* him. We also tell him that the relaxation will be a major activity of the entire treatment and that he will not be introduced to the biofeedback until the third session. The patient is also introduced to the laboratory as a setting in which some or much of his treatment will take place.

After introduction to the laboratory the patient sits in a soft recliner chair and the appropriate electrodes are attached to him in as efficient a manner as possible. As soon as an electrode pair is attached, the therapist begins to record from it, so as to gain an overview of instrument performance. When all electrodes are attached, the patient is asked to rest for a few minutes while initial data are collected. After a period of 3 to 10 minutes, when a reasonably stable sample of the variables has been collected, the patient is instructed that a relaxation session will be carried out by tape recording. This is done to ensure close comparability of the administered relaxation session from patient to patient. (During the establishment of a new facility when practice at giving the exercise was needed, it could be personally spoken by the therapist or other training therapist. However, once past this phase we recommend using a tape recording for uniformity.)

The patient is told that we wish to evaluate his particular response to relaxation by observing his physiological parameters, that we wish him to make himself as comfortable as possible and to follow the relaxation instructions. The tape is then played and the measurements are taken while the patient is relaxing. As soon as the exercise is over, the patient's electrodes are removed and he is given a tentative overview of what was found.

Because we have a fully equipped research laboratory we measure several parameters: four channels of EEG (O_1-C_3, C_3-F_7, O_2-C_4, C_4-F_8), two channels of EMG, GSR, toe pulse plethysmogram, finger temperature, heart rate, and blood pressure. However, as indicated above (Sec. 8.8), a modified profile is possible as long as a particular biofeedback laboratory has several good quality feedback instruments available. We recommend that a clinic have both EMG feedback and temperature feedback instruments. Then pulse rate, blood pressure, and respiration should be taken before and after the relaxation exercise. Thus, a measured profile of five variables is available. In addition, many clinics will have GSR and alpha and theta EEG instruments available for further measurements.

§8.10 Selecting Feedback Treatment Parameters. The primary reasons for collecting the psychophysiological profile in the baseline session are to have a picture of the patient for differential diagnostic purposes to compare with after treatment progresses, and to select the best feedback treatment parameters with which to work. Selection of feedback parameters is based upon a combination of factors, some of which were reviewed in Sections 3.10 and 3.11. These factors include the specific nature of the patient's complaints, the specific nature of his perception of the variables available for feedback, the results of the baseline session and the clinical judgment of the necessity of keeping the maximum number of options open during treatment. We will not give a precise formula for choosing parameters, nor do we believe such is apt to emerge in the next few years. Rather, we can indicate some limiting factors which can help in choosing treatment parameters.

This mainly involves a common sense approach. If a patient is unusually tense, for example, and does not have much movement of any parameter in a baseline session, it may be worthwhile to have him work with forearm EMG for a while before going to other parameters. An unusually tense patient who has movement in the direction of relaxation by one parameter, but not others, should probably be started on that parameter. Patients who are unusually tense might anticipate the need to work with several parameters, while those who are more relaxed, but have localized muscle tension problems, might do quite well by only using EMG.

The major options to consider in a clinic which has both EMG and temperature feedback as available parameters are between a single parameter for the entire treatment or a progression through several parameters. When there is to be a progression through several parameters, it is usually best to start with one which may show movement. This is forearm EMG for the most tense patients, but might be either forehead EMG or finger temperature for a less tense patient. After the easier parameter has been satisfactorily controlled. the patient may then shift to the more difficult parameter.

Budzynski (1976) has worked out an algorithmic flow diagram for deciding on biofeedback parameters. We have not yet tried his schema and so are unable to compare that procedure with our less precise method of choosing parameters.

GOAL-SETTING SESSION

§8.11 Introduction. After a patient has been evaluated for biofeedback treatment (Secs. 8.2–8.4), been given some initial information about the treatment (Sec. 8.5), had a baseline recording session (Secs. 8.6–8.10), and received initial instructions in the home practice of relaxation exercise, he returns for a third session (the first two having been the initial evaluation session and the baseline session). This third session can be termed a *goal-setting* session because that is the main work to be accomplished. If the goals can be easily set and there is time, it is usually the first session in which the patient experiences biofeedback.

This part of the chapter is organized into four main sections which follow the flow of the goal-setting session. The *appraisal of home practice* since the initial assignment in the previous baseline session is first (Sec. 8.12). This enables the therapist to determine the *working equilibrium* to be expected (Sec. 8.13). Using this information, *psychophysiological goals* (Sec. 8.14) and *symptom goals* (Sec. 8.15) are set. Then the patient will, as just mentioned, begin biofeedback training.

It is to be noticed that the patient does not actually experience biofeedback until the third session. We do not believe this is necessarily better than other methods in which the patient would begin biofeedback training immediately. We have found that some structure is better than too little structure and this is the particular structure at which we have arrived. Also, it is a good idea for the therapist to have ample opportunity to contemplate the patient's initial responses to home relaxation assignments and to the baseline measurement session before trying to reach closure with the patient on goals, and the first two sessions provide plenty of time for this. Finally, we believe that a beginning therapist will learn more readily when not forced to decisions and closure prematurely. Therefore, we recommend that our procedure be followed closely until the therapist has acquired the confidence to structure the sessions differently. This assumes, of course, that our procedure is reasonable in the particular setting.

§8.12 **Appraisal of Home Practice.** The goal-setting session follows the baseline session in which the patient had been first introduced to the home relaxation exercise with cassette tape recorder. Sometimes this may be introduced in the initial session, but either way it is now the therapist's task to question the patient concerning his experience with home practice, using the techniques described in Sections 5.9, 7.6, and 7.11. This is the first extended opportunity for contact between patient and therapist regarding the patient's performance at an assignment and the information elicited must be rapidly assimilated into the therapist's decision about a working equilibrium in order to decide how to set goals.

§8.13 **Working Equilibrium.** After assessing home practice the therapist must intuitively decide on the best way to work in harmony with the particular patient. This not only depends on the therapist's particular repertoire of styles but also on what will help the particular patient to accomplish the most in his work. Some patients need encouragement, others need prodding; some need challenge, others need protection; and some need the therapist's identification with their situation while others need for the therapist to be capable of coping with their contentiousness. The actual framing of therapeutic goals must be in the context of the working equilibrium established.

§8.14 **Physiological Goals.** Using the result of the baseline session, physiological goals are set for the patient to work toward in the treatment. The first decision is which parameters should be fed back. After that is decided, a goal for that particular parameter needs to be arrived at. In describing the feedback parameters below considerable specific information is given concerning what to expect of that parameter (EMG in Sec. 8.17; temperature in Secs. 8.23 and 8.24; alpha in Secs. 9.6–9.11). In addition, the assessment of the patient's needs helps set goals. Thus, some patients can set a goal for the whole treatment—these are usually people who are secure, independent, and well motivated. For other patients who are insecure and not likely to tolerate frustration well it may be better to set short term easy goals and to progress through more difficult goals in a series of steps. With some patients, goals can be implicit and need not be spelled out, whereas for others they need to be completely spelled out. We advise the beginning therapist to learn to set explicit goals with all of their patients and then as confidence is acquired by the therapist less of this needs to be done when indicated.

§8.15 **Symptom Goals.** The same principles used to set physiological goals are also used to set symptom goals, except that this is often a more urgent issue for the patient. Occasionally, the patient is asymptomatic, as in some cases of hypertension. Then the therapist must attempt with the patient to define degrees of relaxation or stress tolerance in a mutual experiential language and set goals with these. When setting goals with a headache patient, one typically takes into account the current frequency of headaches and sets a goal of a reduced frequency. For instance, if someone has headaches twice a week, a suitable initial goal might be to go 2 weeks without a headache, whereas in a patient with daily headaches, a initial goal might be to have 2 consecutive days without a headache.

Goals are always set with the provision that they can be revised if necessary. When a goal appears to have been set which is unrealistic for short term attainment and the patient is discouraged, it is usually important to set an easier goal. The wise therapist will learn to recognize that goal setting is a way of mobilizing patient expectations.

ELECTROMYOGRAPHIC FEEDBACK

§8.16 **Introduction.** Although there are earlier uses of EMG feedback reported (see Secs. 1.1–1.3), the use of it as we describe here evolved out of the work of Green, et al. (1969 a,b), and Budzynski, et al. (1973). It has become one of the most widely used and standardized techniques. Widespread clinical experience has led to fairly clear-cut expectations of treatment and a quite good understanding of the likely course of treatment and its variations.

We will first describe some of the uses of EMG feedback and our recommendations for its use (Sec. 8.17). We will then describe the preparatory steps the patient goes through before treatment (Sec. 8.18) and the establishment of a therapeutic contract (Sec. 8.19). This will be followed by discussion of training sessions (Sec. 8.20) and the process of termination (Sec. 8.21).

§8.17 **Uses of EMG Feedback.** Among the original clinical uses of EMG feedback was the treatment of tension headache (Budzynski, et al., 1973). However, this rapidly broadened into use for the general purpose of teaching and verifying relaxation in the broad category of stress-related conditions. Our own experience has shown it to be very useful when the training is given as we recommend in the context of therapeutic training, with therapeutic goals agreed upon to constitute a therapeutic contract, with home practice of relaxation provided, with attention paid to progress in all areas, and with sensitivity in handling termination. Again we caution against seeing the EMG feedback as an entity in itself apart from the rest of the treatment and deciding whether or not "it" is "the" proper treatment for "a" condition. Experience seems to be leading in the direction of using the physiological profile response to relaxation as a fairly important indicator of when and how to use EMG feedback. In general, for patients whose frontalis EMG readings are already within normal limits, there may not be too much point to using the technique. On the other hand, for those patients whose EMG readings are very high and when they are not appreciably lowered by a relaxation exercise, frontal EMG feedback would be premature and unwise until after a period of work with forearm EMG and possibly with the elementary concentration exercise (Sec. 9.5), and home practice of relaxation (Secs. 7.7–7.13). Another important consideration is whether there is a clear relationship between the patient's symptoms and muscle tension. Thus, one is particularly drawn toward EMG feedback for tension headaches, neck muscle pain, lower back spasm, torticollis, writer's cramp, and similar conditions where there seems to be an especially clear connection between the symptoms and increased muscle tension. Likewise, when the general complaint of anxiety, excessive stress responsiveness, and nervousness is accompanied by abnormally high EMG activity on the psychophysiological profile, this is also an indication for considering EMG feedback, assuming that there is some lowering of the EMG during relaxation.

§8.18 **Preparation for Training.** When we speak here of treating a patient with EMG feedback, we are assuming that the patient has already been through the routine procedure of initial assessment (Secs. 8.2–8.4), has had initial briefing as to the nature of treatment and expectations (Sec. 8.5), has been introduced to the laboratory and instrumentation for the baseline session in which a psychophysiological profile is collected (Secs. 8.6–8.10) and has been introduced to the home relaxation practice (Secs. 7.7–7.13, 8.11–8.12). The parts of the treatment having to do with EMG feedback then include goal setting in the therapeutic contract related to the feedback performance (Sec. 8.19), the EMG training sessions (Sec. 8.20), and the termination (Sec. 8.21).

§8.19 **Therapeutic Contract for EMG.** The therapeutic contract in the EMG treatment, as with any treatment, will have a *physiological training goal* and a *symptom change goal*. We will go into each in order, describing how they would be managed in a goal-setting session.

Before considering the physiological training goal, however, we will briefly take up levels of EMG activity to be expected at various muscle sites. Levels are usually described as either peak to peak microvolts, peak microvolts, average microvolts, or root-mean-square (rms) microvolts. Table 12.2 (Sec. 12.2) lists conversion factors to change from one to the other. However, microvolt levels to be expected do not only vary because of being reported on different units, but also because particular EMG amplifiers have their own special characteristics, especially band pass width and noise level. Therefore, the results for EMG levels from different laboratories and clinics are not easily comparable, even if converted to the same definition of measure. We wish to emphasize that this is not necessarily a sign of poor technique or improper instruments, but may be strictly due to technical differences in the instruments and will not be settled until a standards committee standardizes criteria for noise, band pass, and similar variables.

When measuring frontalis EMG, our particular instruments reach a level of about 5 μv rms when the subject is fairly relaxed, while deeply relaxed subjects reach 3 μv rms and tense subjects are at 10 μv rms and above, up to about 30 μv rms. Forearm EMG values at rest in a tense subject can be about 5 to 10 μv rms, while most subjects can relax until there is no EMG activity and the instrument will reach its own noise level. Measurements from the trunk and neck have to be specified for the particular instrument and the electrode placement because EKG pickup is likely to override other considerations in a particular result. The above gives some idea as to EMG levels to be expected, but it should be emphasized again that having EMG levels quite different from these does not mean anything is necessarily wrong with the equipment, the technique, or the patient. Each clinic should expect to set its own values based on its experience with its particular apparatus.

Physiological goals may be set progressively in a series of steps. Therefore, the patient's particular situation will be considered in setting the first goal and it will often be followed by other goals afterward. The easiest EMG goal in the most tense patient is the task of quieting the forearm of the dominant side. That may either be followed by working with the other forearm or with frontalis EMG. Less tense patients may start with frontalis EMG. A good goal to set is to work toward an average level of relaxed EMG in our clinic of about 5 μv rms. If the patient reaches that very easily it may be worthwhile to work toward even deeper relaxation—about 3 μv rms in our clinic. For some very tense patients, it may be better to work progressively toward an average EMG level by setting goals at each session about 20% below their current starting level.

Symptom goals have already been considered in Section 2.13. We would merely stress that their progression should be coordinated with the physiological goals as the stages unfold.

§8.20 **Training Sessions.** Each session has certain parts which have already been considered in detail elsewhere. These include greeting the patient, re-assessing his current status and learning about home practice at the beginning of the session, giving interim instructions, and parting at the end of the session. These are described in Chapters 4 and 5 and Sections 7.9 through 7.11. The therapist will need to review those parts to coordinate with the EMG training itself.

The EMG training per se consists of that part of the session, usually about 30 minutes, in which the patient is connected to the EMG feedback and able to work at the task of controlling EMG level. This may be approached in different ways, of which we will describe one in detail and mention several others. However, whatever approach is used, it is important that the patient be given tasks at which he feels success, that the therapist be available as needed during the session, that the patient's fears and frustrations be acknowledged and responded to appropriately.

When the patient can tolerate it and when the therapist's immediate schedule allows, we have the therapist stay in the room with the patient while practicing and remain in a low keyed dialogue with long silences. On the other hand, if the patient is made uncomfortable by the therapist's presence or if immediate needs demand the therapist's attention elsewhere, the therapist will leave the room for an appropriate time. We do not usually follow a special training trial protocol during a session, with feedback and no feedback trials of prescribed length alternating, as we feel that would be appropriate only to a particular stage of treatment unless there were a rule for otherwise determining the trial structure. In addition, we feel that the extensive home practice routinely prescribed results in a carry-over of learning to the no-feedback condition and to a variety of other settings.

When patients mention particular problems during a training session, we try to respond in a practical way which will help them past the obstacle presented. Much of the typical situations of importance here are taken up in Chapter 5. Using our approach, we are usually able to achieve a steady progression toward physiological goals accompanied by symptomatic improvement at the same time.

§8.21 Termination. Assuming that physiological goals are being met, the termination of treatment is usually decided upon other criteria, such as the meeting of symptomatic goals, the patient's confidence in maintaining these gains, the patient's progress in making concomitant changes in his life, etc. These have been dealt with elsewhere (Secs. 2.19; 4.17; 7.12; 8.33). If there is no progress with physiological goals in spite of all efforts on the therapist's part there is usually a problem which cannot be solved. It is then best to discuss this with the patient and terminate the use of something which is doing no good.

When a patient meets physiological goals but has no symptomatic improvement it is necessary to change to another parameter. This is often a sign of poor motivation or an extreme degree of secondary gain and the patient is apt to stop treatment at this point, since a continued campaign toward symptom control is contrary to his wishes in spite of superficial compliance.

SKIN TEMPERATURE FEEDBACK

§8.22 Introduction. Skin temperature feedback may have been developing as an experimental procedure in several laboratories, but seemed to get its major thrust into a central position as a feedback modality through the work in the laboratory of the Greens (Sargent, et al., 1972) in treating migraine headache with finger temperature training. In that particular use it not only gave good results but also had a useful rationale to explain the results (see Sec. 3.11). Following the success in its use in migraine, it has begun to be used more widely as another method of training relaxation, although it obviously operates through different mechanisms than EMG feedback.

Aside from operating through a different presumed mechanism than EMG (lowering level of sympathetic nervous system activity instead of lowering level of voluntary muscle activity), skin temperature feedback also differs in having an unavoidable long time lag from the time of occurrence of the event causing finger temperature change (arteriolar change) and the actual registration of the change. This means that whenever the actual change in blood vessel diameter occurs, it takes several seconds more for the actual temperature change to become very evident. In addition, it may be that the temperature change systems tend to operate more in a manner of "mass movement," with an apparent inertia to change and an inertia which continues a change once started. This gives a different kind of experiential work for the patient to attend to. It has been termed "passive volition" by Green, et al. (1969a), to reflect the subjective need of passivity in order to accomplish the task.

This part of the chapter will be organized the same as the last. First we will review some of the uses that have been made of skin temperature feedback and our own particular recommendations for its use (Sec. 8.23). Then we will describe our preparation of the patient for the training (Sec. 8.24), and the therapeutic contract at which we arrive (Sec. 8.25), followed by a description of the training sessions (Sec. 8.26), and termination (Sec. 8.27).

§8.23 Uses of Skin Temperature Feedback. Aside from the treatment of migraine, there are a number of other areas in which skin temperature feedback has been used. As mentioned above, there are a growing number of clinicians who have developed partiality toward the general use of finger temperature feedback as a general method for the treatment of stress-related syndromes and who may not use other modalities as a result. Their good results seem to validate their taking this position, although thorough comparative studies are not yet available. These clinicians have often commented on the dimension of "warmth" not only as an objective quality of the fingers and hands of the trainee, but also as a necessary quality to be possessed by the therapist. Their clinical experience is that therapists who do not show warmth and inspire trust have a hard time training subjects or patients to raise their finger temperature whereas those who do show warmth and inspire trust rarely fail to be able to teach their patients to raise their finger temperature.

In certain specific conditions there is a good rationale for using skin temperature feedback. This would include Reynaud's phenomenon and Buerger's disease where spasm of the small arteries causes cold hands and feet. Our own use of finger temperature feedback is based upon a number of different criteria, including the patient's characteristic finger temperature, his response in the psychophysiological profile test of relaxation, and the nature of the condition being treated. When the patient's finger temperature is already characteristically quite warm there is less dynamic range within which to work upon change. Thus, if initial readings are already above 90° F (32.2° C), we are less likely to use finger temperature feedback than if the temperature is between 75° F (23.8° C) and 90° F (32.2° C). Likewise, if a patient shows little change in finger temperature from a low reading (near room temperature), we are also less likely to use skin temperature as the initial feedback modality. Generally, when the patient's condition is related in a direct or indirect way to finger or other area's skin temperature or where the condition has been treated by others with temperature feedback successfully, we will be more likely to choose it. As mentioned above (Sec. 8.17), we may use such criteria to decide to *begin* treatment with a particular modality, but then after either success or evident difficulty with that modality we will shift to another.

§8.24 **Preparation for Training.** As with EMG feedback training we are assuming that the finger temperature training patient is prepared for training by having been through the routine procedures of initial assessment (Secs. 8.2–8.4), initial briefing as to the nature of treatment and expectations (Sec. 8.5), introduction to the laboratory and instrumentation for the baseline session in which a psychophysiological profile is collected (Secs. 8.6–8.10), and has been or will concurrently be introduced to the home relaxation practice (Secs. 7.7–7.13). There are some special aspects of the training related to the briefing and expectations of skin temperature feedback which will be gone into briefly now.

Many patients, more commonly women than men and more commonly in cold climates or where air conditioning is used extensively, will be quite aware of cold hands and feet as general subjective symptoms. Many readers, themselves being aware of this condition, will be able to identify with the perception of the symptom. On the other hand, those who do not possess the condition may find this hard to do. However, it is of value to reassure patients who have cold hands that it is not in and of itself a sign of an abnormality, that there are no particular standards that define the level at which the temperature of the hands and feet is abnormal, and that they should not worry about the condition. Also, they should be told to begin to notice when their hands are warm and when they are cold, to notice the general association of warm hands with feelings of being at home and comfortable in a given situation and cold hands with being tense. They can notice that room temperature and bodily activity also have an effect and they can be taught to look for orienting responses during temperature feedback sessions. An orienting response is a lowering of finger temperature within a few seconds whenever a sudden noise or other novel stimulus suddenly takes the attention away from where it had been. Thus, a telephone ringing will almost always produce a degree or two drop of finger temperature in all of us and it is our inability to discriminate such a small change that makes us unaware of it (Sokolov, 1963).

Even though cold hands and feet are signs of tenseness, we will also see many patients who are obviously quite tense who do not have this relationship, so that it is obviously not invariant. When a patient who might have been given finger temperature training is treated with another parameter – such as a migraine patient with high hand temperature being given EMG feedback – this can be explained to the patient in case he wonders why the treatment modality he may have heard of is not used.

After the patient has been prepared for treatment, the sequence then unfolds of establishing a therapeutic contract related to skin temperature training performance (Sec. 8.25), going through the training sessions (Sec. 8.26), and of preparing for and undergoing termination (Sec. 8.27).

§8.25 Therapeutic Contract for Skin Temperature Feedback. The therapeutic contract in skin temperature feedback training also involves the same setting of physiological training goals and of symptom change goals as with other treatments. This is done in the goal-setting session (Secs. 8.11–8.15). Each goal will be gone into in order now, but first some more details of the ranges of skin temperature changes to be expected will be given.

Skin temperatures of the hands and feet have the potential to be the coldest of the body, with the distal ends of the finger and toes being the coldest part of the hands and feet. Generally every other region of the body will be closer to core body temperature. The temperature can range from several degrees below room temperature, apparently as a result of evaporation and vasoconstriction, to core body temperature or slightly above if warmed by an outside source. Even among the tense, few will often have temperatures below room temperature; while even among the very relaxed, few will ever have finger temperatures above about 96° F (35.5° C).

The tremendous dynamic range of arteriolar dilation and constriction in the distal limbs has important adaptive survival value to the species. If the hands did not cool in cold weather, there would be a very large heat loss which would require compensation by caloric intake. Both Australian aborigines and the Indians of Tierra del Fuego at the tip of South America have the capacity to sleep outdoors nearly naked in near freezing temperatures, which they accomplish in part by restricting heat loss through vasoconstriction of the limbs.

The recent popularity of the "mood ring," a color detector of temperature, has made the public more aware of finger temperature as a sign of internal state. However, the erroneous idea of assuming that the finger temperature reflects specific moods is often made. Instead, the temperature reflects a general state of sympathetic arousal and cannot differentiate anger from fear for instance. The importance of the finger temperature is that it clearly reflects movement along a dimension of sympathetic arousal and is a reactive system.

In order to set psychophysiological goals with finger temperature training it is necessary to consider the total activity of finger temperature responsiveness. This includes habitual levels of activity, reactivity to specific stress, reactivity to "safe" situations, the learning of the capacity to inhibit reactivity to stress, the learning of the capacity to warm the hands voluntarily, the learning of the capacity to cool the hands, and the reactivity to cold and warm environments. It must be borne in mind that usually symptomatic goals can be reached without having been able to effect all of the above dimensions of finger temperature control, but that the therapist and practitioner need to be aware of these dimensions and able to discuss them with patients to be able to interpret the meaning of change of these dimensions both for themselves and for the patient. Table 8.1 lists the dimensions and how to detect change in them. The therapist may make use of this information in setting special goals for the patient in whom it is important to achieve a particular result.

Usually, however, the goal will be for the patient to acquire the capacity to raise and lower the finger temperature several degrees voluntarily. It is not possible to specify the limits of the goal for several reasons, one of which is that in patients who already have a high finger temperature there is much less of the dynamic range upward left for

TABLE 8.1
Dimensions and Change of Finger Temperature

Dimension	Possible Positive Change
Habitual level of activity	From habitual cold hands to habitual warm hands
Reactivity to stress	From cold hands in stressful situations to not getting cold hands in stress
Reactivity to security	From slightly warm hands to very warm hands in secure situations
Capacity to inhibit stress reactivity	Become able to inhibit cold hands in stress consciously
Learning voluntary warming	Being able to warm hands voluntarily
Learning voluntary cooling	Being able to cool hands voluntarily
Reactivity to cold	Having warmer hands in a cold environment

them to work upon. In other words, when a patient's finger temperature is 75° F (23.8°C) there is over 20° F (11° C) rise available, whereas in the patient whose finger temperature is 92° F (33.3° C) only a 4° F (2.2° C) rise is even possible. This means, as with many other psychophysiological measures, that there is not equivalence of units over the entire dynamic range.

The capacity to raise the finger temperature several degrees voluntarily, then, must be evaluated in terms of the place from which the patient starts. It also must be evaluated in terms of when this capacity exists — whether only in the laboratory or on a few occasions, whether consistently in the laboratory or most occasions, whether both with and without feedback, whether during home relaxation practice, and whether accompanied by a subjective cue (see Secs. 5.6; 5.10; 5.12; 5.13). The patient need not be coached into the complete appreciation of all of these dimensions of the task, but the therapist must know them. Ordinarily it suffices to set with the patient the explicit psychophysiological goal of being able to raise and lower finger temperature several degrees in the laboratory with and without feedback. The other dimensions can be evaluated by the result of casual questioning and a specific task added to the goal as indicated. Implicit in our approach is the idea of the therapist gradually learning about the range of normal variations of finger temperature trainings and outcomes from their routine discussion and questioning with a number of patients.

The above discussion of the goal allows for the alternatives of reaching the goal by progressing through a series of sub-goals or tasks and of setting a new psychophysiological goal once a particular goal has been reached. Much of the decision about this may be based upon the general progression of treatment and upon the progress toward the symptom goal (Secs. 8.11–8.15). This symptom goal must of course be reached before a successful treatment can be concluded.

§8.26 **Training Sessions.** We have already detailed how each training session must include those particular parts which have little to do with the biofeedback training (Chaps. 4; 5; Secs. 7.7–7.13), such as greeting the patient, reassessing his current status and learning about home practice at the beginning of the session, and giving interim instructions, and parting at the end of the session. The therapist will need to review these parts to coordinate with the temperature training itself.

We approach the training with skin temperature basically the same as with EMG and suggest re-reading Section 8.20. The 30 minutes or so of training time is divided by the therapist's assessment of the patient's progress rather than by fixed time trials. The therapist is able to be in the room or out as indicated, to use feedback and no-feedback trials as indicated, to give "time out" breaks when task effort is ceased, and to ration the patient's frustration in tolerable doses.

§8.27 **Termination.** Section 8.21, discussing the termination process with EMG biofeedback, can be reviewed and followed, since there are no special differences to be considered.

REVIEW OF BIOFEEDBACK TREATMENT FLOW

§8.28 **Introduction.** Under this heading we will summarize an entire treatment, in all of its steps, in one place. This is done so that there is one place in which an entire treatment is described and serves as a summary of a treatment. The steps in a treatment are: initial evaluation (Sec. 8.29), baseline session (Sec. 8.30), goal-setting session (Sec. 8.31), training sessions (Sec. 8.32), termination (Sec. 8.33), and follow-up (Sec. 8.34). This overall picture can be schematized in the block diagram of Figure 8.1.

§8.29 **Initial Evaluation.** The initial evaluation of patients can usually be done in a single session in which the practitioner may be joined part or all of the time by the biofeedback therapist. The main presenting problem is reviewed and discussed, the pertinent past medical history is taken, and permission is obtained to review past treatment with primary physicians and others consulted. A tentative decision may be made to undertake treatment, in which case the patient is given an overview of treatment and how it might be relevant to his presenting problem. The next session (baseline session) is then explained to the patient and an appointment for the next session is made. The patient is also asked to fill out the relevant questionnaires and test forms at this time. Sometimes the patient can be introduced to the home practice at this point, although we do not recommend this for beginning therapists.

More extensive discussion of the initial evaluation sessions may be found in Chapter 3 and Sections 8.2 through 8.4.

§8.30 **Baseline Session.** This is the second visit by the patient. After going through the initial greetings and learning of important intervening events, the patient is introduced to the treatment room, physiological measurement transducers are put on, about 5 minutes of resting baseline measurements are collected, and then measurements are made while a relaxation exercise is presented, usually from a tape recording.

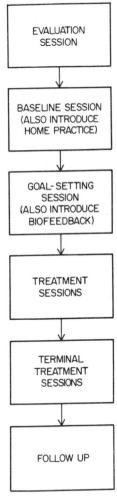

Figure 8.1. Block diagram of a biofeedback treatment structure.

Depending upon the complexity of the instrumentation, the physiological measurements may either be evaluated by the therapist at the time if simple or evaluated later if extensive. After finishing the baseline measurement, the transducers are removed. Then the patient is given complete instructions in carrying out the home practice relaxation procedure with a cassette tape recording. Finally patient and therapist part until the next session. More extensive discussion of the baseline session is found in Sections 8.6 through 8.10.

§8.31 **Goal-Setting Session.** This is the third treatment session. After the patient has been greeted, the session begins with a discussion of the experience with the home practice exercises. After this has been satisfactorily dealt with, the therapist will present some general observations about the baseline session and indicate a tentative biofeedback parameter with which to work. Possible physiological and symptomatic goals are presented to the patient and discussed. After agreement is reached, these goals are noted by both for future reference in judging progress. Usually there is time then for the patient to have the appropriate transducer applied and to practice with the biofeedback parameter for the remainder of the session. Before leaving, the home practice assignment is reviewed. More details of the goal-setting session are given in Sections 8.11 through 8.15.

§8.32 **Training Sessions.** Following the goal-setting session, the patient enters into the remaining series of the bulk of the sessions. These sessions always begin by the therapist greeting the patient and making inquiry into the progress of home practice and of self-observation of symptoms. The therapist carefully evaluates both and discusses progress with the patient. When satisfactory closure is reached, transducers are applied and the patient begins the practice work with the biofeedback parameter, which is usually carried on during much of the rest of the session. After the electrodes are removed, the next assignment is reviewed and the patient leaves. These training sessions are discussed extensively in Chapters 4 and 5 and in Sections 8.20 and 8.26.

§8.33 **Termination.** When it becomes evident that the treatment goals are being reached and that symptoms are satisfactorily managed, the topic of termination can be introduced into the dialogue. This is usually at least two or three sessions before the last one planned. The patient's reactions to this are noted and responded to as indicated and when the time arrives treatment is terminated. The topic of termination is discussed at greater length in Sections 2.19, 4.17, 4.29, 7.12, 8.21, and 8.27.

§8.34 **Treatment Follow-Up.** Whether to have treatment follow-up and in what form are decisions dictated in part by the needs of the individual patient and of the treatment facility. Until more clinical data are available, we have an obligation to do follow-up studies to learn about the long term effects of our treatments. Questionnaires can be routinely sent after set periods following treatment or routine follow-up visits can be scheduled. A suitable questionnaire is given in Appendix B.

§8.35 **Summary.** The foundation of biofeedback treatment is training sessions with a biofeedback instrument. This chapter describes in detail how to carry out this training with the parameters of EMG and skin temperature. When combined with the relaxation training of the preceding chapter, a complete method is available.

The physician has two sleeves, one containing a diagnostic and the other a therapeutic armamentarium; these sleeves should rarely be emptied in one move; keep some techniques in reserve; time your maneuvers to best serve the status and special needs of your patient.

Albert R. Lamb

From the basic error that specific remedies were created for particular diseases came the notion that the whole course of a disease, or even its separate stages, could be annihilated by a single remedy. It was reserved for the ablest physicians of all time to perceive that identical remedies are good only for identical phases of different diseases and that for different phases of the same disease, different remedies are necessary.

Rudolph Virchow

Nothing hinders a cure so much as frequent change of medicine; no wound will heal when one salve is tried after another.

Seneca
Moral Epistles to Lucilius

CHAPTER 9

Advanced elements of treatment

§9.1 **Introduction.** In the last chapter we gave complete details about how to use the basic elements of a treatment program — home practice of relaxation, EMG feedback, and skin temperature feedback. These will enable practitioners and technicians to learn the basic skills necessary to use this treatment method. Although these suffice for most cases it is sometimes necessary to use additional techniques in order to succeed when difficulties arise. After the mastery of the basic skills, then, it is possible to assimilate the additional techniques presented in this chapter. We have not gone further into the art of managing the therapeutic relationship but have restricted ourselves to technical procedures. Those who wish to gain greater mastery of managing the therapeutic relationship are referred to Haley's (1967,1968) compilations of Milton H. Erickson's work as one fruitful source.

The first section will dissect the dimensions commonly covered in a tape recorded relaxation exercise (Sec. 9.2). Next we will describe how to tailor a tape for a particular patient (Sec. 9.3), and how to achieve progression in a series of tape recordings (Sec. 9.4). Elementary concentration exercises are recommended in a few instances for unusual distractability (Sec. 9.5). Alpha brain wave training is then described (Secs. 9.6–9.11), and finally the special techniques of mental imagery (Sec. 9.12).

ADVANCED USE OF TAPE RECORDINGS

§9.2 **Dimensions of a Relaxation Tape.** Under this heading we are going into more detail concerning the use of relaxation tapes than was done in Chapter 7. There the learning therapist was introduced to the basic knowledge necessary to be able to use simple relaxation tapes as a therapeutic adjunct. This included the giving of a simple relaxation exercise and the extension of the technique into a training series which attempted to bring the patient to a certain level of proficiency in a circumscribed period of weeks. The first consideration we will take up in describing the advanced use of tape recordings is a more detailed study of the dimensions of the tape which can be varied. We will describe 20 such dimensions in order.

Tailoring a tape. The tapes we have described to this point are meant for general use and in no way are designed for the special needs of a particular patient, but rather for the general needs of the average patient. It is possible to make a tape especially for a particular patient. This will be described in detail in the next section (Sec. 9.3).

Progressive series of tapes. So far we have described a simple technique involving a single relaxation tape which is the only one used throughout the course of treatment. Another alternative is to utilize a series of different tapes which carry the patient through a progression of stages. This major dimension of the use of tapes will be described in detail in a following section (Sec. 9.4).

Length of tape. So far we have recommended a recording of about 20 minutes length. This is designed for the needs of an average patient, but there are others for whom a longer or shorter tape might be more appropriate. Also, at different stages of the treatment, the patient's needs might change. In the extreme situation of a patient who was especially distractible, a very short tape of perhaps 5 minutes might be appropriate as an introduction. Likewise, the patient who had mastered the tape and needed only to be able to reach a relaxed state rapidly might do well with a 5-minute tape which helped to ensure his consistently going into a relaxed state. Other patients who have more time available or who have symptoms which do not change rapidly—such as hypertension, long standing chronic anxiety or tension headache—may find it useful to work as long as 30 to 45 minutes with a tape recording. Obviously there is a point of diminishing returns after which fatigue, boredom, and weakening of motivation must be expected to provide an upper limit to the time of practice.

Source of voice. The voice on a tape recording can be chosen for a number of qualities, some of which will presently be described. A major consideration is the relationship between the patient and the person speaking on the tape. Among the likely possible choices are the therapist, the practitioner, the patient himself, or a stranger. Which to choose is largely governed by the situation and there are not yet any clear cut guidelines beyond those suggested by common sense.

Tonal quality of voice. Voices differ in their tonal quality along such dimensions as pitch (high versus low), resonance (rich versus thin), and effect (soothing versus strident). As far as possible we wish to choose qualities which enhance the patient's relaxation and therefore favor low, rich, soothing voices. On the other hand we also wish to avoid some of the extreme qualities which could be associated with this kind of a voice such as seductiveness and pseudo-confidentiality.

Hypnotic quality. A number of characteristics enhance the hypnotic quality of a voice – the low, rich, soothing voice is hypnotic, but the qualities of slowness, with a definite pace, with slow movement of attention to different places, with optimal authoritativeness and suggestion also contribute. Some patients enjoy the hypnotic quality and respond positively. Others find it aversive and react against it.

Authoritativeness. The content of a relaxation tape will differ in the degree to which it is structured in an authoritative manner versus the degree to which it is permissive, unstructured, and ambiguous. Rebellious and contentious patients will resent definite statements and dependent and passive patients will expect structure.

Suggestiveness. Relaxation tapes differ in the degree to which they suggest different thought perceptions and ego states. Thus, some will mention little of this and others a great deal. When the particular suggestions can be achieved by the patient and are generally pleasant and positive they may enhance the treatment, whereas when they are outside the patient's realm of current experience or are aversive they may slow it down.

Male versus female. For particular patients the sex of the speaker may be important and this must be considered. Generally, however, it appears that the speaker's sex is only one aspect and usually not the major one.

Dialect and vocabulary. Social distance or closeness is conveyed by these qualities and we must ensure that we do not create an undesired effect. Thus, some lower-class patients might be intimidated by large words and an upper-class accent or racial and regional prejudices might be incited by a particular dialect.

Background sound. We have a choice as to what background sound is on a particular tape. Thus, we may generally wish to avoid distracting noises such as telephones, automobiles, trains, airplanes, conversation, laughter, etc. On the other hand we may choose to add the beat of a metronome, simulated breathing, soothing music, or other steady rhythms. These steady rhythms would generally add to the relaxing and hypnotic qualities if well chosen, but we wish to avoid aversive qualities as much as possible.

Focus on breathing. Many techniques refer to breathing – a major interface between the physiological and the psychological (Christiansen, 1972). Although this is a preferred technique for relaxation it can be overdone, especially when there is no possibility of outside monitoring of performance as with a tape.

Focus on muscle relaxation. Through a variety of chains of attentional focus, the muscle sensations of relaxation can be progressively scanned as in the simple exercise we presented (Table 7.1; Sec. 7.5). This is another preferred method which can be used in a variety of ways –

part by part in sequence, limb by limb, part by part randomly, or in diffuse wholes.

Focus on muscle tensing. The classical Jacobson (1938) technique involves alternate tensing and relaxing muscles. For special purposes the tensing is useful. However, as a general method it may fail to demonstrate a clear purpose unless the therapist's own experience carries conviction of its worth. Also, although useful in early stages, later on it may be unnecessary. Further, some patients who are used to sedentary life may have painful muscle spasms after practice. Finally, the technique was designed originally to be administered by a therapist who is present rather than by tape. We sometimes use it early in treatment, but will drop it after a few weeks of practice.

Focus on body parts. Different from focusing upon the muscles in the arm is to focus upon the arm itself. Any part can be focused upon, even internal parts such as heart, lungs, stomach, kidneys, as the special circumstances require. Discussion of anatomical drawings or special models can help in this focusing.

Focusing on sensations. The mind can attend to the attempt to discriminate certain sensations in a particular body part or in general. Thus, warmth and heaviness in a limb can be focused upon, or a sensation of the body floating or of the body being inert or comfortable. A sensation of dissociation in which the part is not attached to the body can be sought.

Focus on body imagery. There is a distinct subjective difference between focusing upon a body part and focusing upon imagining that body part. The first instance is more of sensory perception, the second more of thought or imagery. Thus, instead of trying to feel warmth in the arm, one can imagine healing energy going to the arm.

Focus on mental imagery. Here one may imagine any scene desired. The use of this technique is explained in greater detail in Section 9.12.

Focus on subjective cues. Tapes may focus upon the subjective cue which tells the patient that he is entering the relaxed state (see Sec. 5.4). This may be done in a general way or specific to the particular patient's cue. The value of this is to strengthen and enhance the development of the subjective cue.

Focus on differentiating or integrating systems. If indicated, it is possible to ask the patient to focus on producing a differentiated response where one system goes in a particular direction and another system goes in a different direction. Schwartz (1975) has described how cardiovascular functions can be differentiated so that heart rate goes down and blood pressure goes up. The same principle can attempt to make one arm cool and the other warm or whatever is indicated. We do not personally have much experience with such a technique and mention it more because it is used by others [e.g., autogenic warmth of limbs and coolness of forehead (Schultz and Luthe, 1959)] and because it is hypothetically of great interest.

It can readily be appreciated that the subject of simple relaxation tapes may be quite richly complex and that there are many options open to the therapist in tailoring the tape to the particular patient and in building a progression of tapes.

§9.3 **Tailoring a Tape Recording.** The most common kind of situation requiring the special tailoring of a relaxation tape involves a patient for whom the regular tape is not suitable for some particular reason. Ordinarily, one attempts to take this reason into account and adjust to it. Thus, if the tensing of Jacobson's (1938) technique causes painful spasm or pain in a weak area of the body, it is better to not include tensing in the exercise. If the patient finds the voice on the tape objectionable one may change the tape toward what is desired. If the tape is too "hypnotic" this aspect can be lessened. If the patient is judged unusually ready for suggestion this may be emphasized.

One situation frequently encountered is the patient who has a particularly intractable symptom in a particular area of the body which the regular tape does not focus upon. Thus, painful spasm in an area of the body such as genitourinary, anal, esophogeal, or intestinal can be focused upon. This can be done in a number of ways — by imagining the pain lessening, by imagining the pain transferred to another part of the body or by imagining pleasant sensations taking over. Once a tape is tailor-made for a patient it becomes even more important to monitor the progress of the practice, since a special focus has been placed upon the method at this point and to neglect the outcome is to undermine one's own choice of emphasis.

§9.4 **Progression in a Tape Series.** One of the weaknesses of the use of a single relaxation tape throughout a treatment is that the method does not have a natural end point which consolidates the gains made. In describing the method (Secs. 7.7-7.13), emphasis was placed upon weaning the patient from the tape and training him to get along without it. This may require considerable skill on the part of the therapist and may not always work out well. Some patients may also become bored with a single tape repeated over several months. A straightforward answer to these problems is to progress through a series of tapes which introduce new ideas as the series unfolds and which anticipates the termination as it approaches.

Such a series is very much attainable at the current state of knowledge but does not yet exist in a well perfected form. The best we know of the series presently available is that produced by Lazarus (1970). However, experience with that series readily suggests a number of improvements. This kind of a series probably can best be generated either by a busy clinic which sees a large number of patients or by a study group of clinicians who periodically meet. The task is one which lends itself well to group effort.

SIMPLE CONCENTRATION

§9.5 Elementary Concentration Exercise. This particular very simple technique can be used in special situations when the patient is having difficulty with his home practice exercises because of unusual distractibility. This most often happens to a patient who is unusually nervous, but where the nervousness takes the form of rapid ruminative thoughts which are hard to get out of the mind. Typically, the patient has been given instructions in home practice with a relaxation tape, but reports that when he is using it he cannot keep his mind focused on the instructions. For such a patient the best course may be to interrupt the home practice with the tape temporarily and ask him to practice the elementary concentration exercise for a week or two. After he has done this he will then usually be able to go back to a relaxation tape, but it may be better to give him a different tape to work with than the one with which he had trouble.

To do the elementary concentration exercise, the patient is instructed to sit quietly in a comfortable chair three times a day. (The number can be four or five times a day if desired.) On each occasion he is to close his eyes and repeat the phrase "peaceful, one; peaceful, two; peaceful, three; . . . . etc." until he is interrupted by a distracting thought. Then he is to note how high he had been able to count and mark it down on a piece of paper for the therapist. This is then repeated two more times. Therefore, at the end of the day the patient has done three series of three rounds of the exercise and has nine numbers to report.

Some patients will demand an elaborate definition of what exactly constitutes a distracting thought. Practically, a precise end point is not essential and one patient's distracting thought may include different things than another's. It is important not to get trapped into trying to give a precise definition. Instead, one can ask the patient to practice, ask what distracted him and define the end point somewhat in his own terms. There are several purposes behind asking the patient to do the exercise. One is to release him from a difficult task and replace it with a simpler one. Another is to give therapist and patient some experiences to examine out of which they can draw tentative conclusions about how the patient's mind is working and develop a common language for describing what they observe. A third is to give the patient a rudimentary understanding of the mental dimension of the focus of attention and meditation. It is also important for the patient to see the exercise as a means to an end and not as an end in itself and to see it as something to be done for a short while before going on to do other things. Although basically similar to Benson's (1975) method, it is easy to see that the aims and use of this exercise are quite different.

ALPHA FEEDBACK

§9.6 Introduction to Alpha Feedback. Alpha wave feedback is the most widely used method of EEG feedback, followed by theta wave feedback. The other methods (mentioned in Secs. 11.6 and 12.8) are not yet used by us nor by most other general clinics and may be considered more experimental and specialized than alpha and theta. Further work will be needed to establish their overall place in the biofeedback armamentarium.

Alpha feedback work was begun by Kamiya (1969), soon to be followed by others such as Barbara Brown (1974), Hart (1968), and Mulholland (1968). Most of the work with alpha has been with non-patient experimental subjects. There is considerable controversy over the meaning of alpha production in a feedback setting and what it may be associated with. We will not discuss these issues here, but refer the interested reader to the excellent review by Travis, et al. (1975). Along with the scientific controversy about alpha, its clinical use has been inhibited by the fact that there was no clear-cut and concrete rationale to explain why it should help patients, as discussed for other parameters in Sections 1.38 and 3.11. Even so, it has been used empirically in several settings by a number of investigators with good results (McKenzie, et al., 1974; Montgomery and Ehrisman, 1976). However, little of the clinical use has been reported in the literature.

Our description of alpha feedback will begin with a discussion of the clinical uses of alpha (Sec. 9.7). Then we will discuss the preparation for training (Sec. 9.8), the therapeutic contract (Sec. 9.9), the training sessions (Sec. 9.10), and termination (Sec. 9.11).

§9.7. Uses of Alpha Feedback. Clinicians have used alpha for the treatment of tension headaches, migraine headaches, and general tension states (McKenzie et al., 1974; Montgomery and Ehrisman, 1976). Since there are not enough large case studies available to make the data comparable, there is only clinical impression to go by, and it is our clinical impression that therapeutic results using alpha training are similar to those with EMG or temperature training for a variety of conditions. We would not consider small scale comparison studies to be particularly convincing because of the impossibility of adequately controlling for patient's subjective bias, therapist's experience with a particular parameter, therapist's preference, difference between therapists, and similar independent variables which are probably of greater consequence than the parameters compared. Although this position may appear nihilistic, we believe it will ultimately prove more fruitful for research as well as for the advancement of clinical efficacy.

Although therapeutic history is full of instances where a supposed rationale for an effective treatment is later found invalid and the true explanation was entirely unexpected, nevertheless it would be almost unprecedented to use a treatment without a rationale. One of the major factors we believe may explain the efficacy of alpha training, no matter what the mechanism of alpha production, is that alpha training (as for that matter EMG or temperature training) is a method of inducing the patient to focus his attention upon an internal process. This is a universally used meditation technique—to focus attention upon a bodily process—and is well known for its effectiveness in teaching meditation. Furthermore, it is well known that the plethora of meditative techniques produce results which, on the one hand, have not been clearly demonstrated to be more easily obtained with one technique than another, while on the other hand, there are definite qualitative differences in the physiological outcomes of different forms of meditation. We do not consider it an adequate explanation to attribute the efficacy of alpha training solely to suggestion and placebo effect, since this leads to a circular argument in which suggestion and placebo effect are not clearly defined.

Another way of understanding the efficacy of alpha training is to consider it to be undertaken in relation to a symptom and the patient's attitude toward the symptom, to work toward a change of state, to focus attention away from the symptom, to be associated with relaxation as a change of state, to mobilize the patient's hope of relief, to offer the patient a collaborative relationship with a goal of symptom relief, to follow steps toward the goal, to mobilize the patient's other resources for treatment, and to expect change. No explanation of treatment can ignore these factors, and the deeper understanding of alpha training must await the deeper understanding of the therapeutic endeavor. However, in describing alpha training, these factors will receive particular emphasis.

We feel that alpha feedback training can be offered to most patients with most stress-related conditions for which EMG and finger temperature feedback have been used with about the same expectation of success. This has been our own experience with the technique. Adequate controlled studies have yet to be designed to test such an assertion and the assertion must partially be weighed in the context of the general reliability of what we present. We have no reason to assume that alpha feedback is better than the other methods, but experience with over 100 patients using alpha feedback has shown it comparable to the other methods. Because the other methods have a clearer rationale and have been more widely used in clinical treatment, we now give them preference over alpha training. However, we do not feel it would be justified to abandon the clinical use of alpha feedback and are describing the way in which we have used it.

§9.8 **Preparation for Alpha Training.** When we treat a patient with alpha feedback we are assuming that the patient has already been through the routine procedures of initial assessment (Secs. 8.2–8.4), has had initial briefing as to the nature of treatment and expectations (Sec. 8.5), has been introduced to the laboratory and instrumentation for the baseline session in which a psychophysiological profile is collected (Secs. 8.6–8.10), and has been or will be introduced to the home relaxation practice (Secs. 7.7–7.13). The parts of the treatment related to alpha feedback then include those parts of the therapeutic contract concerning the feedback performance, the alpha training sessions, and the termination. In preparing the patient for alpha feedback, we emphasize even more than with other modalities the importance of associating the desired symptomatic goals with the training. This would be counter to the design of some research in which one works to dissociate possible interactions as far as possible so as to dissect the elements of a procedure.

§9.9 **Therapeutic Contract for Alpha Feedback.** Alpha feedback training criteria are more like those for temperature training than those for EMG training. In EMG training there tends to be a relatively uniform criterion of very low activity for which everyone works, whereas with both alpha and temperature training subjects vary widely in where they start on the scale of typical activity levels and can be expected to make less movement along that scale in the course of achieving satisfactory symptom relief in a typical treatment of typical time course.

The amount of alpha activity present in the baseline session has dimensions of both amplitude of alpha activity and per cent of time alpha is present in various amplitudes. Different equipment gives different measures of this, so that it is not possible to give universally usable figures to be applied in different clinical settings. Also, a particular change in alpha activity is usually less intelligible to the patient than are changes in muscle tension or finger temperature. We cannot give specific recommendations of actual levels of change of alpha activity because of these and other varying factors. However, when it is possible to measure alpha amplitude we usually work for a 100 to 200% increase in alpha amplitude present a given amount of time, usually about half of the time. The symptom goals are set as for other conditions.

§9.10 **Alpha Training Sessions.** Even more than with other feedback modalities, it is important that alpha training be done in a pleasant, quiet setting without distractions. Since scalp electrodes are used, these need to be applied in an efficient, unobtrusive, and non-threatening manner. The other elements of a training session have been discussed elsewhere—greeting the patient and learning about home practice at the beginning of the session and giving interim instructions and parting at the end of the session (see Chaps. 4; 5; Secs. 7.7–7.13). These should be reviewed before planning sessions.

The alpha training itself usually involves about 30 minutes of continuous work in a quiet room, with the task being to keep the alpha tone on as much of the time as possible and at as loud an amplitude as possible. We have an intercommunication system with microphones and loudspeakers so that the therapist can be in the other room during a session, and we have found that that works well.

Presumably, if the patient finds any of the details of the setting not to his liking, that is a problem to be dealt with. Since other feedback modalities are available, these can be substituted either temporarily or throughout the treatment, as indicated.

§9.11 Termination of Alpha Training. The same principles apply at the termination of treatment as with other modalities, as discussed elsewhere (Secs. 2.19; 4.17; 4.29; 7.12; 8.21; 8.27).

MENTAL IMAGERY

§9.12 Mental Imagery. Mental imagery can be thought of as pictures in the mind or ideas. It may be used as an adjunct to relaxation and as a tool to facilitate the biofeedback task. Mental imagery techniques are used as diagnostic and therapeutic aids in psychotherapy when the images are guided to a degree and allowed to flow freely (Hammer, 1967; Biddle, 1969; Kosbabs, 1974). A less intense and more controlled approach is presented here where the patient is encouraged to re-acquaint himself with his capacity for imagery and to use it to develop only good and pleasant images.

Although Sheehan (1969) states that imagery is a universal phenomenon in both man and animals, the extent to which it is consciously experienced by the individual varies. Some people report quite active and vivid images while others report not having the experience at all. Images can occur in all of the sensory modalities, but the usual is visual imagery—images which occur in the visual mode. Most children experience imagery, but that capacity diminishes in many as they grow older and use imagery less. In some adults the experience of imagery can be revived by means of simple mental exercises designed to enhance the image experience. Very often through such exercises, some discover that they do experience imagery even if they thought not when first asked. In others, the ability to image is not as great, and the experience may be a sensation of the shape, or color without actually "seeing" the image. At the extreme are those who cannot relate to the experience of images in any sensory mode or with any measure of vividness or sensation. These are often people who report very few dreams and when dreams do occur, they are usually remembered in black and white rather than in color. The literature on imagery is not extensive compared to other psychological subjects and the topic is not recently popular (Horowitz, 1970; J. L. Singer, 1974).

The vividness of the image is not as important as whether the patient can relate to the image. A patient who senses rather than sees an image, but who also senses the changes when they are suggested is just as able to use imagery as the patient who sees the image as clearly as if his eyes are open and he is experiencing the scene.

One aid to ehancing the vividness of mental imagery is something upon which to project the images. A surface, such as a screen in the mind's eye can be suggested to the patient as the mental imagery skill is introduced and can be maintained throughout the work with imagery. The images are then projected onto the screen, manipulated on the screen and removed from the screen when complete. This not only anchors the image in the mind's eye, but avoids any tendency for the image to linger when it is to be removed.

Another aid to the manipulation of mental images is a signal such as a gesture or noise that indicates the exact moment that the image is to change in the desired way. This facilitates the rapid manipulations often useful in biofeedback tasks and signals the imagery apparatus when to cause changes. It can serve the same purpose as a message which says, "I'm going to go to the store now" as opposed to "I'm going to go to the store . . . ". In the first message, there is no doubt when the event is going to happen, while the timing is not as clear in the second message. The same is true of manipulating mental images and without the "now" in the form of a gesture or sound, there is sometimes a tendency for images to change slowly. Any gesture or sound will do, but it is preferable to use one that is easily accomplished and that can be done without attracting too much attention if the exercises should ever be practiced in public. Tapping the foot is an example of a good signal. Some use snapping the fingers, but one disadvantage is that when done in public, the patient may fear that others are looking at him and wondering what he is doing. An exercise to re-acquaint the patient with his imagery and enhance its usefulness may be found in Appendix C.

Mental imagery can be a useful adjunct to biofeedback therapy and to the relaxation task. In biofeedback, the patient may be asked to develop an image of the aspect of physiology that is being fed back and imagine it changing in the desired way. Very often a change is observed in the actual measurement. One example of such an application is in the case of EMG biofeedback, when the frontalis muscle is instrumented and is resistant to change, such as may be the case in the early treatment sessions. The patient can use imagery to visualize the muscle at its tense level and then manipulate the image to represent a change toward relaxation. The manipulation could be in the form of imagining something which represents tension flowing out of the muscle. If the image is successfully manipulated, usually there is an actual reduction in the amount of tension present in the muscle.

In the case where the muscle to be relaxed is one which has a counterpart on the other side which is not hyperaroused, visualizing the bilateral muscles simultaneously and mentally comparing them is often helpful in giving the patient a mental reference for developing an awareness of the feeling of tension in the aberrant muscle. Further, when a tense and a relaxed muscle are visualized simultaneously, the relaxed muscle can serve as a reference for manipulating the image to achieve relaxation in the tense muscle. This can take place simply by asking the patient to note the differences in the two muscles, paying attention to size, shape, texture, and color and allowing him time to do so. Once the differences are noted, then changing whatever is different about the tense muscle to resemble that of the relaxed muscle often brings about a change in the EMG level.

Sometimes patients who are not anatomically sophisticated become concerned that they cannot visualize muscles or other aspects of physiology. This fear can act as a block to progress if not allayed by stating that the image of the aspect of physiology suggested will be the image of the mind's representation of that structure and may not be anatomically correct, nor does it need to be. Sometimes, muscles are seen as stripes or dots and the images are just as functional as for those who see muscle tissue or who recall the pictures of muscles straight out of the pages of an anatomy text.

When using mental imagery to bring about a change in actual physiological functioning, it is important to see first the level of functioning as it is at the moment that the image is called up and then manipulate a change in the desired direction. Seeing only the change or trying to imagine the function at a level other than what it actually is at that moment will result in slow acting or ineffective manipulation of the physiological levels.

As an adjunct to the relaxation task, mental imagery can be employed to visualize passive and relaxing scenes and thus bring about a lowering of tension or arousal for the time that the image is held in the mind's eye. Patients can be encouraged to visualize favorite scenes after a few appropriate ones are suggested. Some scenes often suggested are a walk through the woods or a day out fishing, with elaborate attention to the detail that may be encountered with the experience being suggested. Guided imagery helps the patient develop his own favorite passive scene that he will learn to visualize whenever he wishes to relax and avoid momentary tension. It is not necessary that the content of the scene be shared with the therapist for if it is indeed a relaxing and passive scene changes in the level of tension observed will tell the therapist that the patient has developed an effective peaceful scene. It is useful, however, for the therapist to suggest that the scene be passive and that it not contain other people. When other people are in the scene, the relaxing quality of the scene is subject to changing feelings about the person in the scene, and scenes with others are simply not relaxing to patients who respond a great deal to social stimulation.

The therapist who enlists mental imagery in his treatment should do so with utmost respect for the tool in his hands. Mental imagery can be a powerful technique and the therapist without psychotherapy training should be sure to keep the content always within the framework outlined here.

§9.13 Summary. Basic techniques of relaxation training and biofeedback of EMG and skin temperature can be supplemented when indicated by more advanced special techniques described in this chapter. One of these techniques is to elaborate upon the simple use of relaxation tapes by specially tailored tapes or by progressive series of tapes. Another technique can help the especially distractible patient by an easy step into meditation. Alpha feedback is another standard method which deserves continued use at this time, whereas mental imagery is a special method of working toward the recapture of this elusive mental capacity.

I would wish the young practitioner especially to have deeply impressed on his mind, the real limits of his art, and that when the state of his patient gets beyond these, his office is to be a watchful, but quiet spectator of the operations of nature, giving them fair play by a well regulated regimen, and by all the aid they can derive from the excitement of good spirits and hope in the patient.

Thomas Jefferson

CHAPTER 10

Biofeedback in the treatment of neurological disease

§10.1 **Introduction.** This chapter will be different from other chapters of the book for several reasons. One has to do with what we are trying to say to various audiences to whom we write. Another has to do with our own particular experiences with the use of biofeedback in the treatment of neurological disease. A third has to do with the differences between the patients seen with neurological disease and other patients typically treated with biofeedback.

It is an advantage in writing not to have more than one major audience addressed in a particular piece. However, we have chosen here to attempt to meet the needs of two types of readers: the biofeedback clinician who wishes to become informed about the use of biofeedback in the treatment of neurological disease, and the clinician working in the rehabilitation of neurologically diseased patients who is unfamiliar with biofeedback. In order to extract what is of importance to them from this chapter, each group must overlook the oversimplified information from their own field which is presented to orient briefly the non-expert into a complex subject.

Our own experience with biofeedback in rehabilitation has been gained while working in close coordination with physiatrists. Our patients are treated by physical therapists and occupational therapists working together in our laboratory with an experienced biofeedback therapist whose major contributions are to supply technical expertise in the use of equipment, to modify biofeedback displays to meet the situation, to structure biofeedback tasks, and to evaluate the patient's psychological involvement in treatment. This is a combination research and clinical program whose usefulness has well been established for the clinicians involved, but where the procedures to be ultimately used and their place in overall treatment are still unclear.

The differences between neurologically diseased patients and the other patients with whom biofeedback is used will be described in detail in the next major heading (Secs. 10.2–10.8). After that, the nature of the pathology will be elaborated in a simplified version of control theory (Secs. 10.9–10.15). Finally, some of the special techniques used in rehabilitation will be described (Secs. 10.16–10.20).

This chapter will not go as far as the rest of the book in completely readying a clinician to treat patients. The complexity of the subject and the newness of the techniques do not allow this. Instead, the reader will be given the tools with which to start, but will then have to find his own way.

SPECIAL PROBLEMS IN THE TREATMENT OF NEUROLOGICAL DISEASE

§10.2 Who Should Do Treatment. Patients with neurological disease present special problems requiring special techniques. Although there are occasional specific cases where conventional treatment has been exhausted with poor results and biofeedback is undertaken with a spectacular outcome, there are many more cases where this would not happen. Also, as we will describe below (Secs. 10.4–10.5), these patients are often desperately clutching at the false hope of complete recovery and are particularly susceptible to the pursuit of new methods in the hands of enthusiastic amateurs.

Undoubtedly, there will be important new technical contributions made to the rehabilitative treatment of neurological disease by people who have no formal training in the disciplines usually responsible for these treatments, and we do not wish to discourage those unusual serious minded and thorough clinicians who cross disciplinary boundaries to acquire competence in the management of some of these patients. We feel strongly, however, that the average biofeedback clinician who has no special experience in the rehabilitative treatment of neurologically diseased patients should not treat these patients with biofeedback except in close collaboration with rehabilitation professionals using conventional methods. We see biofeedback as an adjunct to conventional methods and not as a technique to replace them. It appears likely that within the course of a few years most rehabilitation treatment with neurologically damaged patients will use biofeedback to monitor and enhance the use of conventional methods. Therefore, the major professional groups to use biofeedback techniques will be those already responsible for these treatments—physiatrists, neurologists, neurosurgeons, orthopedists, physical therapists, occupational therapists, speech therapists, corrective therapists, and nurses. The biofeedback clinician who attempts to treat these conditions without close collaboration with an appropriate specialist must consider thoroughly the hazards of such undertakings, some of which we will bring out below, and must have ample justification from the special circumstances of the situation before going ahead.

§10.3 **Unavailability of Equipment.** Currently anyone undertaking the treatment of patients with neurological disease will find a major problem is the unavailability of the appropriate equipment. Unlike the situation with the equipment discussed elsewhere in this book, the appropriate clinical instruments for use have not yet been developed and made available on the market. Surface electromyography is the main technique to be used and multi-channel recorders are necessary. The simple use of two separate modular EMG units is not satisfactory because the signal display (see Secs. 1.40, 12.3) is not easily deciphered by the patient. The instrument of the clinical electroymyographer, with needle electrodes and special measurement capabilities, is not designed for biofeedback work and lacks the necessary flexibility. It may be used by rehabilitation therapists to get started, but is not ideal. However, it seems likely that within a few years biofeedback capability will be added to new models of this equipment.

In institutional settings where consultation and collaboration between departments can be arranged, it is possible to do pilot work with a standard multi-channel polygraph with two to four channels of EMG displayed on a four-channel storage oscilloscope and then a treatment program can be organized around a duplication of this equipment when found effective. Such equipment is cumbersome and over-engineered for the purpose and not efficient relative to its cost, but until the proper instruments become available, it is the best that can be had. Most private clinical settings will probably still find it hard to justify such a purchase. A few instruments for special purposes are starting to become available, such as for the treatment of foot drop as described by Basmajian, et al. (1975) and the special EMG used by Brudny, et al. (1974b). Since we have used neither, we cannot comment on their efficacy.

§10.4 **Impact of Devastating Illness.** In the rest of this book we have discussed the treatment of conditions which can frequently be completely cured and which can at worst sometimes not interfere drastically with normal living. This is in marked contrast to the neurological diseases which are likely to be treated with biofeedback. Stroke is a typical example. Here we are hard pressed to identify with the patient's situation as it really is and if inexperienced are apt to make the mistake of identifying with the patient as being capable of normality and encouraging him to think of himself this way also. A stroke victim's future life is usually irreconcilably altered. He will usually never be normal again, and his future depends in part upon how he reconciles himself to this fact. The usual stroke victim who seeks out biofeedback treatment has one aim—complete recovery. He will often seem to acknowledge his limitations while secretly nourishing the idea that the right treatment can lead to cure. Whatever hope is held out to him will be eagerly embraced.

If this type of patient brought this same attitude to the treatment of a less serious condition it would be ideal. He will work hard and persist in treatment on the strength of his hope, even in the face of failure—up to a point. He is willing to accept knowingly the experimental nature of what is done and to follow a difficult routine of practice as required.

However, what is required of the patient for serious treatment to begin is to go through the process of grieving for *what was* and giving it up to accept *what can be*. Typical situations involve businessmen in their 60's who have strokes. Before the stroke they were active, interested, physically involved in life, and enthusiastically manipulating automobiles, boats, airplanes, and telephones with ease. After the stroke they may walk with great difficulty and be unable to use even eating utensils with the affected hand. The goals set with such a patient must be as harshly realistic as possible.

The patient has a burden to accept that is many times greater than what most of us are likely to face until old age. If we present a dim prognosis and we are asked by the patient if we could be wrong, we are caught in a trap. If we acknowledge our fallibility, this keeps alive the hope of the million in one chance of complete recovery. If we insist on the certainty of our prognosis, we may lose the patient who cannot respect rigidity.

Once the patient becomes reconciled to his condition, his life takes on a different meaning, with which it is hard for us to identify. As discussed in Chapter 4, all living takes place within a structure, which is in part a structure of meaning derived from activities. Thus, an active businessman may be gratified by decision making, driving his boat, etc. After a stroke he must make major efforts to do poorly things which were formerly automatic and effortless, and meaningfulness may come to rest in being able to learn to use a spoon. In order to treat such a patient we must learn to share with him his abandonment of the healthy world behind him. We must learn to recognize where meaning can be put into his new life with activities he may have first mastered before he started school.

Specialists in rehabilitation have to do this every day in order to carry out their work and learn to live with the particular burdens imposed. Other biofeedback clinicians are likely to misjudge dramatically the treatment situation with these patients if they fail to consider the issue of the psychology of devastating illness (Cohen, 1976).

§10.5 **Mutual Withdrawal with Failure.** Every therapist with every type of patient and every form of treatment has to learn to cope with the occasional failure of treatment. Work with the severely neurologically damaged patient is apt to present this situation in a prototypically pure form worth considering in detail. This is immediately relevant to the treatment described in this chapter because the situation can usually be avoided or its traumatic impact minimized. It is more widely relevant to all treatment as a process to be understood and utilized.

Consider again the example from the last section of an active businessman who has had a stroke. Assume that he has retained most of his intellectual functioning and determination but has lost the use of one arm and leg and has stabilized to his expected level of recovery with conventional treatment. Also assume that he has not given up his hope of recovery and wishes to enter a biofeedback program. It seems a cruel and unnecessary infliction of pain to take away a man's hope, and most clinicians do not wish to be cruel.

If this man is treated without dealing with his hope for complete recovery, his treatment will inevitably fail because it will not reach his hidden goal of complete recovery. Treatment will often go along well for several months, and the patient may make considerable progress. However, eventually this will be exhausted, and he and the therapist will begin a process of mutual withdrawal. The patient will lose hope that the therapist has anything further to offer, but rather than voice this disillusionment will be silent to the question. The therapist will need to make the internal emotional transition from dealing with a positive, enthusiastic patient to a guarded and uncommunicative patient. One of the least painful ways for both to cope with their feelings is through a mutual withdrawal. Usually when this happens the patient's progress is lost after the termination of treatment, and he returns to the same state he was in before the treatment began or even worse. Often other calamitous events soon intervene to end the travail. Obviously, this chain of events is to be guarded against, and all experienced therapists will recognize the inevitability of sometimes being a part of a mutual withdrawal in spite of their best therapeutic efforts. Analogous situations also develop when the treatment of less serious conditions fails, which accounts for the universality of the experience for therapists. The latent acknowledgment of failure is even something which can be transcended and not interfere with the rest of a treatment relationship. Thus, a tolerant patient may remain with a doctor for the treatment of heart trouble even after finding his sinus medication is ineffective. Also, it is inevitable that failure and mutual withdrawal will happen often to the ineffective therapist treating curable conditions and seldom to the effective and experienced therapist.

It is important to consider this situation in the treatment of the neurologically diseased patient because its frequent occurrence is inevitable if the patient's expectations are not correctly defined and the proper therapeutic goals set.

§10.6 **Exceptional Patient.** The above examples of mutual withdrawal and failure, although valid where applicable, can give a skewed picture if an opposite situation is also not appreciated. Neurological disease is often irreversible, but in some cases the remaining residual capacity can be assiduously trained by an exceptionally strong willed patient. The physical training undertaken by such patients puts them in a situation compared to other patients with identical damage which is analogous to the acrobat as compared to an untrained normal person.

There are enough examples of such patients that it merits the awareness of therapists to be alert to recognize them. To fail to respond to the needs of such a patient is as great an error as to fail to recognize unrealistic expectations. Usually, these are patients for whom the game is more important than the prize – the challenge of doing the most that they can with what they have means more to them than whether they become able to return to normal functioning.

Those unfamiliar with such patients can find an interesting example described by Haley (1967) of a strong willed physician who was twice stricken by polio and twice taught himself to walk again in spite of severe damage. That particular self-treatment did not involve biofeedback, nor are we aware of specific instances of biofeedback being used by such patients. However, we urge that the potential role of biofeedback in the lives of such patients not be lost sight of. For them, the meaning of life may be found in their throwing themselves into the challenge provided by the obstacle of their illness, and they will not be disheartened by failure as long as there is still something ahead for which to work. This is quite different from the patient who cannot tolerate failing to become normal again.

§10.7 **Goals of Treatment.** By now it should be clear to the clinician unfamiliar with rehabilitation that both the art and the science of its practice lie in the selection with the patient of proper goals. To go further into this subject would be beyond the scope of this book. We have explored some of the pitfalls of poor choice of goals (Secs. 10.4–10.5) and have considered an instance where the patient may only use the therapist as a consultant in setting goals (Sec. 10.6). We have also made clear that the use of biofeedback training is only part of a treatment undertaken in conjunction with conventional techniques and with other non-biofeedback techniques being tried. The principles we abbreviate here derive mostly from conventional rehabilitative training and less from the special aspect of biofeedback. The first principle has been described in Section 10.4 – that unrealistic goals must be given up by the patient and that the hope propelling the treatment must be carefully conserved. The next is that realistic forms of more practice must be utilized. A third principle is that goals must relate when possible to the activities of daily living. When we are unable to define a goal of daily life which the patient can obtain or wishes to obtain, we are likely to be unsuccessful. Biofeedback goals which can be specific and related to a specific pathology are preferred over those which are general and aimed at an unspecified malfunction. Goals must be subdivided into tasks necessary to reach the goal and sequenced into the proper chain (algorithm).

§10.8 **Structuring Treatment.** The treatment consists of the proper interleafing of biofeedback with conventional techniques and other procedures. Hope must be rationed to restrain the patient from overenthusiasm and sustain him through despair. Goals must be consensually shared, and the tasks into which treatment is divided must be monitored to keep track of progress. The general principles of Chapter 4 apply to the design of treatment, but it must be assumed that the therapist possesses knowledge of how rehabilitation treatment is structured.

NATURE OF PATHOLOGY

§10.9 **Introduction.** More so than with other conditions treated with biofeedback, neurological diseases usually present the need to aim at a number of problems with a number of techniques. Thus, a typical patient may face component elements of spasticity, loss of sensory awareness, loss of motor control patterning, and motor weakness to be overcome before the return of potentially realizable functioning has been attained. This is in contrast to treatment of a condition such as migraine where home relaxation training and a single feedback modality training may constitute the whole of treatment. Each section under this heading will consider a particular part of some of the problems typically presented by patients – loss of motor control and weakness (Sec. 10.10), loss of sensory feedback (Sec. 10.11), flaccidity and spasticity (Sec. 10.12), the hyperarousal syndrome (Sec. 10.13), cerebral palsy (Sec. 10.14), and torticollis (Sec. 10.15).

Before taking up these particular problems, however, we will examine briefly the use of control theory as a model for describing neurological diseases. A system block diagram such as Figure 1.3 (Sec. 1.11) can be further expanded to include more systems and to break into subsystems, and in doing so, the communicating arrows come increasingly closer to representing specific efferent and afferent nerve tracts. A particular neurological lesion will have caused damage to one or more of these tracts to a greater or lesser degree and has specific consequences which stem from the disruption of the information flow. This is a highly specific process whose results should be easily predictable from the control system changes produced. Instead, since we do not yet have a good idea of the dynamics of the control systems involved, we fall back upon empirical expectations based on our knowledge of similar cases (Twitchell, 1951).

Biofeedback provides an opportunity to diagnose the dynamics of a particular control system malfunction by artificially re-introducing lost information over a parallel channel. How useful this will ultimately prove to be remains to be seen. At this point we can use the schematization of control systems to conceptualize some of the component elements in a simplified way. In this we will utilize Figure 10.1 as an elemental conceptualization of the main parts of the nervous system with which we are concerned. Figures 10.2 through 10.7 will use the same basic diagram to describe some specific control system malfunctions and the correction provided by EMG biofeedback. It should be understood that these simplified diagrams are not always completely accurate in their portrayal of the pathology involved, but are used because they allow a clear understanding of the relationship between the particular malfunction and the corrective action biofeedback undertakes. Part of their purpose is also to introduce new modes of thought.

§10.10 Loss of Motor Control. A number of neurological lesions primarily damage the motor system—the nerves or information channels carrying impulses or commands to the muscles. These include damage to the motor cortex, the motor portion of the internal capsule, the anterior brain stem, the anterior spinal cord, anterior spinal roots, and many peripheral nerves. Figure 10.2 illustrates this by a dotted line indicating the malfunctioning motor system channel. Damage to any of the above anatomical pathways represents loss of motor system capacity, but each may have different consequences.

Biofeedback cannot directly supplement this disrupted channel; rather, as shown in Figure 10.3, biofeedback augments the sensory

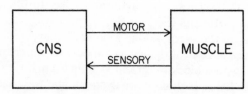

Figure 10.1. Simplified motor control system. This diagram is homomorphic with the normal motor control system. The box on the left represents the central nervous system, and the box on the right represents not only the muscular system but all other sources of information about the muscular system, especially proprioceptive receptors. The upper arrow represents the information channel from the central nervous system to the muscles, while the lower arrow represents the sensory information returning.

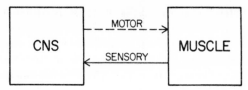

Figure 10.2. Motor control loss. In this diagram the dotted line from the central nervous system to the muscle system represents a loss of channel capacity to carry information to the muscle system.

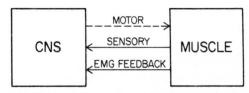

Figure 10.3. Biofeedback treatment of motor loss. Here it can be seen that the channel provided in treatment does not augment the lost function, but only augments an intact system. However, to the extent that it can increase the capacity of the intact system, it may provide previously indiscriminable information needed to use the remaining motor ability.

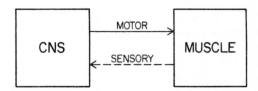

Figure 10.4. Sensory feedback loss. In this diagram the dotted line represents a loss of channel capacity in the returning feedback of information about the muscle system.

return pathway. Presumably the value for this situation would lie in giving more useful information to the patient than could be immediately obtained with the natural sensory pathways. For example, if a very weak muscle has so little activity that none of the natural proprioceptive or exteroceptive sensory channels can detect activity, it will still be detectable by EMG, and training could be successfully initiated. This is one rationale of how biofeedback might help in treating foot drop from partial anterior spinal cord injury.

§10.11 **Loss of Sensory Feedback.** In many neurological diseases, the primary deficit results from sensory loss. This includes lesions of the sensory cortex, sensory portion of the internal capsule, posterior and central brain stem, posterior spinal cord, posterior nerve roots, and many peripheral nerves. Brudny, et al. (1974b) in particular have brought out how this disrupted control channel is supplemented by biofeedback. Figure 10.4 shows by the dotted line how the sensory channel is attenuated, while in Figure 10.5 the supplementation of the parallel EMG biofeedback channel is demonstrated. Generally we have not found that severe sensory disruption has been overcome by biofeedback. Thus, little return of function with biofeedback training has been found in limbs showing the neurological sign of astereognosis. An exception has been the special instance where feedback provided by a foot switch triggered by the foot striking the ground has caused marked improvement of gait in patients with unilateral anesthesia of the foot. With lesser degrees of loss, a greater return of function can be expected. A typical instance is a mild stroke where the sensory portion of the internal capsule is the primary site of damage.

§10.12 Flaccidity and Spasticity. Flaccidity and spasticity are regular secondary accompaniments of neurological damage. In flaccidity, a particular muscle is loose and lacking in tone, whereas in spasticity, it is tightly contracted, pulling upon the attached body parts. Each has different significances in different conditions and helps both diagnostic and prognostic evaluation. Figure 10.6 crudely depicts the situation in flaccidity if the dotted arrows are taken to represent underactivity of the motor and sensory channels, but without implication of whether there is loss of channel capacity. The pathology can be considered a negative feedback loop, because the lack of activity on the two channels does not constitute the necessary matrix to maintain muscle tonus. In this situation, biofeedback attempts to enable a positive feedback loop (see Sec. 1.6) to operate through the feedback display of muscle activity

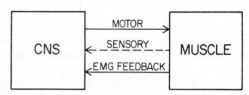

Figure 10.5. Biofeedback treatment of sensory loss. The use of EMG feedback directly augments the lost sensory channel capacity, and may provide a specific replacement in this instance. Hypothetically this should be the most powerful method of using biofeedback.

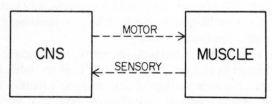

Figure 10.6. Schematization of flaccidity. Here the dotted lines represent relative inactivity of a channel rather than necessary loss of capacity of the channel. The immediate problem is the failure of activity rather than the lack of means to transmit activity.

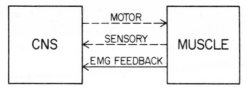

Figure 10.7. Biofeedback treatment of flaccidity. The biofeedback can attempt to provide a positive feedback loop. An increment of motor activity is detected and fed back by the EMG feedback with the intent to increase the activity even more by use of the feedback.

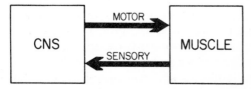

Figure 10.8. Schematization of spasticity. The heavy arrows represent an overactivity of the two channels, resulting in spasticity of the muscle and hyperarousal of the nervous system.

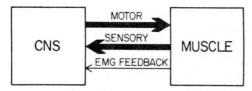

Figure 10.9. Biofeedback treatment of spasticity. The biofeedback channel can attempt to provide a negative feedback. The intent is to use the feedback information to decrease the amount of muscle activity and, by breaking a vicious circle, to lower arousal level as well.

being a stimulus for more muscle activity (Fig. 10.7). Spasticity often results in a hyperarousal syndrome which is described further in the next section.

§10.13 **Hyperarousal Syndrome.** Spasticity in a particular muscle is a specific instance of a process which, when widespread, produces a hyperarousal syndrome. This can be accurately conceptualized as a vicious circle or a deviation amplifying positive feedback system (see Sec. 1.6), as illustrated in Figure 10.8 where the heavy arrows indicate an overabundance of activity in both the motor and sensory channels. In control theory this is a clear-cut instance of a stabilizing system malfunction. This syndrome is common in spastic strokes and spastic cerebral palsy (to be described in the next section).

The role of biofeedback treatment in a hyperarousal syndrome is to provide a negative (stabilizing) feedback (Fig. 10.9), which can allow the quieting of the overactivity (see Sec. 1.40). As described below (Sec. 10.17), the treatment of hyperarousal can often produce the marked change of allowing the patient to become much more quiet and less reactive to stimuli.

§10.14 **Cerebral Palsy.** The kinds of damage in cerebral palsy can cover all of the problems in the preceding sections. There are a number of typical pictures encountered among these patients for which biofeedback is particularly to be considered. One instance is the common combination of spasticity and hyperarousal in which biofeedback treatment can be used as a negative feedback (see Sec. 1.6) to reduce the excessive activity. A number of clinics are gaining experience in treating this condition (Harris, et al., 1974; Finley, et al., 1976). Our own experience has mainly been with hyperaroused and spastic patients using the strategies of general relaxation, reduction of spastic activity, and training in inhibiting spillover spastic activity during the carrying out of regular activities. These are all described below (Secs. 10.16–10.20).

§10.15 **Torticollis.** This is a peculiar condition of unknown cause in which the neck muscles twist the head, usually to one side, against the patient's will. The condition appears in various degrees of severity from a slight twist easily overcome to severely incapacitating rotations far to one side. Biofeedback training with EMG electrodes attached to the neck appears promising, especially with good results obtained in a few mild cases. However, success rates in more severe cases are not as high, and it is unclear what sort of training procedure has the most to offer (see Cleeland, 1973; Brudny, et al., 1974a; and Russ, 1975). Our own treatment has been primarily based upon feedback training in inhibiting the overactive muscles and activating the opposing muscles, both while the patient is seated in a chair and walking about the treatment room using extra-long leads to the EMG electrodes.

SPECIAL TECHNIQUES

§10.16 **Introduction.** In this section we will review a few of the special techniques addressed to specific problems which we have used in the treatment of neurological disease. These techniques need to be evaluated within the appropriate context to decide whether or not they should be used. On the one hand there are only a few controlled studies showing the value of such techniques; on the other hand, the techniques merely offer a better way of doing what is already being done. When biofeedback is used it becomes possible to tell precisely what is going on in a particular muscle, as some later examples will show (Sec. 10.17). Since biofeedback in rehabilitation is not a definitive total treatment, but merely an adjunct to regular treatment, it appears justified to use piecemeal studies to evaluate its efficacy. For example, one may compare the efficacy of conventional treatment versus the efficacy of conventional treatment plus biofeedback in the objective reduction of muscle spasticity in stroke victims as described in the next section. The results of such a study can be more easily objectified than the results of the entire series of steps of a complete treatment chain.

§10.17 Severe Restrictive Spasticity. A frequent situation encountered in stroke victims, especially those who have been inadequately treated or who have left treatment a long time ago, is an extreme degree of spasticity, especially in the affected arm and hand. Often the fingers, hand, forearm, and upper arm are pulled tightly down over their respective proximal joints in hyperflexion. When the condition is long standing and severe it is often difficult to treat with conventional methods. Using EMG biofeedback from both flexor and extensor muscles, the spasticity can frequently be relieved almost completely within three to six sessions. Before treatment, the patient may be unable to work on gaining motor control because the spasticity overrides the situation. Occasionally the spasticity leads to pain. The limb is worse than useless because it interferes with the activity of the rest of the body and contributes to general hyperarousal. The patient has always lost the ability to discriminate degrees of spasticity as conceptualized in other situations by Jacobson (1938).

Treatment focuses upon "putting the mind into the arm" and relearning to discriminate degrees of tension with the aid of EMG feedback. During treatment there is a progressive decrease in the muscle activity, with the last activity to drop out being the rapid single spike firing detectable on the oscilloscope at medium sweep speeds. Part of the training is to discriminate particular degrees of difference in muscle tension. After treatment, the formerly spastic limb is much more relaxed and ready for further training, and the patient has regained awareness of tension and relaxation in the limb. We have rarely had a patient with this condition fail to improve markedly upon undertaking treatment. Of course, it must be realized that the result is only the relief of a sometimes painful and annoying secondary symptom, and that the motor function may be no better after treatment. But this is only one step of treatment and for its purpose it works well.

Others who have reported on the use of biofeedback to control spasticity include Swaan, et al. (1974), who treated spasticity of the peroneus longus muscle, and Amato, et al. (1973), who treated spasticity of the gastrocnemius muscle.

§10.18 Reduction of Hyperarousal. The hyperarousal syndrome described above (Sec. 10.13) is a frequent bothersome and disabling condition found in patients with neurological damage. Thus, cerebral palsy patients often have generalized spasticity which causes them to draw up spastic limbs with the least excitement, such as a stimulating conversation. Sometimes stroke patients are unable to use a walker because the effort of moving a leg may cause the spastic arm to pull up the walker. Forehead EMG relaxation training as described in Chapter 7 will directly bear upon this condition. The amount of this training needed and its outcome will vary according to the condition treated. Thus, the type of stroke patient mentioned may use the training a few times and receive maximum benefit, while a spastic cerebral palsy patient may continue to improve slowly over months of training and might in some instances consider semipermanently incorporating training into the life routine.

§10.19 **Agonist-Antagonist Relations.** A major part of most biofeedback training in rehabilitation work is to attempt to restore motor functions to a damaged limb. It is here that the multi-channel oscilloscope system described above (Sec. 10.3) comes into full use. A typical instance is in the training of the use of the wrist joint and hand in a stroke victim. Skin surface electrodes are placed on the extensor and flexor surfaces of the affected forearm, and the resultant EMG signal is displayed on two channels of the oscilloscope. A number of specific tasks become possible with this system, including quieting all activity in both channels (Sec. 10.17), extending the wrist while keeping flexor activity minimal, quieting flexor activity while the flexor muscles are under stretch, and practicing reducing the time it takes for muscle activity to abate after using a muscle. These are all parts of routine rehabilitative exercises. However, the gain for the rehabilitation therapist is in having immediately available information which could otherwise not be obtained. As an example, the therapist will frequently ask a patient to use a muscle, and after a short use to cease effort. Usually the patient then stops the movement, such as wrist extension, the hand drops, and the muscle appears to relax. Although recognizing that the damaged muscle does not relax as fast as normal, neither patient nor therapist has precise information available on exactly when the muscle relaxes. With biofeedback, however, they can see the failure of relaxation, see how long it lasts, and work together to overcome it.

Brudny, et al. (1974b) have reported upon this type of training in a variety of cases. Andrews (1964) used the methods with 20 hemiplegic patients. Kukulka, et al. (1975) have used EMG to re-train finger function after tendon repairs. Because of motor pattern disruption, this presents the same training problem as neurological damage. Johnson and Garton (1973) have also reported on the use of biofeedback in muscle re-training.

§10.20 **Treating Flaccid Muscles.** Foot drop is a specific syndrome of flaccidity in the muscles innervated by the peroneal nerve used to raise the foot. Electrodes placed over this muscle allow the detection of minute amounts of activity which otherwise would not be known to be present. Once this activity is detected it is possible to build upon it and sometimes reach the point where function is recovered. Basmajian, et al. (1975) and Takeba, et al. (1976) have described specific treatment procedures. They initially treated a group of 10 patients with foot drop with both biofeedback and physical therapy, and a control group of 10 patients with physical therapy alone. All of those treated with both methods showed significant improvement in strength and movement, whereas only half of those treated with physical therapy alone showed improvement.

§10.21 **Summary.** Neurological diseases represent a particularly fruitful field in which to apply biofeedback. However, there are special problems which make the clinical practice different. In particular, the patients have experienced a devastating illness which they must face, and there are many more stages of treatment than with the other uses of biofeedback described. For these reasons, treatment of neurological conditions should be done by the rehabilitation specialist.

There can be no adequate technical education which is not liberal and no liberal education which is not technical.

Alfred North Whitehead

The telescope, the microscope and the test-tube have made sceptics of us all. We have changed wisdom for an exact knowledge of strains, precipitants, reactions and refractions, and put it, for this generation at least, beyond recall.

Oliver St. John Gogarty

CHAPTER 11

Instrumentation techniques

§11.1 **Introduction.** The aim of this chapter is to provide the biofeedback therapist with a step by step instrumentation procedure for each of several biofeedback parameters. This includes applying electrodes to the patient's body, putting the signal into the biofeedback instrument and setting the biofeedback device to produce clear, meaningful feedback of the physiological signal under observation. Section 11.2 will describe general considerations which apply to all parameters and explain terms which will be used in each of the parameter sections which follow. Section 11.3 will describe EMG biofeedback instrumentation. Finger temperature instrumentation will be described in Section 11.4, while Section 11.5 will take up EEG alpha. In Section 11.6, some biofeedback parameters which are used less often will be described.

The reader who is interested in more detailed instrumentation information is referred to the following works, some of which stress psychophysiology, and some which are more technically oriented and would interest engineering-minded readers. A basic introduction to psychophysiology can be found in Sternbach (1972), while psychophysiological methods are described in greater depth by Brown (1967) and Greenfield (1972). Venables and Martin (1967) give both psychophysiological methods and a discussion of electronic background, while Cromwell, et al. (1973) and Geddes and Baker (1975) provide an in-depth discussion of electronics and instrumentation. Davis (1959) has described surface electrode technique for EMG in detail.

§11.2 **General Considerations.** Most of the physiological signals to be discussed in this chapter result from changes in ionic membrane potentials within the body and are detectable on the skin's surface by means of appropriate electrodes. Electrodes have metal surfaces which, when correctly applied to the proper body site, detect the physiological signal to be observed, and convert the ionic membrane potential to an electrical potential which can then be carried through the electrode's cables to an electronic device which can respond to the electrical signal. In the case of biofeedback devices, the machine's purpose is to amplify the signal, condition it, and indicate its presence by providing a feedback signal, usually a tone, a light, or a dial reading (see Secs. 1.8; 1.38; 1.41). This is the general sequence which will be followed in each of the following sections which will take up individual parameters.

Steps of instrumentation include: (1) choosing the correct body site from which to record the signal; (2) selecting an electrode capable of detecting the signal; (3) applying the electrode in such a manner as to maximize its efficiency; (4) getting the signal into the biofeedback machine; and (5) setting the biofeedback device so that the patient receives clear, meaningful feedback of the selected values of the signal. Each of these will be taken up next.

Choosing the correct body site involves knowing the source of the signal to be recorded and where on the body it can be detected with a minimum of contamination from other body signals. In the case of EMG, a muscle site would be selected, whereas in EEG, a scalp location is necessary. Anatomical considerations for locating the correct placement for each parameter will be described.

Adequate electrodes vary with the signal, and in some types of signals the therapist is able to choose among a variety of types. With EMG, for example, either surface or needle electrodes may be used. In this chapter, the application of surface electrodes will be described for all parameters since most portable biofeedback equipment manufacturers provide this type with their machines. Application of electrodes usually requires particular attention to the quality of contact between the actual metal electrode surface and the source of the signal. Most surface electrodes are constructed so that the metal surface is recessed within a holder of some other material such as a type of plastic. Figure 11.1 illustrates a typical surface electrode. When the electrode holder, the plastic, is affixed to the skin, there is a space between the skin and the effective electrode which must be filled with an electrolyte or conducting gel or cream. Furthermore, the skin itself has insulating properties which

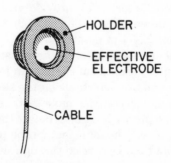

Figure 11.1. Diagram of a standard surface electrode.

must be diminished so that good contact can be made to record the physiological signal within the body. The reduction of the skin's insulating properties for this purpose is termed "reducing the impedance." Each parameter section will take up the matter of reducing the impedance to an acceptable level for that parameter, along with considerations of electrolytes and methods of affixing electrodes to the skin.

Most biofeedback instruments have characteristics in common such as sensitivity and threshold, regardless of the manufacturer. These characteristics will be referred to by their function without reference to any particular manufacturer. These functions are usually on labeled knobs or switches on the front of the biofeedback machine. "Input" is the term usually used to label the place on the machine where the electrode cables from the patient attach. Sometimes there are three holes or jacks into which the cables must be plugged. When three jacks are provided, there are usually two recording electrodes and one ground electrode required of that parameter. "Sensitivity" pertains to the size that the signals are amplified by the machine. It works like the volume on a radio, in that the more sensitive the setting, the smaller the signals that the machine can detect. The "threshold" is like sensitivity in pertaining to the size of the signals that are detected, but refers to the feedback signal processor mechanism of the machine and not the input signal amplifier (see Fig. 1.5; Sec. 1.38). It works like a hurdle, in that the greater the threshold, the greater the signals must be to influence feedback. Threshold is the setting that is manipulated by the therapist when the physiological learning task is to be slowly changed to allow the patient a gradual increase in his skill.

An "artifact" is a signal that may influence the feedback device, but is not the physiological signal about which information is sought. It is sometimes called "noise." One way to reduce artifacts is to apply the electrodes so that the impedance levels are within tolerable range for the parameter and the biofeedback device. Another way to reduce the effect of artifacts on the feedback task is to be aware of the common ones that affect the particular parameter and learn how to recognize their influence on the feedback signal. The common artifacts likely to influence any particular parameter will be discussed in the section dealing with that parameter. With any particular biofeedback instrument the technician must learn to recognize the specific signs that the instrument is not functioning correctly. Signs of malfunction include any failure of the instrument to do what is expected. Sometimes a particular instrument which is malfunctioning may be closely simulating its normal function so that alertness is required to detect trouble. Artifacts are most common with alpha feedback. At other times the malfunction is obvious. The most common cause of malfunction is weak batteries. The next most likely cause is a transient disturbance due to poor electrode application, electrical interference, or a broken electrode wire. Less common are instrument component failures. An oscilloscope is invaluable in detecting the cause of malfunction, but a trouble-shooting trial-and-error approach often suffices. Special local conditions also need to be considered, such as nearby heavy electrical equipment or nylon clothing or rugs causing electrical disturbances.

Other general considerations affecting the use of any particular biofeedback machine are usually set out in the manufacturer's booklet which accompanies the machine when purchased. The therapist should read the owner's information very carefully to determine what he must do to ensure the best possible performance of his machine and the function of each of the various dials and switches on the machine. Few things unnerve an anxious patient faster than being electrically attached to a strange machine by a therapist whose cues indicate a lack of familiarity with the device. The therapist should, therefore, be completely familiar not only with his machine, but with the instrumentation procedure required for the parameter he intends to introduce to the patient.

Once instrumented, the patient's task is to attend to the feedback signal and use the feedback information to gain control of the physiological system being monitored, moving it in the desired direction to achieve the physiological goal set out in the therapeutic contract. Although the subjective cue has been discussed with the patient at other times, it should be re-emphasized here. As the biofeedback task is being practiced, the subjective cue should be developing. The patient should be encouraged to attend to the feelings or sensations anywhere in his body that appear to accompany success with the biofeedback task. These feelings will serve as a built-in feedback signal once the skill is developed and the cue is validated with the feedback signal (see Sec. 5.2).

§11.3 Electromyographic (EMG) Instrumentation. Biofeedback applications from the musculoskeletal system can be broadly divided into feedback to diminish electrical potentials present in the muscle as in relaxation-related biofeedback (see Secs. 8.16–8.21) and feedback to enhance potentials as in neuromuscular re-education (see Chap. 10). Surface electrodes are almost always used except for special applications (Smith, et al., 1974). Davis (1959) has given an extensive discussion of surface electrodes in EMG work. EMG instruments are discussed in Section 12.4.

When a task is to reduce muscle activity and bring about a state of lower arousal or relaxation, the frontalis muscle is often chosen as recording site. The frontalis muscle is located in the forehead and has several advantages from the standpoint of relaxation training: it is often a direct expressor of stress within the musculoskeletal system; it is not a postural muscle and therefore can be reduced to very low potentials without regard for positioning the patient; it is readily accessible for instrumentation. The source of the signal from the frontalis muscle is the electrical activity in the muscle itself. The proper surface electrode for recording the frontalis EMG is any standard skin electrode such as is provided with most biofeedback devices. Placement of the electrodes is on the forehead, approximately 1½ inches above the center of each eyebrow. The sites should be located and marked with a skin-marking pencil. Skin preparation should include procedures to reduce impedance and facilitate attachment of the electrode to the skin's surface. The skin oil may be removed with alcohol, and the area allowed to dry. A cotton-tipped applicator should be used to "twirl" a small quantity of conductive gel with an abrasive material (such as quartz crystals) on the site with the end-most surface of the cotton tip. Care should be taken to confine preparation to a size not exceeding the center opening of the electrode. Twirling the cotton tip against the skin while applying moderate pressure for 20 or so twirls is usually sufficient to remove most of the surface material which, if left on the skin, would cause high impedance readings. Surface electrodes are usually affixed to the skin in one of two ways: either holding them in place with an elastic band, or sticking them on the skin with an adhesive collar designed for that purpose. The adhesive collar has the advantage of preventing small movements of the electrode against the skin and causes less discomfort than the elastic band. Furthermore, once applied, the therapist can rely on the electrode either remaining in the correct position or falling off all together; there is never any concern about slipping, or recording potentials from other than the optimum site. When using an adhesive collar, it is helpful to place the collar on the electrode prior to filling the electrode cup with electrolyte gel, as the gel will prevent the adhesive from sticking if it gets under the collar. The electrode should be filled with enough gel to make contact with the skin when the electrode is applied, but not so much that the gel will spread, preventing the collar from sticking to the skin. A little practice will soon indicate how much electrolyte is best for the particular electrodes being used. The electrode can then be applied to the skin so that the center of the electrode is directly over the prepared site. For most frontalis biofeedback procedures, two recording electrodes and one ground electrode are required. The ground electrode may be placed midway between the two recording electrodes by preparing the skin in the same manner as for the recording electrodes. Following application, the electrode impedance should be measured. For most recording instruments, impedances less than 30,000 ohms are required for accurate recordings – i.e., there should be no more than 30,000 ohms of resistance between any two electrodes in the system. Some instruments require as low as 10,000 ohms for best function. The impedance of each pair of electrodes should be measured, including the two recording electrodes together as one pair and then each recording electrode with the ground electrode as a pair. When all three electrodes have been checked and are within tolerable resistance limits, they are ready to be plugged into the biofeedback device. Manufacturers usually indicate tolerable impedance with their particular instrument.

The device will indicate where the electrodes are to be plugged in and whether the ground electrode has a special place designated for it. With the electrodes plugged in, turn the machine on. Some machines have logarithmic scales and usually do not require sensitivity or threshold settings. On this type of machine, the task is simply to move the needle of the meter in the direction of the lower number until the goal is reached and maintained. On this type of machine, there is never a need to consider the sensitivity and threshold settings from one session to the next, and the readings on the face of the dial are directly comparable. On machines with linear scales, there is usually a choice of sensitivity ranges and threshold settings which the therapist may use. In such cases, the therapist should always make careful notes about the settings so that they are the same each time, and the readings comparable across sessions. Early in the patient's biofeedback experience, he will require less sensitivity and greater threshold because the muscle signals will be large compared to the size after some relaxation has been learned. The therapist should set the sensitivity sufficient to allow small reductions in muscle activity to be detected, but insensitive enough to prevent the dial from reaching the top of the scale often in a session. As the patient learns control of muscle activity and is able to reduce it at will, the therapist will need to reset the machine to detect levels close to the goal.

Other muscle sites sometimes selected for relaxation tasks are the forearm, the thigh, the back of the neck, the jaw muscles of patients who brux or jaw clench, or the stump in phantom limb pain. For each of these sites, the electrodes should be placed approximately 2 inches apart over the most prominent part of the muscle or the most tense ridge. The skin preparation and method of attachment are the same as for the frontalis muscle.

Some artifacts that affect the EMG signal are: (1) movement which can affect any EMG site. Movement can usually be detected by the therapist and often a simple reminder to the patient of the need to remain still will suffice. (2) EKG which can be a problem in most EMG sites other than frontalis. EKG artifact is recognizable by the electrical signal of the heart beat, causing the feedback signal to fluctuate in a detectable rhythmic way. The most effective means of reducing this type of artifact is to place the two recording and ground electrodes on a straight line from the heart to the distal most electrode. Where this is not possible, or in cases where the artifact remains in spite of the move, the therapist must decide whether the artifact can be tolerated. Some patients are able to disregard the rhythmic fluctuations and reduce the average between-beat levels, while others are too distracted by the beats to use the feedback signal at all. In the latter case, the therapist should select a "quieter" muscle site, confident that he is feeding back information meaningful to the patient's stress response, in that it is within the aberrant system.

Goals in EMG feedback are determined by the pretreatment resting levels and the choice of muscle sites. When the frontalis is used, an average of 5 μv is usually sought as the ultimate goal. It may be set as an initial goal also when the resting baseline level does not exceed 20 μv. When 20 μv are exceeded, the initial goal is usually to reduce the activity to one-half of the baseline levels. When using portable devices where microvolt levels are not available, an initial goal might be to reduce the dial reading to one-half of its level in the initial session and then revise the goal downward until an average of 5 μv is reached.

When biofeedback is used to reinstate muscle function as in neuro-muscular re-education, the biofeedback task is to increase levels of muscle activity, and the goal is some level above the baseline readings. This situation is just the opposite of the one described immediately above. In this case, selection of the target muscle must be based on the desired movement. Instrumentation is applied in the same manner as with relaxation, and all of the same considerations apply. Settings on the biofeedback machine are also the opposite of relaxation training, in that at the beginning of treatment, the machine is set very sensitive, and the threshold set low so that very small increases in muscle potential can be detected. The task is to increase the meter reading, and movement of the muscle will take place as a by-product of that increase—the task need not be to move the muscle. The same artifacts apply in this application, but the movement that is likely to contaminate the feedback signal may be from some other part of the body. EKG artifact can be managed in the same manner as described above for the relaxation task. EMG biofeedback goals for this application are often set by instrumenting the same muscle on the opposite side of the body and determining the normal functional level for that muscle. Setting goals in this manner helps prevent arbitrarily setting an unrealistic goal and structuring a frustrating biofeedback experience.

§11.4 **Skin Temperature Feedback Instrumentation.** Changes in blood flow at the skin's surface result in temperature variations detectable with temperature-sensitive instrumentation. The special biofeedback techniques used with skin temperature are discussed in Sections 8.22

through 8.27, and the instrument is discussed in Section 12.5. The finger is the site most often selected for biofeedback tasks, but sometimes the palm of the hand or the forehead is used. The transducer is usually a thermistor which is easily fixed to the skin surface over the selected site. When the finger is to be instrumented, the thermistor is placed along the side of the finger and held in place with a length of tape. The tape should be wrapped around the finger at an angle rather than like a ring in order to reduce the possibility of restricting blood flow with the tape. The thermistor is then plugged into a biofeedback machine which registers temperature differences and feeds back the information in the form of a change in the meter reading or tone. Sensitivity of the device refers to the value in degrees of the total visible scale. Some devices allow for a variety of ranges so that in order to move the indicators over the entire range of the scale, a temperature variation of 2° might be required at one setting, while 20° might be required at another. When the patient is beginning the temperature task, the most useful setting is the most sensitive one, so that small changes are rewarded. Once instrumented, the patient should not be given access to the feedback information until the thermistor has adjusted to the patient's skin temperature and stabilized at that level, and the patient's own adjustment to the situation is complete. A period of about 10 minutes is sufficient. Then, with the meter visible, the patient should be instructed to observe the meter face. If the needle moves in the direction which indicates that the temperature is decreasing, the patient should say to himself, "*that's cooler.*" By the same token if the needle moves in the direction which indicates that the surface is getting warmer, the patient should identify that event to himself. After a short period of identification, the patient is ready to begin learning to control temperature variations. When the needle moves in the desired direction, the patient should be encouraged to reward himself by suggesting that the result is good and is what he wants to do.

Goals for temperature biofeedback may be set conservatively at first and later revised. Ultimately, the patient should be able to move the temperature easily at least 1½° in either direction with subjective awareness of when the task is accomplished. The need for control in both directions is not emphasized by some clinicians, however, it obviously requires a greater degree of control, and the skill is likely to be better developed when bi-directional goals are reached.

Common artifacts which influence temperature are: (1) climate and ambient temperature. When the outside temperature is cold, the patient should be allowed sufficient time to warm his hands after arriving in the laboratory. The laboratory temperature should be held relatively constant from one session to the next. (2) Whether the hand is rested against some part of the body or whether it is rested on a table or armrest can influence the surface temperature. Once a resting place is designated, it should be used each time so that the learning experience is constant over the sessions. (3) Arm position: when the arm is held so that the hand is high relative to the rest of the body, the hand tends to cool. When the hand is held low, the surface tends to warm. The level of the hand should remain constant through the session. (4) Finger position: when the fingers are together, less air circulates around them and they tend to warm. They can be cooled artificially by positioning them so that air flows freely around them. The position of the fingers relative to one another should be held constant during all feedback sessions.

§11.5 Electroencephalogram (EEG) Alpha Instrumentation. The signal source in electroencephalography is the electrical activity within the brain. Alpha feedback techniques are discussed in Sections 9.6 through 9.11, and instruments are described in Section 12.6. The signal can be detected from the surface of the scalp by applying EEG electrodes. The surface electrode used in EEG is different from the surface electrode illustrated earlier in this chapter, but some of the same basic principles apply. The electrode is usually flat or cup-shaped and not contained within a holder. The metal surface is exposed and applied directly against the scalp. Such electrodes are supplied with the biofeedback instrument and additional electrodes may be obtained from any instrument manufacturer offering EEG equipment.

Alpha frequencies within the EEG are most abundant over the occipital cortex. Thus, the active recording electrode should be placed in the occipital region, determined by locating the external occipital protuberance (the bony process at the lower back portion of the skull) by moving the fingers up the center of the back of the neck until the most prominent point is found. From that point, a distance of 1 inch upward and 1 inch to the left will locate the site for the left occipital electrode. If the right side is preferred, it may be located in the same manner, but by moving 1 inch to the right of center. The site of second recording (or reference) electrode may be located by first imagining a line from the bridge of the nose across the top of the head to the external occipital protuberance, the prominent point located earlier. A second line should be imagined running from the external auditory meatus (the hole in the ear), on one side across the top of the head to the same location on the opposite side of the head. Where these two imaginary lines cross at the top of the head is called the "vertex." Starting at the vertex and moving 2 inches along the imaginary line toward the left external auditory meatus will locate the site for the reference electrode if it is to be located on the left and recorded against an electrode placed at the left occipital location. Do not place the active and reference electrodes on different sides of the head. The two hemispheres of the brain do not usually emit the same electrical activity and the EEG signal could be distorted by this tendency to asymmetry. The ground electrode may be placed on the ear lobe or the bony mastoid process behind the ear or on any other electrically quiet place on the head. As each site is located, the skin must be prepared for electrode application. Surface oil may be removed by wiping the area with alcohol and allowing the area to dry. Next, the site must be scrubbed with abrasive gel by twirling it against the scalp with the end of a cotton applicator as was described in the section on EMG instrumentation. Remember that the cotton tip should be held with moderate pressure against the scalp and 20 or so twirls made by turning the applicator stick between the thumb and forefinger. The gel can be any substance with an abrasive quality. Some EKG gels contain quartz crystals and do a good job of scrubbing or some commercial acne preparations available from druggists are as good. EEG paste or cream should next be applied to the prepared site – a tongue depressor works well as a spatula. The size of the mound of EEG cream should be no greater than the size of a quarter and should be uniform from one electrode site to another. It should also be uniform from one application to another as it affects the inter-electrode distance which is an important consideration in reproducing similar quality signals from one recording session to another. The electrode should be pressed into the mound of cream so that the cup of the electrode is filled with cream and the metal surface of the electrode is pressed firmly against the skin of the scalp. Care must be taken to ensure that the electrode is placed against the scalp rather than the hair. Each of the recording electrodes as well as the ground electrode should be applied in this manner. Various methods of further securing the electrode are sometimes used, such as fastening an elastic band around the head over the electrodes or using short lengths of masking tape over the electrode and the mound of cream in which it is buried. If a choice is available, the elastic band should be avoided as it tends to become uncomfortable over the length of the recording session and sometimes causes the electrode to slip away from the chosen recording site.

With the electrodes in place, impedance should be measured between each pair of electrodes. One pair is made up of the active and the reference electrode and the other two pairs include the ground electrode and each of the two recording electrodes. Tolerable impedance values for EEG vary according to the biofeedback instrument and the limit for any particular instrument may be found in the instruction book for that instrument. A valid impedance level for any instrument in current use is less than 10,000 ohms, which is easily achieved with good application technique. However, many instruments do well with as much as three times this level.

Electrode cables should be plugged into the biofeedback machine and the machine adjustments made. Adjustments usually required include setting the filters to detect only frequencies within the alpha band width of 8 to 12 cycles per second (Hz). This is accomplished by a single adjustment on machines with pre-set band widths. Several ranges are usually labeled around the indicator, so that by setting the indicator to "8–12," this adjustment is complete. Some machines allow independent setting of the upper and lower frequency points. In these machines it is necessary to set the lower frequency point to 8 and the upper to 12. When frequency adjustment is accomplished by either of these two means, the machine will ignore all parts of the EEG that do not fall within the alpha band. The sensitivity adjustment is sometimes labeled "amplitude" on an EEG machine. This refers to the size of the signal that the machine can recognize. When sensitivity is increased, the machine is able to recognize smaller signals coming from the scalp electrodes. Early in the biofeedback therapy, the required sensitivity is greater than in later sessions when EEG control is better established. The threshold adjustment determines how much of the alpha that the machine is detecting is to be considered for feedback. Proper setting of this control is vital to the success of the biofeedback task. In the beginning, the patient must experience some success but room must be provided for progress within the task. Consider for a moment that there is alpha being recognized by the machine 100% of the time, but that that alpha is occurring at various amplitudes or heights, some tall peaks and some short peaks, and the tasks are to increase the number of tall peaks and to make the tall peaks taller. If the threshold is set so low that all of the alpha present is rewarded no matter how tall the peaks, the patient has no opportunity to distinguish between greater and lesser heights. Further, there is no way that he can progress in the task since the device is feeding him back reward signals constantly. If, on the other hand, the threshold is set so that only the peaks of average or greater height are rewarded with the feedback signal, then it appears to the patient that half of the peaks are as desired and half need improvement. This is a good level. At this level, there is enough reward to give the patient early feelings of success and still allow him to see that there is room for improvement. If, on the other hand, the threshold is set too high so that only the very tallest peaks are rewarded, the patient is likely to see the task as a source of frustration and react in a stressful manner to it, thus defeating the purpose of the entire biofeedback program. By setting the threshold so that 50% of the total effort is rewarded in the early phases, and adjusting the threshold each time the patient reaches 70% feedback, a balance can be maintained and the physiological skill can be shaped in the desired direction. Thirty minutes of feedback is the optimum amount for any one feedback session, and sessions should be planned so that during the course of treatment, the patient receives a total of not less than 300 minutes of EEG alpha feedback. EEG control is not likely to be learned well enough in less than 300 minutes to enable the patient to maintain control when regular laboratory visits are terminated.

Goals for the alpha biofeedback must be set in light of the machine's method of quantifying EEG alpha abundance. If the machine reports per cent time, then the goal may be to achieve 99% time over a specified number of minutes. If the machine quantifies in a standard unit of measure, such as the microvolt, then the goal should be in the range of achieving 140% over baseline amplitudes. In either case, it is important to continue the feedback sessions until 300 minutes of feedback time have been exceeded whether or not the amplitude goal has been reached.

EEG alpha is especially vulnerable to artifacts. Movement results in muscle signals which are so much greater than the EEG signal that the EEG is lost within them. For some people eye position is an important factor determining EEG alpha abundance. Alpha is increased in many people by simply closing the eyes, and when the eyes are strained in any position away from center, there may be a muscle twitching that occurs in the same frequency range as alpha and influences the feedback. If the patient is especially bothered by wandering thoughts, the alpha is reduced, as it is when he becomes drowsy. Alpha is enhanced as the patient is able to maintain himself in a relaxed, but alert state.

§11.6 **Other Biofeedback Instrumentation.** Within the short history of biofeedback, many physiological parameters have been explored as potential biofeedback tasks. Those that have come into wide acceptance have been described above in sections devoted to them. Some others which have not been used as widely will be described here.

Heart rate and **heart rhythms** are sometimes fed back to the individual producing them by applying electrodes to the chest and putting the signal into a device which produces a feedback signal. Such devices are designed to provide feedback when the heart rate is increased, decreased, or maintained within a pre-determined range. Standard clinical EKG electrodes can be used and the sites often selected include placing the active recording electrode on the chest in the space between the third and fourth ribs just to the left of the sternum. The reference electrode may be placed on the patient's left side, midway between the front and back of his body, in a space between two ribs. The ground electrode may be placed on the arm or leg. Skin preparation is not a major consideration, but the quality of electrode contact should be assured by application of an electrode gel between the electrode and the skin. The EKG signal is especially strong and slow compared to many other physiological signals, and there is very little that can create artifacts in it. Major movement by the patient can cause momentary interruption of good quality signals, but as soon as the movement stops, the signal is re-established. Feedback of heart rhythms may be done in a number of ways depending upon the goal in mind. The feedback signal may be a light or tone that tells the patient when he is doing the task or sometimes the actual EKG complex is shown to the patient on an oscilloscope. Goals of heart rate feedback depend upon the particular condition being treated and the strategy used. Goals must be conservative as no reliable basis for predicting individual ability is yet available.

Blood pressure is instrumented in several ways. One instrument manufacturer has developed a feedback device which detects changes in blood pressure through a microphone which rests over the radial artery pulse in the wrist. Another method relies on changes in the Karotkoff sound (heard by a stethoscope or microphone only at pressure levels between systolic and diastolic pressure) to indicate changes in the pressure. A blood pressure cuff is applied in the usual manner and inflated from 3 to 5 mm below diastolic pressure so that the Karotkoff sound is not detectable. In this type of instrumentation, the patient's task is to turn the sound on. To do so, the patient must cause a drop in diastolic pressure to below the inflation level, thus allowing the Karotkoff sound to be detected. This parameter is undergoing extensive investigation in several laboratories and the interested reader should refer to the literature to update information as it becomes available.

Galvanic skin response (GSR) is fed back in some clinical settings. The signal source is change in resistance of the skin resulting from a change in the autonomic nervous system. The signal has two characteristics: a slowly changing resistance level (sometimes called the tonic level) that is thought to indicate general arousal level at any particular time, and shorter, abrupt changes (sometimes called phasic changes), usually in response to a short term stimulus such as a thought or an event. The longer lasting aspect of the GSR is potentially the more amenable to feedback of the two, since it is a much more stable signal. However, it is more common to feed back the abrupt phasic changes. Standard surface electrodes are used and are affixed to the palm of the hand in two places on the palmar side of two non-adjacent fingers. No ground is usually required and no skin preparation needed. A slight current is presented through one of the recording electrodes and the resistance across the skin is continuously measured. When a change occurs in the autonomic nervous system arousal level, a drop in resistance across the skin occurs allowing the current to flow more freely from one electrode to the other and an increase is seen in the "response" or potential of the skin. An increase in the galvanic skin response indicates an increase in emotional arousal, a condition contrary to relaxation.

TABLE 11.1

Trouble-Shooting Guide for Common Problems

Problem	Probable Reason and Solutions
1. No response by machine when power turned on.	1–8 can all be due to weak or non-existent power. Check batteries and replace if necessary.
2. Indicator level drops after short period on.	
3. Indicator range not as great as usual.	
4. Sensitivity diminished.	
5. Threshold not allowing usual amount of feedback.	
6. Machine's response slower than usual.	
7. Light signal dim.	
8. Audio signal diminishes.	
9. Rhythmic signal influencing feedback (EMG, EEG).	EKG interference – move electrodes to site less influenced by heartbeat.
10. Erratic fluctuations of feedback signal.	1. Poor electrode contact. Check all electrodes and re-apply if necessary.
	2. Interference from nearby electrical equipment. Check for source by unplugging other equipment one piece at a time.
	3. Static electricity. Check whether patient is wearing nylon clothing or nylon rug is in room.
	4. If two or more machines in use, be sure both are on same patient ground. *Do not* use two separate grounds on patient.

The major artifacts affecting the long term tonic GSR signal are short term increases in GSR due to phasic responses. Goals of GSR biofeedback center around enhanced awareness of internal arousal levels so that the patient learns to realize when he is physiologically stressed and can recognize the need to calm himself.

EEG frequencies other than alpha are sometimes fed back, including theta (4–7 Hz), sensory motor rhythm (12–16 Hz) and 40-Hz rhythms. For each, EEG surface electrodes are applied in the same manner as described in the section on EEG alpha over appropriate scalp locations for optimum detection of the various frequencies. The same artifacts effect these frequencies as those impinging on EEG alpha learning and a reliable basis for goal setting in these frequencies has not been determined. Instruments are described in Section 12.8.

§11.7 **Summary.** The special aspects of applying electrodes or other sensors and of preparing the instruments and the patient technically for the feedback session are described in this chapter. Finger temperature, EMG, and EEG instrumentation are described in detail, while other, less often used parameters are described in more general terms. Major issues discussed include: (1) location and preparation of the electrode sites; (2) selection and application of electrodes; and (3) introducing the signal into the feedback machine and adjusting the machine for the feedback session. Ways to determine whether the biofeedback machine is functioning as expected are discussed along with suggestions as to what to do if it is not (see Table 11.1).

This chapter is directed to the technician and may be followed quite literally while he is in the training phase.

Caveat emptor

CHAPTER 12

Biofeedback equipment

§12.1 **Introduction.** This section will concern itself with helping the practitioner with relatively little electronics background in the selection of equipment for clinical use. We will attempt to explain the elementary functions of a particular kind of equipment, the nature of the component parts, some of the specifications of the components, and useful features to be sought. We will not recommend specific manufacturers, since the available instruments are rapidly changing and recommendations would soon be obsolete, but will attempt to provide guidelines which will allow the reader to make his own discriminations.

Before discussing specific equipment, we will take up general considerations (Sec. 12.2) about biofeedback equipment. Then we will discuss research grade equipment (Sec. 12.3). This will be followed by discussion of electromyographic (EMG) feedback equipment (Sec. 12.4). After this there are sections on skin temperature feedback equipment (Sec. 12.5), electroencephalographic (EEG) feedback equipment (Sec. 12.6), galvanic skin response (GSR) feedback equipment (Sec. 12.7), and finally other feedback equipment (Sec. 12.8).

§12.2 **General Considerations.** There are a number of general considerations to be weighed concerning biofeedback equipment which we will take up in order. These include the basic types of equipment available, the manufacturers of the equipment, the specifications of the equipment, whether to use battery-operated equipment, what basic instruments a clinic should purchase, whether to buy equipment with complex special features, and what cost will be. We will briefly describe our experiences with each of these questions below.

Basic types of equipment. Biofeedback equipment is currently available in three major forms—portable units, modular components, and polygraphic.

Portable units are the type for most clinical practices. These are the self-contained complete portable units which carry out a particular kind of measurement and then have a feedback display of that particular measurement available for the patient. They include the typical EMG unit, the typical finger temperature unit, and the typical alpha and theta unit. When well designed, they offer the clinician the ideal instrument for his practice. In terms of cost, ease of operation, simplicity, and fulfillment of function, the portable unit is far ahead of the alternatives.

Modular component biofeedback equipment has not yet been reduced to a form where it will appeal to many clinicians, although it is very useful for research. Those unfamiliar with electronics can best understand this equipment as analogous to component high fidelity equipment, in which a user selects a number of optional building blocks out of which to build a particular high fidelity set. A number of single function modular components are held in an equipment rack and interconnected in the desired way by wires. The user must purchase a number of modules, but once they are purchased, he can use them to "build" particular biofeedback instruments by interconnecting the modules. Besides amplifying and displaying signals in auditory and visual modes, the modules can perform such logical functions as analog-to-digital or digital-to-analog conversion, filtering, and/nand gating, or/nor gating, timing, integrating, etc. The equipment is particularly useful for the programming of complex experiments.

Polygraphic equipment represents the standard used by researchers trained in the era when the quality of amplified signals was of great concern because of the uncertainty of electrode technique, unreliability of amplifiers, and the need for complete electronic shielding. Advances in modern equipment technology lessen the need of these concerns. However, the polygraph may still be justifiably viewed as the work horse instrument of the psychophysiologist and is the basic starting point of many biofeedback laboratories. Both research grade types of equipment are generally offered by older, larger, and more established manufacturing companies, many of whom have long standing reputations of deep concern for the quality of their products. Most of these companies have not yet entered the portable unitary equipment market, whose manufacturers will be considered next.

Manufacturers. Currently, there are less than a dozen manufacturers making clinical portable biofeedback equipment of quality worth considering. We and our engineering staffs have examined equipment and specifications from all of these and have not found a single manufacturer whose entire line of equipment is so complete and outstanding that it can be recommended without reservation. It appears justified to conclude that the portable biofeedback instrument manufacturing industry has not yet stabilized and may not do so for a number of years. It began and has continued with a number of small firms recognizing a demand and meeting it by providing the needed instruments. It has passed beyond the hand-to-mouth stage for the larger firms, but has not yet reached the stage where the manufacturing is profitable enough to stabilize the companies, or are any companies known by us to have been bought out by larger firms to provide stability in this way. Some of the current firms operate marginally; others have well financed backers and advertise extensively. Some firms provide good value for the dollar; others are overpriced. Some firms have imaginative engineering; others follow the pack. Some firms provide basic fundamentals; others feature gimmicks, appendages, and attachments. Some of the best do not advertise well, while some of the more dubious merit their main praise for promotion. Some have good repair policies; others not. Some have instruments which can be repaired by competent electronic workshops; others have epoxy-potted components which must be replaced by the manufacturer. Some provide complete schematic diagrams of their instruments; others maintain a veil of secrecy because the components are epoxy-potted and diagrams are not available.

Recent government regulations of biofeedback devices will provide some help by eliminating firms who make extravagant claims. It will also improve the quality control of instruments, but will not address many of the problems considered above. The only reliable guideline in instrument selection is *caveat emptor*.

Three methods of choosing a manufacturer can be recommended. The first is for the clinician to obtain complete specifications for instruments under consideration from as many manufacturers as possible, examine the specifications, talk to manufacturer representatives when they are available, and then make his own choices. The main disadvantage of this method is that it does not provide unbiased authoritative guidance. The next method is to talk with other clinicians who have used equipment and get their opinions. The disadvantages of this method are that the clinician's opinion may not be informed and that the clinician may have no experience with a particular good line of equipment. The third method is to consult with an electronics engineer regarding equipment purchases. The disadvantage of this method is that it may be difficult and costly to find the right engineer, who must fully understand the clinician's needs, should have knowledge of the product's internal circuits, and ideally should know most of the companies by reputation. All of these methods can also be combined. When possible, the clinician purchasing equipment should seek to buy it on approval and once it has been obtained, to have it inspected by an electronics engineer or qualified electronics technician, to use it as much as possible during the trial period, and to compare it with units owned by colleagues.

Specifications. In describing biofeedback instrument specifications, we will use the technical terminology of electronics without explaining the meanings of all of the terms. Table 12.1 reviews a few of the basic units. Further information on electronics in psychophysiology can be found in standard texts on psychophysiological methods, such as Brown

(1967), Venables and Martin (1967), Sternbach (1972), Cromwell, et al. (1973), or Geddes and Baker (1975). Some of the specifications we recommend are routinely supplied by manufacturers in their advertising material. Other specifications can only be determined by electronic tests—this applies particularly to EEG feedback equipment. Manufacturers often give noise levels and input voltage ranges in different forms. Therefore we have provided Table 12.2 to allow conversion of AC voltages to the root-mean-square value, which is the most accurate form for complex physiological signals.

Battery operation. For the sake of safety and simplicity, we make the general recommendation that all portable clinical biofeedback equipment be battery-powered unless it is to be used by someone quite familiar with electronics or is in a research setting where electronic consultation is available. The reason is that it is inevitable with line-powered equipment that eventually there will be accidental shocks received, while with battery-operated equipment mishaps will not occur unless other electrical equipment which is line-powered is connected to the biofeedback equipment. Rechargeable batteries are a convenient, but not essential, feature of a portable unit and should be weighed against other features in making a decision about equipment.

Basic instruments to purchase. We recommend that the clinician contemplating the general use of biofeedback in the treatment of stress-

TABLE 12.1

Simple Definitions

Unit	Measures	Use
Ampere = a	Current flow	Milliampere = 1/1000 a (ma)
Volt = v	Electrical energy	Millivolt = 1/1000 v (mv)
		Microvolt = 1/100,000 v (μv)
Ohm = Ω	Electrical resistance	Kilohm = 100Ω
Hertz = Hz	Cycles per second	Alpha rhythm = 8–12 Hz
Decibel = dB	Logarithmic ratios	Filter design
		Frequency response
Root-mean-square = rms	Wave quantity	Best single measure of complex signals

TABLE 12.2

Wave Measure Conversions for a Sine-Wave Signal*

E (peak) = 1.414 × E (rms)
E (peak to peak) = 2.828 × E (rms)
E (average) = 0.9 × E (rms)

* To be used in comparing instrument specifications of different manufacturers. Usually given in microvolts for EMG and EEG.

related conditions have available portable EMG and skin temperature feedback equipment. After experience with these instruments, the clinician should be able to see from his own situation what further instruments to purchase. Having both instruments available is particularly desirable because of the flexibility it offers in having alternate routes of treatment when a particular method does not work well.

Complexity of instruments. As a general rule we have not found that the addition of special processing options to clinical feedback equipment is necessarily an advantage. Some companies have a series of models for a particular biofeedback function; often their least expensive model is as good as the higher priced line. In some instances, high priced options do not do what is advertised. One particularly useful optional item is the time-period integrator which gives the average score over a pre-set time interval. For trial periods of 10 seconds up to several minutes this can be quite useful, especially in comparing performance from session to session and trial to trial, since the alternative is to try to guess at an average reading from a constantly moving needle on a meter.

Cost. The clinical portable units most clinicians should be considering vary in cost from several hundred dollars to about $2,000 per unit. Generally, the very cheapest equipment may not be satisfactory but one cannot assure quality by purchasing the most expensive. A rule of thumb is to try to shop in the lower-middle price range. Skin temperature instruments are among the least expensive and EMG units are in the middle price range, so that a basic starting package can be purchased for around $1,000. Psychotherapists are generally unfamiliar with instrument costs, but physicians from fields where a great deal of equipment is needed to practice, such as radiology, pathology, ophthalmology, or urology will recognize that the cost of this equipment is very modest indeed if actually used much in patient care.

Special equipment. Every clinician using EEG or EMG equipment needs an ohmmeter in order to measure electrode impedances. In many instances the inexpensive volt-ohmmeter available for about $20 in electronics shops will prove satisfactory. However, these ohmmeters have the disadvantage of polarizing skin electrodes, which can potentially cause signal processing difficulty if the first stage amplifier is DC-coupled with a high gain. Since the meter is inexpensive, it is worthwhile to find out from the manufacturer if there would be difficulties with its use. The alternative instrument is a battery-operated AC impedance meter which prevents polarization of electrodes. This costs more than $100 and is unnecessary if the problem mentioned above is not present.

§12.3 Research Grade Equipment. We are not addressing ourselves in this book to the problems of the psychophysiological researcher attempting to purchase biofeedback equipment, because he is almost sure to have other adequate sources of information available to him through colleagues, through engineering consultants, and through his own past experiences in the field. One of the typical paths chosen by researchers is to purchase a standard 8- or 12-channel polygraph with plug-in modular amplifiers for some of the major parameters of interest, such as EMG, EEG, GSR, heart rate, skin temperature, blood pressure, etc. The output of the modular amplifiers is then readily subjected to signal reduction and display by fairly inexpensive circuits which the researcher or his engineering support personnel can fabricate.

Some investigators will wish to depart from the tradition of the polygraph to record and collect data in other forms. Other types of equipment often help in this process, especially the now widely available modular switching equipment and medium sized laboratory computers, which can simultaneously collect and analyze data as well as control the experimental setting. We have not attempted to provide guidance on these matters.

One particular instrument of great value to any biofeedback research is the four-channel variable persistence storage oscilloscope with widely variable sweep speeds. It is an effective display for many forms of feedback and can be made integral to numerous experiments. When seeking understanding, the way often becomes clear after staring at data at varying sweep speeds for several hours. The four-channel storage scope is also the simplest flexible display for rehabilitation muscle re-training work (see Sec. 10.3).

§12.4 EMG Feedback Equipment.

Function. The portable modular EMG biofeedback unit is designed to detect muscle activity and feed back suitable information to the subject about the activity level of the muscles measured. It thus fulfills the function of feedback arrow 2 in Figure 1.4 (Sec. 1.38). It almost always uses skin surface electrodes as transducer and has the typical component configuration shown in Figure 1.5 (Sec. 1.38) of transducer, signal amplifier, signal processor, and signal display.

Safety. The battery-powered unit does not have the shock hazard of the line-powered units and is therefore recommended. Equipment design must ensure that no more than 5 ma of direct or 500 μa of 60-Hz alternating current would enter the subject in the event of a component failure.

Equipment specifications. Differential (bi-polar) signal input is to be greatly preferred over single ended (uni-polar) input. This permits the use of the EMG in electrically noisy environments such as most offices and homes provide. Impedance of the input circuitry should be at least 1 megohm. The common mode rejection ration (CMRR) at 60 Hz should be

at least 100 dB (100,000:1) measured at the output of the signal amplifier. Notch filters are a valuable asset for additional attenuation of 60-
Hz interference.

A high quality device should respond to signals in the 20-to-1,000 Hz
frequency range having amplitudes of 1 to 100 μv rms. For clinical use,
however, it does not appear crucial to cover the entire frequency spectrum. For monitoring muscle activity in the neck or back region, a lower
frequency cut-off of 100 Hz can help eliminate EKG artifact. Input
equivalent noise (the noise generated by the signal amplifier) should be
less than 1.0 μv rms. The time constant of the output circuits should fall
between 0.25 and 1.0 seconds. A built-in circuit for measurement of
electrode-to-electrode resistance is a worthwhile feature, but should
give a range on a meter and not just consist of an *on* or *off* light.

Feedback modalities. Having both auditory and visual modes of
feedback is to be greatly preferred in an EMG. The most common
auditory feedback used is a clicking sound or tone that increases in
frequency as the input signal increases in amplitude. Visual feedback is
normally given by an analog meter that provides amplitude information
as well as a means for comparing performance during and between
sessions. Those instruments equipped with meters either provide a gain
control, giving several full scale sensitivity ranges, or they incorporate a
non-linear (usually log or semi-log) display that covers the entire range
of input amplitude. The latter method has the advantage of providing a
larger meter deflection for a given change in amplitude at the low end of
the scale where further reduction becomes more difficult. This method
also eliminates the need to change ranges, and therefore to establish
new goals, as relaxation progresses. Digital numerical displays as a
continuous visual feedback are not very practical, since most subjects
find it hard to follow the registered changes in numbers. On the other
hand, a digital readout of average amplitude during a trial period can be
quite useful as mentioned in Section 12.2.

§12.5 Temperature Feedback Equipment.

Function. The portable skin temperature feedback instrument is
designed to measure and display changes in skin temperature from a
selected body site. Since skin temperature is mainly controlled by the
thermal transfer from blood flow to the part, and since blood flow is
controlled largely by autonomically mediated arteriolar changes, the
instrument fulfills the function of feedback arrow 3 in Figure 1.4 (Sec.
1.38). This is one of the simplest of the biofeedback instruments electronically. The temperature is picked up by a thermistor which is
usually taped to the skin with a small piece of adhesive tape. The
temperature measurement is usually read from a simple bridge circuit
by a meter calibrated to read in degrees.

Safety. Most available portable units are battery powered, but since there is no electrical connection directly to the patient there is minimal danger.

Equipment specifications. Most available instruments monitor one location for absolute temperature changes. Some include provisions for measuring the difference in temperature between two parts of the body, but this particular method has been abandoned by most clinicians so the feature is not needed. One reason the feature is not useful is because in following the progress of the subject, it is better to have means of making absolute temperature measurements. The units should have a meter output and sensitivity should be changeable to permit full scale deflections ranging from several degrees Fahrenheit to 10 or 20°. Without the high sensitivity setting the subject may not be able to work as well with the instrument.

The analog meter output is preferable to digital LED readout as trends and small changes are more easily followed. Instruments are also available with auditory feedback in the form of a tone, the frequency of which is usually proportional to absolute temperature.

§12.6 EEG (Brain Wave) Feedback Equipment.

Function. Portable EEG feedback equipment is designed to detect and amplify electrical signals generated by the brain, discriminate among the various frequency components, and give information to the subject concerning the amplitude or frequency of these components. It thus fulfills the function of feedback arrow 1 in Figure 1.4 (Sec. 1.38). Skin surface electrodes are usually used as transducer and the other components are as shown in Figure 1.5 (Sec. 1.38) – signal amplifier, signal processor, and signal display. There are technical problems in making good brain wave feedback equipment which are far greater than for any other feedback instrument that we consider. These are reflected in the details mentioned below. We have only provided details for alpha, theta, and beta feedback equipment, which are the commonly used types. Other brain wave feedback instruments are mentioned in Section 12.8.

Safety. Battery operation is recommended. Input circuitry should be designed to allow no more than 5 ma of direct current or 500 μa at 60 Hz of alternating current to flow through the subject in the event of a component failure. Any accessories used with EEG feedback equipment should also be battery operated or be isolated electrically through the use of optical or magnetic (transformer) techniques.

Equipment specifications. Input to the device should be differential (bi-polar) with an impedance exceeding 2 megohms. Common mode rejection should be at least 100 dB (100,000:1) at 60 Hz. The frequency response of the amplifier alone should be at least 40 dB down at 60 Hz.

Input DC current should be less than 50 na. An equivalent input noise level of 0.5 μv rms or less is recommended. (This measurement should be made at the output of the signal amplifier section, before the filter section, and should be made over the entire frequency range covered by the instrument.)

A calibrated control must be provided to set the threshold amplitude above which feedback is given and it should at least cover the range of 1.5 to 35 μv rms. Some units perform this task by providing an amplifier gain control and comparing the filtered signal to a fixed voltage reference. Another approach is to fix the gain of the amplifier (usually between 2,000 and 100,000) and compare the filtered signal to an adjustable reference. A desirable feature is the incorporation of artifact inhibit circuits to squelch feedback resulting from movement artifact. One of the early stages of amplification should incorporate AC coupling to prevent saturation of the amplifier due to electrode offset potential.

It is recommended that equipment utilize analog filter design with at least -18 dB per octave attenuation of signals outside the passband (e.g., three-pole Butterworth filters). Digital filters have a more ideal frequency response but give poor results if the signal of interest is accompanied by slower waves having amplitudes approaching that of the desired signal. Analog filters, on the other hand, are subject to "ringing" – an output near the center frequency when the filter is excited by spiking activity in the EEG or by movement artifact. This tendency to ring increases as the filter skirts are made steeper. Some manufacturers utilize both types of filters in series, giving improved performance over either type alone.

For alpha and theta feedback, the instrument must respond to signals with frequencies between 4 and 13 Hz. Beta feedback requires an upper frequency limit of 28 Hz. Adjustable upper and lower filter controls allow one device to be used for any of the above ranges. Most devices on the market employing only one frequency range control have filters with undesirable response characteristics. The filter section should have a flat (± 1 dB) response across the band selected, dropping to -3 dB at the upper and lower cut-off frequencies. Use of silver/silver-chloride electrodes is recommended. An internal means of checking electrode-to-electrode resistance is a desirable feature available in some units.

Feedback modalities. Whereas the means by which information is presented to the subject remains somewhat a matter of personal preference, we have found auditory methods preferable over visual since the subject can work with eyes open or closed, as desired. A steady tone which is made to warble when the feedback criteria are met has been found less alerting by some users when compared to techniques in which the tone is either on or off to signal success. Whichever method is utilized, feedback should appear to be instantaneous, lagging the onset of the triggering signal by not more than 0.5 seconds. Devices use different criteria for signaling the presence of the desired brain wave. We feel that it is important for information to come as soon as possible and we prefer that the continuous discrimination of amplitude be given in some way.

§12.7 GSR Feedback Equipment.

Function. The purpose of portable modular GSR feedback equipment is to detect and display changes in the skin resistance (or conductance) caused by changes in the subject's emotional state. It fulfills the function of arrow 3 in Figure 1.4 (Sec. 1.38) because GSR is a reflection of autonomic nervous system activity. Although this is also a very simple instrument electronically, methodological problems complicate the widespread acceptance of its use.

Safety. Instruments should be battery operated and design must preclude the passage of more than 5 ma through the subject in the event of a component failure.

Equipment specifications. Equipment using the constant current method of skin resistance measurement is suggested. These units pass a small controlled current through the skin and measure the resulting voltage drop. Current density should be maintained below 10 μa per cm^2 (calculated by dividing the current output of the device by the area of one of the electrodes). In no case should the current normally passed through the subject exceed 50 μa. The instrument should be capable of accepting skin impedance from 2 to 2,000 kilohms (basal level) and should reflect resistance changes as small as 200 ohms. To display phasic changes adequately, the indicating device should be AC coupled to the input signal through a circuit having a time constant of 3 to 5 seconds.

Feedback modalities. While accurate measurement of the basal resistance level is sometimes done in research work and may someday be important clinically, at present only a relative indication of the amplitude and direction of transient resistance changes is usually provided. This is normally performed by an analog meter and/or changing tone.

§12.8 Other Biofeedback Equipment.
Biofeedback has been used for treatment of a number of specific disease conditions in which special instrumentation is necessary. Here we will briefly mention these uses and the equipment and where to find further information on the subject. It is fairly obvious what the general principles of such instruments are – a bodily function must be measured in real time, the function must have some moment-to-moment variation, and the subject must be shown some indication of this variation. Sometimes this merely means taking an already used instrument and turning it around so that the patient can see the read-out as well as the operator seeing it.

Epilepsy. A number of laboratories are studying the treatment of epilepsy with biofeedback. The methods depend upon special brain wave filtering and differ from most biofeedback in that the length of treatment is very long, with an upper limit not yet having been established. Investigators using the methods do not recommend them for widespread clinical use yet. An introduction to the area is provided by Sterman (1973).

40-Hz brain waves. Besides the usual brain wave frequencies, investigators have recently become interested in studying the properties of a frequency of about 40 Hz. Equipment to analyze the brain waves has been designed and is available. Sheer (1975) is the major investigator responsible for this work, and has described the rhythm in his papers.

Thermography. Modern technology has produced an instrument which operates on the same principles as television, except that it measures infrared radiation instead of visible light. This device can very precisely map the temperature of the surface of any part of the body and presents an alternative to the single probe skin temperature feedback instrument. Currently, the instrument is mainly used diagnostically by radiologists to diagnose blood vessel conditions and screen for breast cancer and is extremely expensive. However, it meets the requirements of a biofeedback instrument mentioned at the beginning of this section and is sometimes available in institutional settings for collaborative work. Its main drawback is lack of sensitivity.

Anal sphincter feedback. The method of this treatment has been well worked out and described. The needed equipment is a special catheter, three pressure transducers, a write-out or display instrument, and necessary tubing and balloons. Engel, et al. (1974) have described the equipment and procedure in detail.

Esophageal sphincter feedback. Nikoomanesh, et al. (1973), have controlled the sphincter between the esophagus and the stomach with biofeedback. The basic equipment is already available in many gastroenterologists' offices in the instrument measuring intra-luminal pressure at several sites on the catheter. Several methods of measurement are used, but as long as continuous measures from several close-by sites on a stationary catheter are obtainable, the procedure is straightforward.

Hypertension. A few words are in order concerning instrumentation in the treatment of hypertension with biofeedback. We have worked with or examined most of the methods of blood pressure biofeedback and feel it is uncertain at present what sort of procedure may eventually be found most useful. The current elaborate methods may not necessarily give better results than very simple ones using standard relaxation parameters such as EMG and skin temperatures. However, this remains to be demonstrated.

Cardiac arrhythmia feedback. The methods of treating cardiac arrhythmias by directly related feedbacks have not yet been reduced to clinical practice and require special equipment as described by Engel and co-workers (see Birk, 1973, for references).

§12.9 Summary. Biofeedback equipment is most readily available for clinical use in low cost portable units which are often of good quality. Many factors need to be considered in making a decision about a particular instrument. A beginning clinical facility should have EMG and skin temperature feedback available and later add other parameters as experience is acquired. Specifications of these and other instruments are described.

BIBLIOGRAPHY

Amato, A., Hermsmeyer, C. A., and Kleinman, K. M. Use of electromyographic feedback to increase inhibitory control of spastic muscles. *Phys. Ther. 53:* 1063–1066, 1973.

Andrews, J. M. Neuromuscular re-education of hemiplegia with aid of electromyograph. *Arch. Phys. Med. Rehabil. 45:* 530–532, 1964.

Ashby, W. R. *An Introduction to Cybernetics*. John Wiley & Sons, New York, 1963.

Bakker, C. B. and Amini, F. B. Observations on the psychotomimetic effects of Sernyl. *Compr. Psychiatry 2:* 269–280, 1961.

Bandler, R. and Grinder, J. *The Structure of Magic*. Science and Behavior Books, Palo Alto, Calif., 1975.

Bandura, A. *Principles of Behavior Modification*. Holt, Rinehart and Winston, New York, 1969.

Barnwell, G. M. and Stafford, F. S. A mathematical model of decision-making neural circuits controlling behavioral mode selection. *Bull. Mathemat. Biol.* In press.

Basmajian, J. V. *Muscles Alive: Their Function Revealed by Electromyography*. Williams & Wilkins, Baltimore, 1974.

Basmajian, J. V., Kukulka, C. G., Narayan, M. G., and Takeba, K. Biofeedback treatment of foot-drop after stroke compared with standard rehabilitative technique: effects on voluntary control and strength. *Arch. Phys. Med. Rehabil. 56:* 231–236, 1975.

Bean, W. B. Address on the history of medicine. The University of Texas Health Science Center at San Antonio, 1975.

Benson, H. *The Relaxation Response*. William Morrow and Co., New York, 1975.

Biddle, W. E. Image therapy. *Am. J. Psychiatry 126:* 408–411, 1969.

Birk, L. *Biofeedback: Behavioral Medicine*. Grune & Stratton, New York, 1973.

Blanchard, E. B. and Young, L. D. Clinical applications of biofeedback training: a review of evidence. *Arch. Gen. Psychiatry 30:* 573–589, 1974.

Bowden, C. L. and Burstein, A. G. *Psychosocial Basis of Medical Practice*. Williams & Wilkins, Baltimore, 1974.

Braatoy, T. *Fundamentals of Psychoanalytic Technique*. John Wiley & Sons, New York, 1954.

Brown, B. *The Biofeedback Syllabus: A Handbook for the Psychophysiological Study of Biofeedback*. Charles C Thomas, Springfield, Ill., 1975.

Brown, B. B. *New Mind, New Body*. Harper & Row, New York, 1974.

Brown, C. *Methods in Psychophysiology*. Williams & Wilkins, Baltimore, 1967.

Brudny, J., Grynbaum, B., and Korein, J. Spasmodic torticollis: treatment by feedback display of the EMG. *Arch. Phys. Med. Rehabil. 55:* 403–408, 1974a.

Brudny, J., Korein, J., Levidow, L., Grynbaum, B., Liberman, A., and Freidman, L. Sensory feedback therapy as a modality of treatment in central nervous system disorders of voluntary movement. *Neurology 24:* 925–932, 1974b.

Budzynski, T. H. On biofeedback procedures: systems approach to biofeedback training. In *Biofeedback Techniques in Clinical Practice*, Vol. 2, edited by J. V. Basmajian and J. Stoyva. Tape cassette series from Biomonitoring Applications, New York, 1976.

Budzynski, T. H., Stoyva, J. M., Adler, C. S., and Mullaney, D. J. EMG biofeedback and tension headache: a controlled outcome study. *Psychosom. Med. 35:* 484–496, 1973.

Butler, F. and Stoyva, J. *Biofeedback and Self-Regulation: A Bibliography*. Biofeedback

Research Society and University of Colorado Medical School, Denver, 1973. (Available through Biofeedback Research Society, see Appendix A.)

Christiansen, B. *Thus Speaks the Body.* Arno Press, New York, 1972.

Cleeland, C. Behavioral techniques in modification of spasmodic torticollis. *Neurology* 23: 1241–1247, 1973.

Cohen, B. S. Considerations in prognosis after stroke. *Md. State Med. J. 25:* 29–32, 1976.

Conant, R. C. The information transfer required in regulatory processes. *IEEE Trans. Syst. Sci. Cybernet. SSC-5:* 334–338, 1969.

Cromwell, L., Wiebell, F.J., Pfeiffer, E. A. and Usselman, L.B. *Biomedical Instrumentation and Measurements.* Prentice-Hall, Englewood Cliffs, N. J., 1973.

Davis, J. F. *Manual of Surface Electromyography.* WADC Technical Report 59-184. Wright Air Development Center, Ohio, December 1959.

Diamond, S. *The Practicing Physician's Approach to Headache.* Medcom Press, New York, 1973.

DiStefano, J. J., Stubberud, A. R., and Williams, I. J. *Theory and Problems of Feedback and Control Systems.* Schaum's Outline Series. McGraw-Hill, 1967.

Dollard, J., Auld, F., and White, A. *Steps in Psychotherapy.* Macmillan, New York, 1953.

Engel, B. T. Behavioral symposium. In *Highlights of the 20th Annual Conference of Veterans Administration Studies in Mental Health and Behavioral Sciences,* pp. 17–23. U.S. Government Printing Office 210-851/608, Washington, D. C., 1975.

Engel, B., Nikoomanesh, P., and Schuster, M. M. Operant conditioning of rectosphincteric responses in the treatment of fecal incontinence. *N. Engl. J. Med. 290:* 646–649, 1974.

Feinstein, A. R. *Clinical Judgement.* Williams & Wilkins, Baltimore, 1967.

Feldenkrais, M. *Body and Mature Behavior.* International Universities Press, New York, 1949.

Finley, W. W., Niman, C., Standley, J., and Ender, P. Frontal EMG biofeedback training of athetoid cerebral palsy patients: a report of six cases. *Biofeedback and Self Regulation 1:* 169–182, 1976.

Fischer, R. A cartography of the ecstatic and meditative states. *Science 174:* 897–904, 1971.

Gaarder, K. A conceptual model of sleep. *Arch. Gen. Psychiatry 14:* 253–260, 1966.

Gaarder, K. Control of states of consciousness. I. Attainment through control of psychophysiological variables. *Arch. Gen. Psychiatry 25:* 429–435, 1971a.

Gaarder, K. Control of states of consciousness. II. Attainment through external feedback augmenting control of psychophysiological variables. *Arch. Gen. Psychiatry 25:* 436–441, 1971b.

Gaarder, K. *Eye Movements, Vision and Behavior.* John Wiley & Sons, New York, 1975.

Geddes, L. A. and Baker, L. E. *Principles of Applied Biomedical Instrumentation,* Ed. 2. John Wiley & Sons, New York, 1975.

Gellhorn, E. and Kiely, W. F. Autonomic nervous system in psychiatric disorder. In *Biological Psychiatry,* edited by J. Mendels. John Wiley & Sons, New York, 1973.

Green, E., Green, A. M., and Walters, E. D. Self-regulation of internal states. In *Proceedings of the International Congress of Cybernetics.* London, 1969a.

Green, E. E., Walters, E. D., Green, A. M., and Murphy, G. Feedback technique for deep relaxation. *Psychophysiology 6:* 371–377, 1969b.

Greenfield, N. S. *Handbook of Psychophysiology.* Holt, Rinehart and Winston, New York, 1972.

Haley, J., ed. *Advanced Techniques of Hypnosis and Therapy: Selected Papers of Milton H. Erickson.* Grune & Stratton, New York, 1967.

Haley, J. *Uncommon Therapy.* Grune & Stratton, New York, 1968.

Hammer, M. The directed daydream technique. *Psychother. Theory, Res. Prac. 4:* 173–181, 1967.

Harris, F. A., Spelman, F. A., and Hymer, J. W. Electronic sensory aids as treatment for cerebral-palsied children: inapproprioception: part II. *Phys. Ther. 54:* 354–365, 1974.

Hart, J. T. Autocontrol of EEG alpha. *Psychophysiology 4:* 506, 1968.

Harter, M. R. Excitability cycles and cortical scanning: a review of two hypotheses of central intermittency in perception. *Psychol. Bull. 68:* 47–58, 1967.

Havens, L. L. The existential use of the self. *Am. J. Psychiatry 131:* 1–10, 1974.

Hefferline, R. F. The role of proprioception in the control of behavior. *Trans. N. Y. Acad. Sci. 20:* 739–764, 1958.

Holmes, T. H. and Rahe, R. H. The social readjustment rating scale. *J. Psychosom. Res. 11:* 213–218, 1967.

Horowitz, M. J. *Image Formation and Cognition.* Appleton-Century-Crofts, New York, 1970.

Houston, W. R. The doctor himself as therapeutic agent. *Ann. Int. Med. 11:* 1416–1425, 1938.

Iberall, A. S. and Cardon, S. Z. Hierarchical regulation in the complex biological organism. *Rec. IEEE Syst. Sci. Cybernet. Conf.* 145–151, 1969.

Jacobson, E. *Progressive Relaxation.* University of Chicago Press, Chicago, 1938.

James, W. *Principles of Psychology.* Dover Publications, New York, 1960.

Johnson, H. E. and Garton, W. H. Muscle re-education in hemiplegia by use of an electromyographic device. *Arch. Phys. Med. Rehabil. 54:* 320–323, 1973.

Jones, R. W. *Principles of Biological Regulation: An Introduction to Feedback Systems.* Academic Press, 1973.

Kamiya, J. Operant control of the EEG alpha rhythm and some of its reported effects on consciousness. In *Altered States of Consciousness,* edited by C. T. Tart. John Wiley & Sons, New York, 1969.

Kaufman, M. R. Hypnosis in psychotherapy today. *Arch. Gen. Psychiatry 4:* 30–49, 1961.

Kiritz, S. and Moos, R. H. Physiological effects of social environments. *Psychosom. Med. 36:* 96–114, 1974.

Koestler, A. *The Lotus and the Robot.* Macmillan, New York, 1961.

Kosbabs, P. A. Imagery techniques in psychiatry. *Arch. Gen. Psychiatry 31:* 283–290, 1974.

Kukulka, C. G., Brown, D. M., and Basmajian, J. P. A preliminary report: biofeedback training for early finger joint mobilization. *Am. J. Occup. Ther. 29:* 469–470, 1975.

Lacey, J. I. Somatic response patterning and stress: some revisions of activation theory. In *Psychological Stress,* edited by M. H. Appley and R. Trumbull. Appleton-Century-Crofts, New York, 1967.

Lain Entralgo, P. *Doctor and Patient.* McGraw-Hill, New York, 1969.

Langley, L. L. *Homeostasis.* Reinhold Publishing Corp., New York, 1965.

Lazarus, A. A. *Daily Living: Coping With Tensions and Anxieties.* Cassette tapes produced by Instructional Dynamics, Chicago, Ill., 1970.

Ludwig, A. M. Altered states of consciousness. *Arch. Gen. Psychiatry 15:* 225–234, 1966.

Margolin, S. and Kubie, L. An apparatus for the use of breath sounds as a hypnogogic stimulus. *Am. J. Psychiatry 100:* 610, 1944.

Mayr, O. *The Origins of Feedback Control.* MIT Press, Cambridge, 1970.

McKenzie, R. E., Ehrisman, W. J., Montgomery, P. S., and Barnes, R. H. The treatment of headaches by means of electroencephalographic biofeedback. *Headache 13:* 4, 1974.

Menninger, K. A. and Holzman, P. *Theory of Psychoanalytic Technique,* Ed. 2. Basic Books, New York, 1973.

Miller, N. Learning of visceral and glandular responses. *Science 163:* 434–445, 1969.

Modell, W. *The Relief of Symptoms.* W. B. Saunders, Philadelphia, 1955.

Montgomery, P. S. and Ehrisman, W. J. Biofeedback alleviated headaches, a follow-up. *Headache 16:* 5, 1976.

Mulholland, T. Feedback electroencephalography. *Activ. Nerv. Sup. (Prague) 10:* 410–438, 1968. Reprinted in: Barber, T. X., Di Cara, L. V., Kamiya, J. Miller, N.E., Shapiro, D. and Stoyva, J. eds. *Biofeedback and Self Control Reader.* Aldine Atherton, Chicago, 1969.

Mulholland, T. B. Biofeedback as scientific method. In *Biofeedback Theory and Research,* edited by G. Schwartz and J. Beatty. Academic Press, New York, 1976.

Murphy, G. and Leeds, M. *Outgrowing Self-Deception.* Basic Books, New York, 1975.

Nikoomanesh, P., Wells, D., and Schuster, M. M. Biofeedback control of lower esophageal sphincter contraction. *Clin. Res. 21:* 521, 1973.

Parsons, T. *The Social System.* Free Press, New York, 1951.

Pascal, G. R. The effect of relaxation upon recall. *Am. J. Psychol. 62:* 32–47, 1949.

Pelletier, K. Diagnosis, Procedures and Phenomenology of Biofeedback. Paper presented at the annual meeting of the Biofeedback Research Society, Monterey, California, 1975.

Polanyi, M. Life's irreducible structure. *Science 160:* 1308–1313, 1968.

Pope, A. T. and Gersten, C. D. A semiautomated system for biofeedback-assisted relaxation therapy. *Behav. Res. Methods Instrument. 7:* 459–463, 1975.

Powers, W. T. *Behavior: The Control of Perception.* Aldine Publishing Co., Chicago, 1973.

Rasmussen, J. E., ed. *Man in Isolation and Confinement.* Aldine Publishing Co., Chicago, 1973.

Razran, G. The observable unconscious and the inferable unconscious in current Soviet psychophysiology: interoceptive conditioning, semantic conditioning and the orienting reflex. *Psychol. Rev. 68:* 81–147, 1961.

Reich, W. *Character Analysis,* ed. 3. Orgone Institute Press, New York, 1949.

Russ, K. EMG Biofeedback of Spasmodic Torticollis. Paper presented at the Conference of the Biofeedback Research Society, Monterey, California, 1975.

Sargent, J., Green, E. E., and Walters, E. D. The use of autogenic feedback training in a pilot study of migraine and tension headaches. *Headache 12:* 120–124, 1972.

Schultz, J. H. and Luthe, W. *Autogenic Training.* Grune & Stratton, New York, 1959.

Schwartz, G. E. Biofeedback, self-regulation and the patterning of physiological processes. *Am. Sci. 63:* 314–324, 1975.

Sheehan, P. W. (ed.). *The Function and Nature of Imagery.* Springer, New York, 1969.

Sheer, D. E. Biofeedback training of 40-Hz EEG and behavior. In *Behavior and Brain Electrical Activity,* edited by N. Burch and H. L. Altshuler. Plenum Publishing Co., New York, 1975.

Singer, J. L. *Imagery and Daydreams: Methods in Psychotherapy and Behavior.* Academic Press, New York, 1974.

Singer, M. T. Engagement-involvement: a central phenomenon in psychophysiological research. *Psychosom. Med. 36:* 1–17, 1974.

Smith, H. M., Jr., Basmajian, J. V., and Vanderstoep, S. F. Inhibition of neighboring motoneurons in conscious control of single spinal motoneurons. *Science 183:* 975–976, 1974.

Sokolov, Y. N. *Perception and the Conditioned Reflex,* (translated by S. Waydenfeld). Macmillan, New York, 1963.

Solberg, W. and Rugh, J. The use of biofeedback devices in the treatment of bruxism. *J. S. Calif. Dental Assoc. 40:* 852–853, 1972.

Spitz, R. A. The derailment of dialogue: stimulus overload, action cycles, and the completion gradient. *J. Am. Psychoanal. Assoc. 12:* 752–775, 1964.

Stanton, A. H. and Schwartz, M. S. *The Mental Hospital*. Basic Books, New York, 1954.

Sterman, M. B. Neurophysiologic and clinical studies of sensorimotor EEG biofeedback training: some effects on epilepsy. In *Biofeedback: Behavioral Medicine*, edited by L. Birk. Grune & Stratton, New York, 1973.

Sternbach, R. A. *Principles of Psychophysiology*. Holt, Rinehart and Winston, New York, 1972.

Stoyva, J. Self regulation: a context for biofeedback. *Biofeedback Self-Regul. 1:* 1-6, 1976.

Stoyva, J. The public (scientific) study of private events. In *Sleep and Dreaming*, edited by E. Hartman. Little, Brown, Boston, 1970.

Stroebel, C. F. and Glueck, B. C. Biofeedback treatment in medicine and psychiatry: an ultimate placebo. In *Biofeedback: Behavioral Medicine*, edited by L. Birk. Grune & Stratton, New York, 1973.

Strupp, H. H. *Psychotherapy and the Modification of Abnormal Behavior*. McGraw-Hill, New York, 1971.

Strupp, H. H. *Psychotherapy: Clinical Research and Theoretical Issues*. Jason Aronson, New York, 1973.

Strupp, H. H., Fox, R. E., and Lessler, K. *Patients View Their Psychotherapy*. The Johns Hopkins Press, Baltimore, 1969.

Swaan, D., van Wieringen, P. C. W., and Fokkema, S. D. Auditory electromyographic feedback therapy to inhibit undesired motor activity. *Arch. Phys. Med. Rehabil. 55:* 251-254, 1974.

Takebe, K., Kukulka, C. G., Narayan, M. G., and Basmajian, J. V. Biofeedback treatment of foot drop after stroke compared with standard rehabilitation technique. Part 2. Effects on nerve conduction velocity and spasticity. *Arch. Phys. Med. Rehabil. 57:* 9-11, 1976.

Tart, C. T., ed. *Altered States of Consciousness*. John Wiley & Sons, New York, 1969.

Travis, T. A., Kondo, C. Y., and Knott, J. R. Alpha enhancement research: a review. *Biol. Psychiatry 10:* 69-89, 1975.

Twitchell, T. E. The restoration of motor functioning following hemiplegia in man. *Brain 74:* 433-480, 1951.

Venables, P. and Martin, I. *A Manual of Psychophysiological Methods*. John Wiley & Sons, New York, 1967.

Watzlawick, P., Beavin, H., and Jackson, D. D. *Pragmatics of Human Communication*. W. W. Norton, New York, 1967.

Wender, P. H. Vicious and virtuous circles: the role of deviation amplifying feedback in the origin and perpetuation of behavior. *Psychiatry 31:* 309-324, 1968.

Wenger, M. A. Studies of autonomic balance: a summary. *Psychophysiology 2:* 173-186, 1966.

Whatmore, G. B. and Kohli, D. R. *The Physiopathology and Treatment of Functional Disorders*. Grune & Stratton, New York, 1974.

Wolpe, J. *The Practice of Behavior Therapy*. Pergamon Press, New York, 1969.

Wolpe, J. *The Practice of Behavior Therapy*, Ed. 2. Pergamon Press, New York, 1973.

Zeeman, E. C. Catastrophe theory. *Sci. Am. 234:* 65-83, 1976.

APPENDIX A

BIOFEEDBACK RESOURCES

This appendix will provide the reader with information on how to delve further into the area of biofeedback. The first section will describe some sources of the biofeedback literature. The second will describe organizations involved in biofeedback. The third will name some journals and newsletters in which equipment is advertised by manufacturers.

§A.1 **Biofeedback Literature.** Although an extensive literature has been developed, it is not necessarily of great practical value to the clinician in many instances. One of the best ways to get a good overview of that literature is provided by the annual collections of reprinted articles published by Aldine Publishing Company, Chicago, under the title *Biofeedback and Self-Control.* Other major collections include Birk (1973) and Brown (1974). The former is an edited work with major papers by many important investigators, while the latter is Dr. Barbara Brown's personal wide ranging view of the field of biofeedback. More complete bibliographies of the field are given by Francine Butler and Johann Stoyva (1973) in their bibliography which was quite complete up to the year of publication, and by Barbara Brown in her syllabus. Journals frequently publishing articles on biofeedback include mainly *Biofeedback and Self-Regulation,* a new journal of the Biofeedback Society, *Psychophysiology, Psychosomatic Medicine, Archives of General Psychiatry,* and the *Archives of Physical Medicine and Rehabilitation.* Other journals to search can be learned from the bibliographies listed above.

§A.2 **Professional Organizations.** The main organization concerned with biofeedback is the Biofeedback Society. The Society, with over 800 members, has its executive offices in Denver. Further information about it can be obtained from the Executive Secretary, Francine Butler, at the Department of Psychiatry, University of Colorado Medical Center, 4200 East Ninth Avenue, Denver, Colorado 80220. The Biofeedback Society devotes itself almost exclusively to the topic of biofeedback, whereas with most of the other organizations, biofeedback is only one of a number of topics of concern. Some of the major professional societies—such as the American Psychiatric Association and the American Psychological Association—have recently had sections of the annual meetings devoted to biofeedback and they have ad hoc committees considering biofeedback from various perspectives. Other more specialized interdisciplinary societies such as the Society for Psychophysiological Research and the several psychosomatic societies are also interested in biofeedback.

On a more local basis several of the larger states now have their own state biofeedback societies. Information about these can be obtained from the national office given above. In addition, a few metropolitan areas have informal groups.

§A.3 **Advertising by Manufacturers.** When buying equipment it is first necessary to learn about what is available on the market. If there are not colleagues available with whom to consult, the practitioner must rely upon advertisements to get in touch with manufacturers. It is now common for several of them to advertise in such places as the newsletters of the American Psychiatric Association and the American Psychological Association, the advertising pages of *Psychophysiology,* the *Archives of Physical Medicine and Rehabilitation,* and similar resources. The smaller and sometimes less reliable companies may advertise in the classified ads of popular magazines such as *Psychology Today.* It is now also possible to contact manufacturers at the annual meeting of the Biofeedback Society and some other conventions and meetings. At the moment they are more likely to be at psychological conventions than medical or psychiatric conventions. A biofeedback manufacturer's association may also soon emerge as another resource for information.

APPENDIX B
ROUTINE CLINIC FORMS

This appendix contains three forms for routine use preceded by an explanation of each of them.

§B.1 **Therapist's Report.** This is a checklist for use by the therapist in each patient session. It reminds the therapist of the areas he should address so that none are overlooked. It provides space for notes on the session as well as planning space for the next appointment. By placing the completed form in the chart, a convenient method of updating the chart after each session is initiated and the form is available for review prior to the next session.

§B.2 **Weekly Clinic Report.** This report is completed each week by the therapist and is given to the practitioner. The practitioner uses information on this form to review the status of each patient quickly. He can detect at a glance whether any particular patient needs special attention.

§B.3 **Biofeedback/Relaxation Follow-Up.** This is a form divided into three parts. Part I is concerned with the symptom status before biofeedback treatment is initiated. This part may also be completed prior to treatment and kept as a baseline of the symptom. When the form is completed by the patient in the follow-up contacts, the similarity of responses to Part I at that time and in the period prior to treatment will serve as an index of reliability of responses.

Part II is concerned with the status of the symptom at the end of the regular treatment sessions. One copy of Part II should be completed at termination and kept in the file for comparison with responses on this part at the follow-up contacts. By comparing Parts I and II, an index of symptom changes may be obtained.

Part III is to be completed at the follow-up periods and a comparison of Part III with Parts I and II will show how well any gains have been maintained and will indicate whether the patient should return to the clinic for a short refresher course. Follow-up periods are suggested in Section 5.13 and a complete follow-up form should be used for each follow-up contact.

These three forms cover the basic procedures and no attempt has been made to supply forms for the variety of situations encountered in various therapeutic situations. Additional forms to meet special needs are best developed within the setting for which they apply.

THERAPIST'S REPORT

NAME_____ DATE_____

SESSION_____ THERAPIST_____

SPONTANEOUS COMMENTS:
Symptom_____
Home practice_____
Relaxation_____
Subjective cue_____
Other_____
_____

PROGRESS:
Symptom_____
Symptom control_____
Relaxation_____
Subjective cue_____
Mental imagery_____
Physiological_____

HOME PRACTICE:
Going well_____
Attitude about_____
Usefulness of_____
Difficulty with_____
Questions_____
Comments_____

TODAY'S PROCEDURES:
Instrumentation
( )EEG (location)_____ Cal:_____
( )EMG (location)_____ Cal:_____
( )Blood pressure_____ Cal:_____
( )Other_____
( )None

RELAXATION PROCEDURES:
( )Physical relaxation
( )Mental relaxation
( )Autogenic exercises
( )Progressive relaxation
( )Other_____
( )None

SPECIAL PROCEDURES:
( )Mental imagery_____
( )Other_____

PLANS FOR NEXT SESSION:
Patient's assignment_____
_____
Next appointment_____
_____
Instrumentation change_____
Feedback change_____
Relaxation_____
Mental imagery_____
Special procedures_____
Other_____

WEEKLY CLINIC REPORT*

Name	Symptom	Visit No.	Therapist	Parameters Fed Back				Parameters Monitored				Overall Trend				Today's Trend				Treatment Problems
				EMG	Temp	EEG	Oth	EMG	Temp	EEG	Oth	W	NC	SI	RI	W	NC	SI	RI	

* Trends key: W: worse (more intense symptom); NC: no change; SI: slowly improving; RI: rapidly improving *(place an "X" in appropriate space)*.

Reviewed by _____ . Date_____

BIOFEEDBACK/RELAXATION FOLLOW-UP

Number:_____

INSTRUCTIONS: Notice that the questionnaire is divided roughly into three parts. Part I asks about the time *before* you had your biofeedback or relaxation. Part II relates to your biofeedback or relaxation sessions themselves and some possible changes that resulted from them. Part III asks about the present time. It is important that you indicate that you have considered every question, so on those questions that do not apply to you, place "NA" beside the number.

PART I: As you read each question in this part, remember that it is asking about the time *before* you began your biofeedback or relaxation visits.

I-1. Describe the condition for which you had biofeedback/relaxation.

I-2. In all, how many months or years had you had the condition?

0 ☐ Less than 6 months

1 ☐ More than 6 months but less than 1 year

2 ☐ More than 1 year but less than 3 years

3 ☐ More than 3 years but less than 5 years

4 ☐ More than 5 years but less than 10 years

5 ☐ More than 10 years

I-3. How often did the condition bother you?

☐ Daily   ☐ Weekly   ☐ Bi-weekly   ☐ Monthly   ☐ Less frequently
0   1   2   3   4

I-4. Would you describe your discomfort at the time from this condition as:

☐ Very mild   ☐ Mild   ☐ Moderate   ☐ Intense   ☐ Almost unbearable
0   1   2   3   4

I-5. At that time, what made the condition better?_____

_____

I-6. At that time, what made the condition worse?_____

_____

I-7. Was the condition worse at a particular time of day?   ☐ No   ☐ Yes
If yes, when?_____

I-8. Once the condition began, how many hours or days did it usually last?

0 ☐ Less than 1 hour   3 ☐ More than 24 hours
1 ☐ More than 1 hour but less than 12 hours 4 ☐ More than 2 days
2 ☐ More than 12 hours but less than 24 hours 5 ☐ More than a week

I-9. How did your condition limit your activities?

0 ☐ Not at all
1 ☐ Mildly; could do most regular activities
2 ☐ Moderately; could do only a few regular activities
3 ☐ Severely; could do only very essential tasks
4 ☐ Completely; had to remain in bed and could carry out *no* regular activities

I-10. On the scale from 0-10, indicate your ability to relax before your biofeedback/relaxation sessions:

No relaxation _____ Very deep relaxation
                00 01 02 03 04 05 06 07 08 09 10

I-11. Use this space for any comments about your condition before any biofeedback and/or relaxation.

PART II: As you read each question in this part, remember that it is asking about the time *during* your biofeedback/relaxation sessions.

II-1. When did you start your biofeedback/relaxation?

☐ Spring   ☐ Summer   ☐ Fall   ☐ Winter   of_____
0   1   2   3   (Year)

II-2. How often were your visits?

0 ☐ More than twice a week   2 ☐ Once a week
1 ☐ Twice a week   3 ☐ Less than once a week

II-3. How many visits did you have?

☐ Less than 10   ☐ 10   ☐ More than 10   ☐ More than 15   ☐ More than 20
0   1   2   3   4

II-4. Did you have home practice?   ☐ No   ☐ Yes
                                   0

If *yes*, was it: ☐ Tape recording   ☐ Exercises   ☐ Other: (specify)_____
                     1   2   3

II-5. What kind of biofeedback did you have?

☐ None   ☐ Alpha   ☐Muscle   ☐ Other (specify):_____
0   1   2   3

II-6. Did you use a:

☐ Tone   ☐ Light   ☐ Other (specify): _____
0   1   2

II-7. On a scale from 0–10, indicate your ability to relax at the end of your visits:

No relaxation   Very deep relaxation

00	01	02	03	04	05	06	07	08	09	10

II-8. At the end of your visits, how often would you say your original condition bothered you?

☐ Daily   ☐ Weekly   ☐ Bi-weekly   ☐ Monthly   ☐ Less frequently   ☐ Not at all
0   1   2   3   4   5

II-9. At the end of your visits, would you describe your discomfort from this condition as:

☐ None   ☐ Very mild   ☐ Mild   ☐ Moderate   ☐ Intense   ☐ Almost unbearable
0   1   2   3   4   5

II-10. Listed below are some statements about the various things which you may feel helped you change your condition. Please check (√) *all* of the appropriate statements *and* rank the three most important ones, *1, 2,* and *3*.

_That you were working on your symptom.

_That you learned to relax your muscles.

_That you were working with someone on your symptom.

_That you learned to control your brain waves.

_That you learned to relax at home.

_That you learned to blank your mind.

_That you learned to avoid the stress that caused the symptom.

_That you learned not to react to the stress that caused the symptom.

_That you learned to recognize early tension.

_That your learned to oppose tension.

_That someone was helping you with your symptom.

_That you expected to feel better.

II-11. Use this space for any comments about your biofeedback/relaxation, including any comment regarding home practice:

PART III: As you reach each question in this part, remember that it is asking about the time *since* the end of your biofeedback/relaxation visits.

III-1. How long has it been since your last visit?

0 ☐ Less than 6 months
1 ☐ More than 6 months but less than 1 year
2 ☐ More than 1 year but less than 2 years

3 ☐ More than 2 years but less than 3 years
4 ☐ More than 3 years

III-2. How often does your original condition now bother you?

☐ Daily ☐ Weekly ☐ Bi-weekly ☐ Monthly ☐ Less frequently ☐ Not at all
0 1 2 3 4 5

III-3. At the present, is your discomfort from the original condition?

☐ None ☐ Very mild ☐ Mild ☐ Moderate ☐ Intense ☐ Almost unbearable
0 1 2 3 4 5

III-4. How often do you still practice your home exercises?

☐ Daily ☐ Weekly ☐ Bi-weekly ☐ Monthly ☐ Less frequently
0 1 2 3 4

☐ Not at all (about how long ago did you stop?_____) ☐ I had no home exercises
5 6

III-5. Has another condition replaced the original one? ☐ No ☐ Yes
0 1

If *yes,* please answer questions a, b, c, and d below:
a. Describe the condition:_____

_____

b. When did this condition begin?_____
c. Would you say this condition bothers you:

☐ Daily ☐ Weekly ☐ Bi-weekly ☐ Monthly ☐ Less frequently

d. Would you describe your discomfort from this condition as:

☐ Mild ☐ Moderate ☐ Severe ☐ Unbearable

III-6. What in your opinion has been most responsible for your present condition? (Use this space.)

III-7. On a scale from 0–10, indicate your *present* ability to relax:

No relaxation _____ Very deep relaxation
00 01 02 03 04 05 06 07 08 09 10

III-8. At the present time, how are *you* generally different from when you had biofeedback/relaxation?

☐ No different ☐ I am generally better ☐ I am generally worse

III-9. How is your *life situation* different now? For example, has there been a birth, a death, a marriage, a divorce, a job or living change? Do you consider things better or worse? (Use this space to describe.)

III-10. Use the remaining space here and on the attached sheet of this form to make any comments you would like or you feel might be helpful in determining the last effects of biofeedback/relaxation for your condition.

THANK YOU FOR YOUR PARTICIPATION

APPENDIX C

MENTAL IMAGERY EXERCISES

This is an exercise that the therapist might use to help the patient re-establish his ability to use mental imagery. It is helpful to record the exercise on tape and allow the patient to work with it on a daily practice schedule for 1 week, making notes about the progression of his re-developing imagination. On the tape, the therapist might begin by allowing the patient a moment or two to relax before beginning the actual mental imagery. Relaxation can be facilitated by suggestions similar to the following: *"Make yourself comfortable. Relax your body completely. Close your eyes. Take a deep breath and let it out slowly while saying to yourself the numbers three, two, one."* This may be repeated once or twice. Then say: *"In a moment, I am going to count from one to three and ask you to tap your foot. At that moment, see in your mind's eye a screen. The screen can be any size or shape. It can resemble a movie or television screen; and it should be light in color."* Then proceed to count: *"one . . . , two . . . , three . . . ,"* and say: *"Tap your foot. See your imaginary screen."* Since it is important that the screen be light in color, the therapist might say: *"In a moment, I am going to count from one to three and ask you to tap your foot. At that moment, please cause your screen to lighten in color so that it becomes either white or light blue. One . . . , two . . . , three, tap your foot. See your screen as white or light blue."* With the screen in mind, and having manipulated it to a functional color, the therapist might say: *"In a moment I am going to count from one to three and ask you to tap your foot. At that moment, please project a shape onto your screen: either a circle, a square, or a triangle. One . . . , two . . . , three, tap your foot. See the shape on your screen. Note the size and color of the shape and note the shape itself. In a moment, I am going to count from one to three and ask you to tap your foot. Change the color of the shape from its present color to red. One . . . , two . . . , three, see the shape as red. In a moment, I am going to count from one to three and ask you to tap your foot. At that moment, change the color of the shape from red to yellow. One . . . , two . . . , three, tap your foot. See the shape as yellow."* Then

219

proceed in the same manner through green, blue, white, and black. Each time suggest the one to three count and ask the patient to tap his foot. This initiates the idea of manipulating the image through colors. Having completed work with any image, it is important that that image be removed from the screen. To do so, suggest to the patient: *"In a moment, I am going to count from one to three and ask you to tap your foot. At that moment, please clear your screen, but keep your screen."* Then say: *"One . . . , two . . . , three, tap your foot and clear your screen."*

The next part of the exercise is for rehearsing movement of images. Suggest: *"In a moment, I am going to count from one to three and ask you to tap your foot. At that moment, please project a ball onto your mental screen. One . . . , two . . . , three, tap your foot. Project the image of a ball onto your screen. Note the size and color of the ball. Now in a moment I am going to count slowly from one to four. With each succeeding number, cause the ball to come closer and enlarge so that by the time the number four is reached, the ball entirely covers the surface of the screen. Begin now, one . . . see the ball come closer. Two . . . larger and closer. Three . . . even larger now. Four . . . the ball should be so large that it covers the surface of the screen."* To reverse the movement, thus gaining more control suggest: *"In a moment I am going to count once again from one to four. As I do so, cause the ball to move away and get smaller with each succeeding number so that by the time the number four is reached, the ball is back to its original size. Begin now; one . . . see the ball move away. Two . . . smaller and smaller. Three . . . the ball should be almost at its original size. Four . . . see the ball at its original size."* A similar series of counts could cause the ball to become very small and then return to the original size. Once again, when the exercise with the ball is over, use the same technique as with the shapes to clear the screen. With size movement and a color of neutral shapes complete, it is advisable to move on to the manipulation of self-images on the screen. Suggest: *"In a moment, I am going to count from one to three and ask you to tap your foot. At that moment, please project an image of yourself, face front, on the screen. One . . . , two . . . , three, tap your foot. See an image of yourself on your screen. In a moment, I am going to count slowly from one to four. With each succeeding number, please cause the image on your screen to turn one quarter turn so that by the time the number four is reached, the image has made a full circle and is once again facing front. One . . . see the image turn to its side. Two . . . see the back of the image. Three . . . see the opposite side. Four . . . see your face once again."* As with the other exercise, once this exercise is completed, clear the screen.

So that the patient may develop skill in using mental imagery to make changes in his level of relaxation, the next exercise is designed to acquaint the patient with the way his muscles will look on his screen. Suggest: *"In a moment, I am going to count from one to three and ask you to tap your foot. At that moment, please see your mind's representation of the muscles of your entire body on your screen. The image may not be anatomically correct, but it will be your mind's representation of the muscles of your entire body. One . . . , two . . . , three, tap your foot. See your mind's representation of the muscles of your entire body."* The patient will report some image if successful. His muscles may be represented in some medium which is familiar to him, such as lines or dots. Suggest: *"Note the size, shape, color, and texture of the muscles of your body. Note whether there is an area that appears different from the rest. If so, you can consider this area one of tension and can relieve the tension by changing the image so that this area appears the same as the rest in every way. I am going to count slowly from one to four and as I do, please cause any tense areas to change in appearance, so that by the time the number four is reached, these areas appear as the majority in every way. One . . . begin to see the changes. Two . . . more and more relaxed. Three . . . almost completely relaxed. Four . . . the tense areas should appear exactly as the relaxed areas in every way. Note how the tense areas looked and how they look now. In the future, when you see areas of your body that appear as the tense areas looked, you can use this technique to change them to resemble the relaxed areas and you will notice a change in the way these areas feel."* The patient has now been given a mental imagery technique for bringing about relaxation in areas of the body that may have been resistant to relaxation. Use the technique for clearing the screen and then remove the screen from the imagination by suggesting: *"In a moment I am going to count from one to three and ask you to tap your foot. At that moment, please cause your screen to disappear from your mind's eye. One . . . , two . . . , three, tap your foot. Cause your screen to disappear from your mind's eye."*

This ends the mental imagery exercise. Give the patient a moment or two with a suggestion that he turn his attention to his surroundings before asking him to return to his regular activities. A copy of the Mental Imagery Practice Notes follows. By asking the patient to complete these notes after each mental imagery practice session, a record is available of his developing skill.

MENTAL IMAGERY PRACTICE NOTES

Each time you finish using your MI practice tape, please take a moment to complete these notes. Bring these notes with you on your next visit.

Date:_____ Day of Week: _____ Time:_____

1. Did you feel relaxed?   ( ) Yes   ( ) No   ( ) Somewhat

2. Was your mental screen vivid?
   ( ) Yes   ( ) No   ( ) Some of the time
3. What color was your screen?_____
4. Did it lighten?
   ( ) Yes   ( ) No   ( ) Changed in a different way
5. Which shape did you project?
   ( ) Circle   ( ) Square   ( ) Triangle   ( ) Other
6. What color was the shape originally?_____
7. Did the shape take on all of the colors?
   ( ) Yes   ( ) No   ( ) Some   ( ) None
   If not, which were difficult?_____
8. What direction was the line on your screen?
   ( ) Horizontal   ( ) Vertical   ( ) Diagonal
   ( ) Curved   ( ) Other: _____
9. What color was the ball?_____
10. Did the ball enlarge?   ( ) Yes   ( ) No   ( ) Partly
11. Did the ball shrink?   ( ) Yes   ( ) No   ( ) Partly
12. Was your self-image vivid?   ( ) Yes   ( ) No
13. Did your self-image change?   ( ) Yes   ( ) No   ( ) Some
14. Was your white frame vivid?   ( ) Yes   ( ) No
15. How many tense areas did you spot?_____
16. Did they improve   ( ) Yes   ( ) No   ( ) Some

Note Comments on the Back Side

INDEX OF NAMES

INDEX OF SUBJECTS